Also edited by John Calder in Picador

A William Burroughs Reader

By Samuel Beckett in Picador

More Pricks Than Kicks
Murphy
The Beckett Trilogy
Company

A Samuel Beckett Reader

edited and introduced by John Calder

 Original
published by Pan Books

Contents

Foreword

The volume contains twenty-one sections drawn from the considerable body of work with which Samuel Beckett has for many
years now astonished, fascinated and puzzled the literary world.
Most of the material comes from the prose works, although there
is one complete short play and there are extracts from several
others, and from the poetry, but nothing has been taken from the
radio plays, TV plays or his one film scenario (all of which are
listed in the bibliography), because the themes they cover are so
well represented elsewhere. The choices are annotated and selec-
ted not only to give the reader a comprehensive picture of what
the Beckett canon is about and how to read it, but to demonstrate
how rewarding and pleasurable reading it can be. But no anthology can take the place of reading the author in his entirety. My
introductory material is designed to guide the reader to what is
most important and what should be read first.

I would like to thank primarily Nancy Webber who helped me to
get the extracts and editorial copy together, Faber and Faber for
permission to include some of their copyright material, the many
friends and acquaintances whose interest in or hostility to the work
of Mr Beckett has given me an insight where enlightenment is
most needed, and finally Samuel Beckett himself for allowing me
to play a small part in communicating to the world the most
demanding and exciting literary adventure of our time.

John Calder

Introduction

It is fifteen years since I last assembled extracts from the work of
Samuel Beckett to make a 'reader', and its considerable sale to the
interested public, as well as its wide use in schools and universities, may have helped to dispel some of the fright that the name
Samuel Beckett still seems to evoke. Today, seventy-seven years
old, a Nobel Prize winner, one of the most internationally performed current playwrights, and the contemporary figure who
attracts more serious academic attention in the arts than anyone
else living, he is still considered by many to be difficult to understand, a pessimist whose view of the world and of humankind is
so black that his relevance can only be to the suicidal, while, in
some quarters, he is still regarded as a charlatan whose alleged
obscurity only hides his lack of anything real to say. These attitudes persist and in some ways are encouraged by the very considerable Beckett industry, created by specialist academics who
meet regularly to read learned papers to each other about their
idol, who tend to find arcane meanings in the writings that are
possibly often created only by themselves, and who would be
quite pleased to keep this fascinating, egregious and universal
writer to themselves.

The purpose of this volume, like the previous reader, is to
demonstrate what enormous pleasure can be found in reading
Samuel Beckett, and how easy it is to involve oneself in his particular world, and to encourage readers to make their own discov-
eries. And it is possible in the 1980s to view him rather differently
from the 1960s, when he appeared to be the most advanced out-
post of modernism in serious writing, a literary equivalent of Anton
von Webern in music, trying to squeeze ever more meaning into
ever fewer words. Miniaturist he may be, but since his seventieth
birthday he has emerged from a narrowing dark tunnel of the
imagination into a metaphorical Elysian field that lives under the
sun and the stars. His latest writing, while closer to poetry than
any other literary form, shows a serenity missing from his earlier
work, offers little difficulty to the reader and is pure joy to anyone
able to appreciate his style.

Samuel Barclay Beckett was born in Foxrock, a suburb of Dublin, on 13 April 1906, a Good Friday. His father was a quantity surveyor who raised his family by comfortable middle-class standards and educated them in good schools. The Becketts were Protestant, probably of Huguenot descent, and Samuel was sent to Portora Royal High School in Ulster and then to Trinity College, Dublin, where he exhibited both academic brilliance and a talent for sport, shining in particular at rugby, golf and cricket. He returned to Trinity to teach French and Italian literature, spent the year 1928–9 teaching at the École Normale Supérieure under an exchange arrangement between the Sorbonne and Trinity, and then turned to full-time writing, although this meant being almost wholly dependent on subsidies from his family. His first collection of short stories, *More Pricks Than Kicks*, was published in 1934 and his first novel, *Murphy*, in 1938; neither made any particular impression on the literary world at the time. During the 1930s he lived mostly in Paris, became a member of the James Joyce circle, and in various ways helped Joyce, although he was never his secretary as is sometimes claimed. A citizen of Ireland, a neutral country, he stayed by choice in France during the war, became a member of the Resistance, narrowly escaped arrest by the Gestapo, and bicycled to the Vaucluse, then part of the Vichy self-governing area of France, where he hid in a small village until the end of the war. For his very dangerous activities in the Resistance he eventually received the Croix de Guerre. His wartime experiences were to make an important contribution to the subject-matter of his post-war work. Believing that a tumour growing in his cheek was probably malignant and that he did not have long to live, he shut himself up in the country for a sustained two-year period from 1947 to 1949 in order to leave behind him the body of work that he felt compelled to write. His reputation depends largely on the products of those two years, the masterpieces of what is now considered his middle period. But happily the tumour, when removed, turned out to be benign, and he has continued to produce plays, fictional texts, poetry, and other work up to the present time.

One of the reasons that Mr Beckett has such an awesome reputation is that no one seems quite able to know where to place him historically in modern literature. His play *Waiting for Godot* was first performed in Paris at the beginning of 1953 and made him instantly famous. It was subsequently produced all over the world to the kind of controversial reception that created arguments and discussion, so that everyone with an interest in the arts and the theatre had to have an opinion about the play and know his name. Since then he has been the outstanding figure of the post-war literary *avant-garde*. With him is associated the 'theatre of the absurd', and many other labels have been coined to describe his novels and other work. Although many have tried to imitate him, he is in fact inimitable, but many other writers have been able to learn from him how to create an atmosphere, set a tone, or create a theatrical effect. Harold Pinter, for instance, has learnt from Beckett how to invest stillness with meaning, and Tom Stoppard, from Beckett's example, to use dialogue.

Beckett is without question a great and original modern writer who has stretched the frames that previously contained the novel and the theatre, but there is another way in which he can be seen that is perhaps more constructive for the new reader. He is really the last of the Romantics, whose work is a link with the European literature that preceded the novel of character (Dickens and Balzac) and the naturalist period. It is no accident that some of his early poems are based on images that attracted him, for instance, in the poetry of Goethe: indeed Beckett's novels can be seen as a modern form of the *Bildungsroman* or novel of development, except that his development is downward. Beckett sees life not as growth but as decline, and the development of his characters is shown as part of a process of decay. His work is probably as much influenced by music as by previous writers, and he has taken much from the *feeling* of Beethoven and Schubert. If he seems to have more affinity with the latter, it is with the former that he can best be compared. Interestingly, in all the many books written about Beckett, nobody has yet properly studied the important role of music in his life and work, both as a model for the forms he creates and as a guide to reading him. In a sense Beckett writes musical compositions with words, and his time markings are there for those who understand music to read, as they would be in a score. This has become more obvious in recent years as literary and dramatic journalists, watching him in rehearsals, have noted the metronome-like beat that he teaches his actors, making them count the pauses between words as a musician does. Musicians indeed are fascinated by his work and were among his earliest admirers, and many have been ambitious to set the plays, the poems, or passages from the novels to music. But nobody has yet succeeded in producing a wholly successful musical work to a Beckett text, and for a very good reason: the music is already there.

Although it is increasingly felt that his most important work is in his novels, Beckett is far better known as a dramatist, and it is through his plays that the revolution he has created in the art of writing is most easily understood. His plays are very exacting, demanding a total discipline on the part of actors who have to approach their parts rather like ballet dancers. Every gesture, inflection, and movement is of importance and preset in rehearsal.

The old-fashioned, easy-going actor, who would paraphrase or change his lines from one performance to the next, has no place in a Beckett play. From the beginning he demanded word-perfect line-readings and tightly controlled direction of every movement, which has in effect brought a new kind of actor into existence. Audiences, as well, instinctively react with greater attention to a Beckett play than to theatre where timing, precision, and line-delivery are less important. The kind of attention that is required is the attention that one devotes to hearing a Schubert song or a Beethoven quartet. In speaking of Beckett, and emphasising his Romantic associations, we are speaking of a fusion of literary and musical imaginative creation, united into an art form that has moved sideways from other literature, and has in a sense invaded the parallel arts.

Beckett is often thought of as a development from James Joyce, and his early work shows many similarities with his great compatriot. His poems in particular sometimes have the same lyrical quality as James Joyce's *Chamber Music* and *Pomes Penyeach*; while *Murphy* has a rich Irish rhetoric that may owe something to Joyce. But his preoccupation is very different, because Joyce wanted to encompass all of life in his work: *Ulysses* may be only the record of a single day in Dublin, but it is a very full picture of an era and its life as a whole; *Finnegans Wake* may be only a dream, but it encompasses a whole history of a race, a nation and a culture as well as the minutiae of Joyce's daily life. Maria Jolas, who with her late husband Eugène supported Joyce financially in the 1930s and published *Finnegans Wake* in instalments in their magazine *Transition*, entertained Joyce to dinner several times a week, and she tells how even the smallest details of conversation at their table went into *Finnegans Wake* the next morning, because Joyce wanted to be the universal writer whose work encompassed all human knowledge and all experience. Beckett on the other hand compresses that same world into the smallest space possible. In doing so he has adopted the techniques of the Romantic poets and those composers through whose work we know their poetry best today, because music is the art through which we are best able to compress joy and sadness, poignancy and human feeling, and the tragedies of life.

Beckett is often criticised for the blackness of his vision, and the question is asked why he feels it so necessary to write to depress us. The same question is not asked of Beethoven's *For the Faraway Beloved* or of Schubert's *Winterreise*, two song cycles of overpowering sadness and perfect beauty, which audiences flock to hear when sung by their most famous contemporary interpreters. If there is a huge sadness in Beckett's work, it is akin to the great

Romantic music of the past in its evocation of beauty, in the way phrases haunt the mind, and in all the other qualities that he introduces, including humour, flashes of joy, moments of contemplative peace.

The comparison with Beethoven is especially close. Beethoven's first period is an extension of the music of the eighteenth century, of the elegance, clarity, and essentially non-political, non-emotional style associated with Haydn and Mozart. His second period contains a new dynamic where emotion constantly breaks out of the framework of form, thereby increasing the possibilities of style and the content that music can express. At the time it constituted a musical revolution, and Beethoven's reputation might be a little different had he died ten years younger. But his third period was a turning away from the world into himself, where he found an introspective peace in which he could escape his own physical suffering and make a statement about the human condition: although this statement is tragic, it has the power to transmute tragedy into art, thereby giving perhaps the greatest pleasure that we can experience from aesthetics. Beethoven was tormented by bad health, physical pain, deafness, and personal unhappiness. Some of his calmest, most spring-like and cheerful music was written at the depths of his depression when, for instance, contemplating, and close to committing, suicide, he brought the Sixth Symphony to life. In his final quartet, the Op. 135, he musically depicts the approach of death, coming ever closer but occasionally pushed into the background with moments of gaiety. This is the way we all live, pushing the unpleasant realities of life, and those spectres we prefer to keep at the back of our minds, temporarily away; people, in T. S. Eliot's phrase, 'cannot bear very much reality'. Yet in music and in painting we bring ourselves, without too much difficulty, to face the realities of suffering and unhappiness in life and the inevitable presence of death, because art is accepted as an alchemist's stone that changes unpleasant reality into an imaginative awareness that we find not only acceptable but positively enjoyable. Samuel Beckett has accomplished the same form of magic in his writing, but is too little appreciated for doing so by the same public that goes to concerts and art galleries.

As with Beethoven, Beckett's work falls into three periods (he is of course still actively writing). His first period was terminated by the war, although some work written or largely conceived during the war really belongs to that time. The early work was an extension of the possibilities open to a writer at the time, portrayals of a hero rather like himself, trying to come to terms with a society with which he was basically out of sympathy, and the victim of many comically described disasters. The post-war second period belongs to: his play *Waiting for Godot*; the three novels *Molloy*, *Malone Dies*, and *The Unnamable*, usually called the *Trilogy*; the four novellas *First Love*, *The Expelled*, *The Calmative*, and *The End*; and the *Texts for Nothing*. These are the fruits of 1947–9 and were written prior to the production of *Waiting for Godot*. They were followed by more plays, most notably *Endgame*, *Krapp's Last Tape*, *Happy Days*, and *Play*, and the novel *How It Is*. There is no perceptible break between the writing that belongs to the second period and that of the third, but most of the work is recognisably on one side of the divide or the other, not by date but by style and content. The late work is distinguished by extreme brevity and concentration, and a perceptible change in tone and atmosphere, most evident since 1975. The play *Not I*, in spite of its fairly late date (1972), really belongs to the second period, while *Imagination Dead Imagine* (1965) really belongs to the third.

Beckett's second period is characterised by great purity of style. Totally fluent in French by the end of the war, he started to write in that language to escape from the over-elaborate use of English that it is virtually impossible for an Irishman to avoid. Irish speech is more ornate and colourful than the language as used elsewhere, and it is more difficult for a direct message to get through it with the economy Beckett wanted to achieve. French, although it can also be used ambiguously and to express nuance, is essentially the language of clarity, and Beckett instantly proved himself a master of French style. In translating his own work into English, as he subsequently did, he recreated that style in his native language. Since the early 1950s he has written in both languages, sometimes starting a new work in one, continuing it in the other until he felt that it was going well, and finishing it in that one, later translating into the other. *Krapp's Last Tape* was his first post-war play written in English, because he had by that time heard the voice of the late Patrick Magee reading the English translation of *Molloy* on the BBC and, fascinated by Magee's voice, with its rasp so perfectly suited to the character, he wrote *Krapp* for an actor he had never met. Some works, mostly plays, have been written in one language or the other because they were a commission from the BBC or a theatre. Of his two most recent prose texts, *Company* and *Ill Seen Ill Said*, the first was written in English after experimenting in both languages, and the second in French. He is almost equally comfortable in German and has spent much time in Germany directing plays for the stage and for television. Although Beckett has perfect knowledge of Italian, which he at one time taught, he has shown little interest in the Italian translations of his work.

Once he had found the right voice, he was able to depict a world, recognisably the real world, but stylised to catch those moments in life that are most important or most revealing. The war left him with an image of suffering humanity that could be depicted only through metaphor and allusion. A scene depicting the horrors of a concentration camp, torture, or execution, however realistic, can never catch the real essence of human cruelty, the despair of those who are trapped, the suffering and universal helplessness of all life in the face of predation and the destructive powers of nature or man. The absence of any divine power able or willing to prevent suffering or improve the human condition, the indifference of nature, and our own limited understanding of the universe in which we live have given modern man, especially in time of war, a sense of helplessness; this helplessness can be countered only with a resigned stoicism, interrupted perhaps with bursts of anger that the world is not the better place we know it could be, so that we should have the intelligence and conscious awareness to perceive the depth of our universal tragedy; if there is a God, why should he treat us so badly or be so indifferent? Beckett has set out to depict this sense of helplessness.

Waiting for Godot is a play set in the same countryside as that in which Beckett spent the war, much of it in company with a Jewish painter who was also hiding from the Nazis. In *Godot*, two tramps, in character not unlike Beckett himself and Henri Hayden, the painter, pass the time waiting for Godot – who may possibly give them a job – to arrive. The day sometimes goes faster, sometimes slower, depending upon what diversions Vladimir and Estragon can think up for themselves in word games, quarrels, or encounters with passers-by. They have nothing to interest them in life except each other's company and the resources of their own minds. They live off any food they can scrounge, and death, they tell each other, would be a relief. Although there are allusions to the beatings they receive from others, their real suffering is cosmic. They are alone in the world, nobody cares what happens to them. The thought that their experience, such as it is, is all a waste, a process of living, dying, and being instantly forgotten – their passage through life ultimately of no consequence – is the greatest cruelty of all. Beckett has discerned in the human condition the need to have an identity and the despair of modern man at being robbed of it. Our time has seen disruptions of whole peoples, diasporas, military conquests, the imposition of inhumane totalitarian systems over much of the world's population. In the more industrialised societies individualism is constantly eroded; increasingly people are displaced by machines, so that no apparent reason for their existence will ultimately be discerned. The break-up of rural society, family continuity, and ancestral records, and the increasing replacement of human and community values by values based on greed, where the greed itself is perpetuated more by machine intelligence than by human, have changed all the certainties of earlier times. Each individual is forced to be more alone in himself, increasingly without religious consolation or the belief that human society can offer an alternative security. Man needs to be needed and to see purpose in his life; nor can he live for ever under the threat of annihilation. But his needs are increasingly ignored. This is a view of the world from which existentialist philosophy begins, and if Kirkegaard, Sartre, and other philosophers have described it in philosophical terms, then Beckett has caught the essence of it in the distilled poetry of his plays and novels. *Waiting for Godot* is about many things, but its central message is the horror of being unknown, unrecognised, and forgotten. At the end of each act a boy appears with a message that Godot will probably come tomorrow. It may be the same boy or it may be his brother, but Vladimir, the more sensitive of the two tramps, is less concerned with Godot's coming than that he should be remembered by the boy.

In *Molloy*, Beckett takes up another aspect of human concern, the delusion, based partly on the expectations created by Hollywood and entertainment literature that all things will turn out for the best, and partly on traditional religion, that we are all in a way protected. *Molloy* is a novel of quest, written in two parts: in the first Molloy is in his mother's bed, not quite sure how he got there, remembering a series of events which led to his being lost in a forest, waiting for help to come; the second part is the narrative of a private detective, Moran, who is sent by a mysterious messenger, Gaber, to find Molloy. The quest is not successful, and when Moran finally returns to write his report he is a broken man. Each of the two narratives is continuous, but the reader never finds out how Molloy got from the forest to the bed of his presumably dead mother. He had faith that he would be saved from the forest and he presumably was, but the arrival of human or divine assistance* is left entirely to the reader's imagination, because it is not important to the author, who is more interested in depicting the condition of two very opposite specimens of humanity, his two protagonists.

Molloy, an itinerant cripple, an outsider from what must have been at one time a conventional background, does not see himself as belonging to the humdrum human society that works, eats

*The names Mr Beckett gives to his characters are frequently significant, and it has often occurred to me that the closeness of Gaber to Gabriel and Moran to Mary may carry an ironic allusion to the Annunciation in the New Testament.

regularly, and has a home to go to – 'their planet' – but views all of life with disgust. He is occasionally taken up by another out of pity or loneliness, but is happier alone, finding perhaps his greatest pleasure in injuring someone even more decrepit and weaker than himself. Molloy meets a charcoal-burner, who tries to detain him.

So I smartly freed a crutch and dealt him a good dint on the skull. That calmed him. The dirty old brute. I got up and went on. But I hadn't gone more than a few paces, and for me at this time a few paces meant something, when I turned and went back to where he lay, to examine him. Seeing he had not ceased to breathe I contented myself with giving him a few warm kicks in the ribs, with my heels. This is how I went about it. I carefully chose the most favourable position, a few paces from the body, with my back of course turned to it. Then, nicely balanced on my crutches, I began to swing, backwards, forwards, feet pressed together, or rather legs pressed together, for how could I press my feet together, with my legs in the state they were? But how could I press my legs together, in the state they were? I pressed them together, that's all I can tell you. Take it or leave it. Or I didn't press them together. What can that possibly matter? I swung, that's all that matters, in an ever-widening arc, until I decided the moment had come and launched myself forward with all my strength and consequently, a moment later, backward, which gave the desired result. Where did I get this access of vigour? From my weakness perhaps. The shock knocked me down. Naturally. I came a cropper. You can't have everything. I've often noticed it. I rested a moment, then got up, picked up my crutches, took up my position on the other side of the body and applied myself with method to the same exercise. I always had a mania for symmetry. But I must have aimed a little low and one of my heels sank in something soft. However. For if I had missed the ribs, with that heel, I had no doubt landed in the kidney, oh not hard enough to burst it, no, I fancy not. People imagine, because you are old, poor, crippled, terrified, that you can't stand up for yourself, and generally speaking that is so. But given favourable conditions, a feeble and awkward assailant, in your own class what, and a lonely place, and you have a good chance of showing what stuff you are made of. And it is doubtless in order to revive interest in this possibility, too often forgotten, that I have delayed over an incident of no interest in itself, like all that has a moral.

Decrepit at the beginning, Molloy becomes more so by the end of the narrative where he seems to merge with Malone, protagonist of *Malone Dies*, the next and second novel of the trilogy, who is, like Molloy, in bed at the beginning of his own narrative. In the meantime, Moran, the detective, a waspish, habit-orientated, conventional individual with a pedantic devotion to religion and whose physical and moral decline is parallel to Molloy's, sets out on his quest. If Molloy is seen by the author as a wild animal in a human world, then Moran is a caricature of civilised man. He demonstrates that life in its implications for the organised and ambitious is in no essential way different from life for the lazy and uninterested, coming to much the same in the end – a central Beckett message that is made many times in different writings; but Beckett also manages to satirise conventional religion and its casuistries, all the panaceas we are offered to ensure conventional respect for society's norms. *Molloy* will probably remain Beckett's central, best-understood novel in that if there is one book that should be read to get the full force of his protest against the order of things, this is it. The Beethoven equivalent would be the Fifth Symphony.

The power of the writing, the insight into suffering, both animal and human, the savage humour, the incredible little humorous asides, the poigancy of the erotic passages, are unlike any other work of its period from any other writer. Inexplicably, it was considered in the early 1950s by some English publishers as too obscene to be published in Britain. It is not a long book but it cannot be read too quickly, because the combination of style and subject-matter makes it difficult not to return constantly to reread every page. The following description from *Molloy* is part of his monologue when, weakened and trying to find his way to the town, he compares himself to a hunted animal.

Morning is the time to hide. They wake up, hale and hearty, their tongues hanging out for order, beauty and justice, baying for their due. Yes, from eight or nine till noon is the dangerous time. But towards noon things quiet down, the most implacable are sated, they go home, it might have been better but they've done a good job, there have been a few survivors but they'll give no more trouble, each man counts his rats. It may begin again in the early afternoon, after the banquet, the celebrations, the congratulations, the orations, but it's nothing compared to the morning, mere fun. Coming up to four or five of course there is the night-shift, the watchmen, beginning to bestir themselves. But already the day is over, the shadows lengthen, the walls multiply, you hug the walls, bowed down like a good boy, oozing with obsequiousness, having nothing to hide, hiding from mere terror, looking neither right nor left, hiding but not provocatively, ready to come out, to smile, to listen, to crawl, nauseating but not pestilent, less rat than toad. Then the true night, perilous too, but sweet to him who knows it, who can open to it like the flower to the sun, who himself is night, day and night. No there is not much to be said for the night either, but compared to the day there is much to be said for it, and notably compared to the morning there is everything to be said for it. For the night purge is in the hands of technicians, for the most part.

They do nothing else, the bulk of the population have no part in it, preferring their warm beds, all things considered. Day is the time for lynching, for sleep is sacred, and especially the morning, between breakfast and lunch. My first care then, after a few miles in the desert dawn, was to look for a place to sleep, for sleep too is a kind of protection, strange as it may seem. For sleep, if it excites the lust to capture, seems to appease the lust to kill, there and then and bloodily, any hunter will tell you that. For the monster on the move, or on the watch, lurking in his lair, there is no mercy, whereas he taken unawares, in his sleep, may sometimes get the benefit of milder feelings, which deflect the barrel, sheathe the kris. For the hunter is weak at heart and sentimental, overflowing with repressed treasures of gentleness and compassion. And it is thanks to this sweet sleep of terror or exhaustion that many a foul beast, and worthy of extermination, can live on till he dies in the peace of our zoological gardens, broken only by the innocent laughter, the knowing laughter of children and their elders, on Sundays and Bank Holidays.

To Beckett, we are all victims; the only right that nature gives us is the right to protest, however vainly. The *Texts for Nothing*, written during the same intensely creative period as *Waiting for Godot* and *Molloy*, are exactly that, thirteen monologues of protest, outbursts where a voice, sometimes plaintive, sometimes strident, questions the meaning of life, identity, and purpose, often answering itself, or imagining an answer, as if from an indifferent God.

Where would I go, if I could go, who would I be, if I could be, what would I say, if I had a voice, who says this, saying it's me? Answer simply, someone answer simply. It's the same old stranger as ever, for whom alone accusative I exist, in the pit of my inexistence, of his, of ours, there's a simple answer. It's not with with thinking he'll find me, but what is he to do, living and bewildered, yes, living, say what he may. Forget me, know me not, yes, that would be the wisest, none better able than he. Why this sudden affability after such desertion, it's easy to understand, that's what he says, but he doesn't understand. I'm not in his head, nowhere in his old body, and yet I'm there, for him I'm there, with him, hence all the confusion.

And the complaint continues, that the 'old stranger' is telling his (the narrator's) story because 'words fail him'.

If at least he would dignify me with the third person, like his other figments, not he, he'll be satisfied with nothing less than me, for his me. When he had me, when he was me, he couldn't get rid of me quick enough, I didn't exist, he couldn't have that, that was no kind of life, of course I didn't exist, any more than he did, of course it was no kind of life, now he has it, his kind of life, let him lose it, if he wants to be in peace, with a bit of luck. His life, what a mine, what a life, he can't have that, you can't fool him, ergo it's not his, it's not him, what a thought, treat him like that, like a vulgar Molloy, a common Malone, those mere mortals, happy mortals, have a heart, land him in that shit, who never stirred, who is none but me, all things considered, and what things, and how considered, he had only to keep out of it.

The voice ends by rephrasing and answering the opening question after describing the state of existence in its life ('What counts is to be in the world').

No point under such circumstances in saying I am somewhere else, some-one else, such as I am I have all I need to hand, for to do what, I don't know, all I have to do, there I am on my own again at last, what a relief that must be. Yes, there are moments, like this moment, when I seem almost restored to the feasible. Then it goes, all goes, and I'm far again, with a far story again; I wait for me afar for my story to begin, to end, and again this voice cannot be mine. That's where I'd go, if I could go, that's who I'd be, if I could be.

Texts for Nothing IV

The *Texts*, written at the same time and in a similar tone to *The Unnamable*, the third novel of the trilogy, are marvellous examples of art drawn out of creative nothingness, the *néant* of Jean-Paul Sartre's philosophical existentialism to which Beckett has so suc-cessfully given a literary framework. He was to return to this form with a collection of *Fizzles*, brief outbursts, but in a more discursive vein, published in Britain under the title *For To End Yet Again*, and first appearing as a collection in 1976. The later texts are partly narrative, the tone quieter, and in the contemplative mood of his later work, nostalgic more than protesting, but essentially it is the same voice speaking.

Old earth, no more lies, I've seen you, it was me, with my other's ravening eyes, too late. You'll be on me, it will be you, it will be me, it will be us, it was never us. It won't be long now, perhaps not tomorrow, nor the day after, but too late. Not long now, how I gaze on you, and what refusal, how you refuse me, you so refused. It's a cockchafer year, next year there won't be any, nor the year after, gaze your fill. I come home at nightfall, they take to wing, rise from my little oaktree and whirr away, glutted, into the shadows. I reach up, grasp the bough, pull myself up and go in. Three years in the earth, those the moles don't get, then guzzle guzzle, ten days long, a fortnight, and always the flight at nightfall. To the river perhaps, they head for the river. I turn on the light, then off, ashamed, stand at gaze before the window, the windows, going from one to another, leaning on the furniture. For an instant I see the sky, the different skies, then they turn to faces, agonies, loves, the different loves, happiness too, yes, there was that too, unhappily. Moments of life, of mine too, among others, no denying, all said and done. Happiness, what happiness, but what deaths, what loves, I knew at the time, it was too late then. Ah to love at your last and see them at theirs, the last minute loved ones, and be happy, why ah, uncalled for. No but now, now, simply stay still, standing before a window, one hand on the wall, the other clutching your shirt, and see the sky, a long gaze, but no, gasps and spasms, a childhood sea, other skies, another body.

Old Earth

Over the years Beckett's protest has become more muted, although it still bursts through the resignation of his recent work in different ways, emphasising the shortness and pain of life, the cruelty of nature, especially human nature, and the waste of it all. This implies an understanding of the possibilities of life, the *douceur de la vie* of Talleyrand's phrase, with its implications of enjoyable creativity, aesthetic appreciation, and love. Beckett is aware of all these things, and sexual love plays a large role in his plays and novels, usually the painful memory of a lost love. In his Platonic dialogues with Georges Duthuit, one of which is given in this volume, he makes it clear how aware he is of the splendour that man can create artistically for his own enjoyment. But he puts the words into the mouth of his opponent: 'Must we really deplore the painting that admits "the things and creatures of spring, resplendent with desire and affirmation, ephemeral no doubt, but immortally reiterant", not in order to benefit by them, not in order to enjoy them, but in order that what is tolerable and radiant in the world may continue?' The need for love, the warmth of human friendship, the regret for lost opportunity, the evocation of sadness for its own sake, all are part of the Romantic view of the world. Many Beckett characters are not far removed from Goethe's Werther and Wilhelm Meister, creations of the German poet's youth and maturity, who lived to suffer and to learn through suffering. Molloy has a memory of love: there was once a little chambermaid whom he never even touched, but whose memory recurs at odd moments of pain and pleasure. He relates his brief meeting and solitary sexual encounter as follows:

It was she made me acquainted with love. She went by the peaceful name of Ruth I think, but I can't say for certain. Perhaps the name was Edith. She had a hole between her legs, oh not the bunghole I had always imagined, but a slit, and in this I put; or rather she put, my so-called virile member, not without difficulty, and I toiled and moiled until I discharged or gave up trying or was begged by her to stop. A mug's game in my opinion and tiring on top of that, in the long run. But I lent myself to it with a good enough grace, knowing it was love, for she had told me so. She bent over the couch, because of her rheumatism, and in I went from behind. It was the only position she could bear, because of her lumbago. It seemed all right to me, for I had seen dogs, and I was astonished when she confided that you could go about it differently. I wonder what she meant exactly. Perhaps after all she put me in her rectum. A matter of complete indifference to me, I needn't tell you. But is it true love, in the rectum? That's what bothers me sometimes. Have I never known true love, after all? She too was an eminently flat woman and she moved with short stiff steps, leaning on an ebony stick. Perhaps she too was a man, yet another of them. But in that case surely our testicles would have collided, while we writhed. Perhaps she held hers tight in her hand, on purpose to avoid it. She favoured voluminous tempestuous shifts and petticoats and other undergarments whose names I forget. They welled up all frothing and swishing and then, congress achieved, broke over us in slow cascades. And all I could see was her taut yellow nape which every now and then I set my teeth in, forgetting I had none, such is the power of instinct. We met in a rubbish dump, unlike any other, and yet they are all alike, rubbish dumps. I don't know what she was doing there. I was limply poking about in the garbage saying probably, for at that age I must still have been capable of general ideas, This is life. She had no time to lose, I had nothing to lose, I would have made love with a goat, to know what love was. She had a dainty flat, no, not dainty, it made you want to lie down in a corner and never get up again. I liked it. It was full of dainty furniture, under our desperate strokes the couch moved forward on its castors, the whole place fell about our ears, it was pandemonium. Our commerce was not without tenderness, with trembling hands she cut my toe-nails and I rubbed her rump with winter cream. This idyll was of short duration. Poor Edith, I hastened her end perhaps. Anyway it was she who started it, in the rubbish dump, when she laid her hand upon my fly. More precisely, I was bent double over a heap of muck, in the hope of finding something to disgust me for ever with eating, when she, undertaking me from behind, thrust her stick between my legs and began to titillate my privates. She gave me money after each session, to me who would have consented to know love, and probe it to the bottom, without charge. But she was an idealist. I would have preferred it seems to me an orifice less arid and roomy, that would have given me a higher opinion of love it seems to me. However. Twixt finger and thumb 'tis heaven in comparison. But love is no doubt above such base contingencies. And not when you are comfortable, but when your frantic member casts about for a rubbing-place, and the unction of a little mucous membrane, and meeting with none does not beat in retreat, but retains its tumefaction, it is then no doubt that true love comes to pass, and wings away, high above the tight fit and the loose. And when you add a little pedicure and massage, having nothing to do with the instant of bliss strictly speaking, then I feel no further doubt is justified, in this connection. The other thing that bothers me, in this connection, is the indifference with which I learnt of her death, one black night I was crawling towards her, an indifference softened indeed by the pain of losing a source of revenue. She died taking a warm tub, as her custom was before receiving me. It limbered her up. When I think she might have expired in my arms! The tub overturned and the dirty water spilt all over the floor and down on top of the lodger below, who gave the alarm. Well, well, I didn't think I knew this story so well. She must have been a woman after all, if she hadn't been it would have got around in the neighbourhood. It is true they were extraordinarily reserved, in my part of the world, about everything connected with sexual matters. But things have changed since my time. And it is quite possible that the fact of having found a man when they should have found a woman was immediately repressed and forgotten, by the few unfortunate enough to know about it. As it is quite possible that everybody knew about it, and spoke about it, with the sole exception of myself. But there is one thing that torments me, when I delve into all this, and that is to know whether all my life has been devoid of love or whether I really met with it, in Ruth. What I do know for certain is that I never sought to repeat the experience, having I suppose the intuition that it had been unique and perfect, of its kind, achieved and inimitable, and that it behoved me to preserve its memory, pure of all pastiche, in my heart, even if it meant my resorting from time to time to the alleged joys of so-called self-abuse. Don't talk to me about the chambermaid, I should never have mentioned her, she was long before, I was sick, perhaps there was no chambermaid, ever, in my life. Molloy, or life without a chambermaid.

Beckett views love with understanding and cynicism, not as a lasting relationship, but as moments of excitement or tenderness doomed in advance to failure except perhaps in memory where it becomes fixed and idealised. In *More Pricks Than Kicks*, his early short stories, his hero Belacqua has many love affairs, all doomed to embarrassing failure, humiliation or worse, as when Lucy, the girl he marries, falls from a horse, is crippled, and eventually dies. Murphy, hero of his first novel, whose life is based very much on Beckett's pre-war experiences and observations, mostly in London, lives with a prostitute, and his relationship to her is more voyeuristic than loving. Molloy's one erotic image is a memory of a chambermaid. The plays sometimes depict marriage, nostalgic love, but seldom sex. Only in *Play*, where a husband, his wife, and his mistress look back from a purgatorial existence on their past relationships, do we get any picture of sexual realism. Krapp, approaching his seventieth birthday which he believes will be his last, playing old tapes back to himself, recalls a long distant love and the memory of a brief moment of happiness, a summer afternoon in a punt with 'Effie'. In later years Beckett has written more about women than about men, usually from their point of view looking back to past love that seems to have been more often brutal than tender. But he understands passion, as is evidenced in his poem *Cascando*:

terrified again
of not loving
of loving and not you
of being loved and not by you

The concept of redemption through love is a strong one in Romantic literature and occurs frequently for instance in the work of Richard Wagner, in most of whose operas the hero is saved (from hell) by the love of a good woman. Although Beckett would hardly claim any affinity with Wagner, there is a strange resemblance in the star-crossed relationships of their heroes and heroines, and the ways they end or can be expected to end. Belacqua, Beckett's *alter ego* in *More Pricks Than Kicks*, whose presence or character is hinted at elsewhere in other books, is borrowed from Dante's *Purgatorio*, where he appears briefly at the end of Canto IV. A Florentine character, known to Dante, he was serving his time in purgatory for indolence and making little effort to get to heaven, believing he would not be admitted. He says:

'For me, shut out, first must the heavens rotate
So long as in my life their circlings were,
Because my good sighs I delayed so late,
Unless, ere that, there succour me a prayer
Rising out of a heart that lives in grace.
What profits pleading that Heaven will not hear?'*

Wagner's Flying Dutchman is released from his divine punishment, which was to roam the world in his phantom ship because of an ill-judged oath, by a girl who loved him enough to die for his sake. Elisabeth in Tannhäuser, Isolde, and Brünnhilde all die for love to bring about redemption, which ill accords with Wagner's real-life history. But Dante's Belacqua too sees himself as only entering Paradise through the intervention of another. Beckett's women, as love images, however tortured, all have some ideal quality requiring sacrifice; the gulf between carnality and the Romantic concept

*Dante, *The Divine Comedy*, tr. Laurence Binyon, Penguin Books.

of purity is a strange hangover from the Romantic age in Beckett's work, the lost love always more real than the possible present one.

I would like my love to die
and the rain to be raining on the graveyard
and on me walking the streets
mourning her who thought she loved me

Collected Poems

If Beckett's attitude to love is close to puritanical idealism, his approach to parenthood is even stranger. He depicts parents as criminals for bringing new life into the world. In *Endgame*, Hamm denounces his father as an 'accursed progenitor!' and Molloy says of his mother:

'I don't think too harshly of her. I know she did all she could not to have me, except of course the one thing, and if she never succeeded in getting me unstuck, it was that fate had earmarked me for less compassionate sewers.'

Molloy's account, given later in this volume, of his visit to his mother, although hilariously funny, is very cruel. Yet it is only by producing descendants that most people can be remembered. In one of his most provocative later plays, *Footfalls*, Beckett puts on stage a woman who may herself be a ghost who invents other ghosts who will remember her in turn, her own function being possibly to remember the mother who bore her, although perhaps not to the point of birth.

Footfalls is one of the more intriguing and indeed haunting of the later plays. The first scene is a dialogue between May, a woman of indeterminate middle age, who paces the stage rhythmically from left to right and back, and her mother, whose voice only is heard. The mother is old and ill but hears the footfalls of the child half her age whom she asks: 'Will you never have done . . . revolving it all?' 'It?' asks May. 'It all. (*Pause*.) In your poor mind,' says the mother. The overwhelming impression given is that May is an imaginary or long-dead child, who nevertheless has to bear the burden of remembering the mother's existence. The second scene discovers May facing the audience while the mother's voice talks of a child, May, creating her life story hesitantly out of details, but unconvincingly, and finally describes her pacing, with the mother quoting May, that 'I must hear the feet, however faint they fall.' In the third and final scene May is still facing the audience and relating a sequel:

'Sequel. A little later, when she was quite forgotten, she began to—

(*Pause.*) A little later, when as though she had never been, it never been, she began to walk. (*Pause.*) At nightfall.'

A description follows of how *she* would slip into a church at nightfall 'by the south door, always locked at that hour'. The presence could be seen in the church by a certain light. May then breaks into telling a story of old Mrs Winter going to church with her daughter who thinks she sees something undescribed, which her daughter Amy (anagram of May) fails to see. And in the final scene there is neither voice nor visible presence; the ghosts are dead. The whole disturbing play is apparently peopled by a series of ghosts who, as long as possible, invent other ghosts to keep alive the mother's memory into the future; the mother may already be dead and remembered by her daughter's ghost at the opening of the play, the daughter who perhaps never existed or was aborted, or else the mother may still be alive, but the daughter imaginary. A clue is given in the footsteps, seven in each direction, which in the original production were nine, later shortened to seven. It is difficult not to draw the conclusion that the reference was to the nine months of pregnancy and that this was shortened to suggest that the pregnancy did not go full term.

Ghosts always play a strong part in Samuel Beckett's work, but they are always memories during his early and middle periods and sometimes phantoms in the later work through which he has found a new way of expressing the need to have an identity, a continuing presence that is remembered. In . . . *but the clouds* . . . , a TV play written not long after *Footfalls*, the atmosphere is again ghostly, a man passing through a circle on stage remembering a woman's face, his voice describing his own spectral presence coming in, going out, 'crouching there, in my little sanctum, in the dark, where none could see me, I began to beg, of her, to appear, to me'. The title of the play comes from a line of Yeats, who in *The Tower*, one of his last poems, refers to

The death of friends, or death
Of every brilliant eye
That made a catch in the breath –
Seem but the clouds of the sky
When the horizon fades;
Or a bird's sleepy cry
Among the deepening shades

This is not just a nostalgia for remembered friends or lovers who have died, but the ghostly recreation of such persons to remember oneself, knowing one's own death is near. In *Ghost Sonata*, which uses Beethoven's music of that name, and where every non-human object in a man's small 'familiar chamber' is coffin-shaped, a man waits for someone, whom a woman's narrating voice calls 'her'. He listens to Beethoven on a cassette, but when someone comes it is instead a fresh-faced boy, who shakes his head, indicating that 'her' will not come, and that he represents future life; also that the man will be remembered after he has ceased to remember 'her'. In one of his most recent plays, *Ohio Impromptu*, so called because it was written for a Beckett seminar given at Ohio State University in 1981, Beckett shows two identical figures on stage: an old man, white-bearded, wearing a 'Latin Quarter hat', reading a narrative from a large book, which describes a person exactly like the reader – there is reference to a past love and 'the dear face'; the other figure at the table listens and occasionally knocks on the table, whereupon the reader goes back to read again the last phrase. The reading concludes with a description of a lonely man being visited by another bringing a message from 'the dear name', who would not come again. Nor would the messenger return. The reading exactly echoes the stage picture:

So the sad tale a last time told they sat on as though turned to stone. Through the single window dawn shed no light. From the street no sound of reawakening. Or was it that buried in who knows what thoughts they paid no heed? To light of day. To sound of reawakening. What thoughts who knows. Thoughts, no, not thoughts. Profounds of mind. Buried in who knows what profounds of mind. Of mindlessness. Whither no light can reach. No sound. So sat on as though turned to stone. The sad tale a last time told.

Beckett's ghost era with its stories within stories, persons within ghosts within memories, the still perfection that radiates within the writing, and his new muted tranquillity, is a long way from the grim and savage world of Molloy, or the almost hopeless stoicism of Vladimir in *Godot* (almost, because Beckett never pushes his pessimism to the absolute limit). But it is also a return in a new guise to that world of classical romanticism with Gothic overtones which Goethe and his contemporaries created, which had appealed to Beckett as a young man, and from which he distanced himself through his awareness of the horrors of war and perception of the nature of human cruelty. The atrocities of the Nazis are only an extension of everyday cruelties that most of us do not have the willingness to face. Goethe himself was much affected by his own near-death at the hands of Napoleon's troops after the battle of Jena, and certainly the disruption of Europe in the early nineteenth century contributed in Goethe's play to Faust's vision of the horrors of the world as he was shown it by Mephistopheles. It would be a mistake to try to draw too many parallels between

Goethe's life and Beckett's, but as young men they had many similarities; if *Wilhelm Meister* is fictionally based on Goethe's own experiences, it has an uncanny resemblance to many aspects of Beckett's life and attitudes. In honoured old age, each has shown an astonishing surge of new creative activity, and has finished or released work previously held back.

A new upsurge of power is evident in Beckett's two most recent prose texts or short novels, *Company* and *Ill Seen Ill Said*. In *Company* 'a voice comes to one in the dark. Imagine.' The voice that speaks is described by the hearer as it tells him about his past: 'Use of the second person marks the voice. That of the third that cankerous other. Could he speak to and of whom the voice speaks there would be a first.' The voice brings up childhood memories:

A small boy you come out of Connolly's Stores holding your mother by the hand. You turn right and advance in silence southward along the highway. After some hundred paces you head inland and broach the long steep homeward. You make ground in silence hand in hand through the warm still summer air. It is late afternoon and after some hundred paces the sun appears above the crest of the rise. Looking up at the blue sky and then at your mother's face you break the silence asking her if it is not in reality much more distant than it appears. The sky that is. The blue sky. Receiving no answer you mentally reframe your question and some hundred paces later look up at her face again and ask her if it does not appear much less distant than in reality it is. For some reason you could never fathom this question must have angered her exceedingly. For she shook off your little hand and made you a cutting retort you have never forgotten.

With the selectivity of memory whereby certain key moments in life, often without apparent importance, constantly come back to the mind's eye, Beckett unerringly sketches out a life and a personality. The inevitabilities of life, of which we are only dimly aware because of the common fallback on banality, such inevitabilities as for instance dawn and dusk, changing temperatures, remembered snatches of reading, the reality of those things the memory contains that the mind re-examines, become the important content of the writing. Ultimately, however real the voices that describe us to ourselves, that tell us what we know, we come to realise that the only reality is the recognition that everything is invented by the mind itself. Wisdom comes with age and it is the wisdom of knowing what to discard that is important, keeping that which is most real. In Beckett's case this means hearing the words diminish while every word acquires more value, like those grapes that German wine-growers leave on the vine to dry out in the autumn sun, which make the finest and sweetest Spaetlese.

Till finally you hear how words are coming to an end. With every inane word a little nearer to the last. And how the fable too. The fable of one with you in the dark. The fable of one fabling of one with you in the dark. And how better in the end labour lost and silence. And you as you always were.

Alone.

Company

Ill Seen Ill Said, the latest book-length short novel, is in one way less complex than *Company*, having only one voice, that of the seeing eye that describes an old woman who, from her bed or sitting in her chair, looks out of the window at the stars or the landscape. 'From where she lies she sees Venus rise.' For, of the three voices in *Company*, the first is listening to the voice, analysing the voice as from outside at a distance; the second is the voice itself telling the subject about himself, the 'company' in fact; and the third, if one heard it, would be answering the second. But all three voices are the same person and all come out of his consciousness. In *Ill Seen* the voice appears to be outside, observing, describing, but could do so only because of inner knowledge, that knowledge which proves the voice without is also the voice within; in other words Beckett is giving the self-observation of someone who does not know that she is observed. So is loneliness for the old: a series of voices that mock, analyse, observe, and carry out dialogues, that are all the same voice.

Loneliness has always been a prime Beckett preoccupation. In his early essay on Proust (1931), he insists that solitude is necessary to the artist. Solitude is not the same thing as loneliness, solitude being perhaps necessary to produce art which may consist of a literary presentation of loneliness that will say something new to the reader. And he has perfectly caught the essence of friendship, particularly in the relationship between Vladimir and Estragon, a mutual need that grows into genuine affection. In *Proust* he writes: 'For the artist who does not deal in surfaces, the rejection of friendship is not only reasonable, but a necessity.' That may be true of the prototype artist, although fifty years later such is Samuel Beckett's own talent for friendship that I doubt if he would still make the point so forcefully today, but his characters are of course not necessarily artists, in which lies much of their tragedy. (Tragedy often consists of the inability of the hero – from Sophocles to Beckett – to perceive the trap that life has set for them.) In *Waiting for Godot* both Vladimir and Estragon long to separate, but as though held by an elastic band are always brought back together because the risk of loneliness is too great. In *Endgame*, where Beckett makes his most potent statement about the rejection of inessentials, and where almost everything except life itself becomes ultimately inessential, Hamm, having thrown away his toy dog, the staff with which he is able to propel his wheelchair, and the whistle with which he can call for help, knowing that his parents have died or are dying, and believing his servant Clov has left him, prepares himself for the long wait for death with no prop left except his thoughts and a pocket handkerchief with which he can still shut out the light. He symbolises that human condition where man as possessor of goods, money, or property, man as enjoyer of technology, man as heir to political and social rights, is becoming increasingly obsolescent. Security is only a mirage; Beckett makes this clear and shows that it is not only possible to live without it, but necessary. If we expect nothing we may receive much more by it becoming possible to live in the world free of its encumbering possessions and becoming aware of its natural resources; aware above all that the greatest riches lie in the ability to use and stretch the mind. We must have the ability to discard, like Hamm facing his end (see page 225), or like the 'she' of *Ill Seen*:

Decision no sooner reached or rather long after than what is the wrong word? For the last time at last for to end yet again what the wrong word? Than revoked. No but slowly dispelled a little very little like the last wisps of day when the curtain closes. Of itself by slow millimetres or drawn by a phantom hand. Farewell to farewell. Then in that perfect dark foreknell darling sound pip for end begun. First last moment. Grant only enough remain to devour all. Moment by glutton moment. Sky earth the whole kit and boodle. Not another crumb of carrion left. Lick chops and basta. No. One moment more. One last. Grace to breathe that void. Know happiness.

This brilliantly poetic passage can be read two ways, as the protagonist savouring her coming last moment and resulting peace, but also as a world apocalypse bringing all life to an end. There is point in the ambiguity – both readings are valid.

I have tried to give some idea of Samuel Beckett's three creative periods as they can be seen retrospectively in his middle seventies, still strikingly productive and expanding in imaginative vocabulary. As a young man he was a mannerist, delighting in an eccentric use of language, portraying the world he observed but did not feel very much part of, exploiting the comic possibilities of human relationships and especially of love. Had he continued in that vein he would by now be a relatively popular, much praised, minority writer, specialising in black humour. The war changed all that and he emerged from it with much *gravitas* as a master of language comparable to Shakespeare, whose characters, with their activities and lives, had the power to carry a universal message. Shakespeare wrote of kings and princes who in their soliloquies reflect on, and enable us to understand, not only the traps that history sets for the strong, the ambitious, and the fortunate, but the innate tragedy that lies at the heart of all human endeavour and of life itself. The fate of kings and that of the common people whose destinies are determined by the activities of their rulers are not so very different in kind.

Beckett also produces characters of universal relevance with whom his readers can identify themselves once it is realised how deceptive is the outer envelope in which he wraps them. Vladimir, Molloy, Hamm, and Krapp are all personifications of twentieth-century man, struck by awareness of what their lives are about and uncannily prophetic as to where they – and we – are going. Beckett deceptively dresses them as tramps, solipsists, and seedy bachelors in solitary rooms. His female characters are women busily keeping up appearances or lying to themselves about their past, trying to find some relevance in memory. The reader will find himself or herself in these creations. Youth passes in a flash, then come the years of counting mistakes and coming to terms with a life that is not what was promised, and without the certainty of a better after-life that gave stability, in some sort, to medieval society. But Beckett does show that there is a consolation in the life of the mature mind that can look at life without blinkers or illusions, and overcome fear.

Between the second and third periods lie two great novels that carry him far above any other imaginative work written until then in technique, and, in content, beyond the shifting prophetic world of Kafka, the psychological under-the-microscope impressionism of Proust, and the all-embracing ubiquitous world of Joyce. *The Unnamable*, the last part of the trilogy, is the bridge between the second and third periods. It starts with a voice asking a series of questions. The voice is not that of Molloy, nor of the reduced, decrepit Moran, nor even of Malone, although all these names are mentioned and well known to the narrator. Probably they are all encompassed in his voice (the author's voice at one remove) as if they were his creation and he has invented their stories and the voices in which they tell them. That is to say, the voices of all the earlier characters have been invented or listened to by the voice in *The Unnamable*, which is the voice that Beckett is inventing while writing the book. Although there is not much incident in *The Unnamable*, there is some, and there are many characters. The whole breaks down in the last pages into complete panic, a thinking mind and a body that are dying or even dead, trying to shut out the silence and oblivion, aware of other silences, other stories, other minds, thinking. After the opening pages there are no paragraphs, and as the work approaches the end with increasing speed, there are no full stops, only commas to indicate the swift intake of breath before pushing out the next phrase. But Beckett never shuts the door totally, and the last three words are positive:

you must say words, as long as there are any, until they find me, until they say me, strange pain, strange sin, you must go on, perhaps it's done already, perhaps they have said me already, perhaps they have carried me to the threshold of my story, before the door that opens on my story, that would surprise me, if it opens, it will be I, it will be the silence, where I am, I don't know, I'll never know, in the silence you don't know, you must go on, I can't go on, I'll go on.

The Unnamable was finished in 1949. It belongs to the second creative period, but moves into the greater abstraction of the third. *How It Is* did not appear until the early 1960s, but it is very close to its predecessor, this time being the monologue of a creature crawling through a sea of mud that will pull him down if his efforts to stay afloat weaken, occasionally coming across others crawling through the same mud with whom some generalised, occasionally sexual, contact is made, while the mind thinks faster and faster, gasps for breath, breaks down into panic as it asks itself if its screams are heard and if the voice it sometimes imagines it hears answering is a real voice or not, finally subsiding into acceptance as no answer comes back. It is a more pessimistic novel than *The Unnamable*, but contains some of Beckett's most magnificent language. It must be read in short bursts of breath, as for instance: 'no more / I'll hear no more / old words / find a few more / not quite so old / . . . *or* wrong / for never twice the same / time / vast tracts / aged out of recognition / no / for often fresher / stronger after than before / unless sickness / follows / they sometimes pass'.

The following passage from Part III of *How It Is* has not only great forward drive that suggests the rhythm of the crawler, but contains powerfully effective imagery:

no more I'll hear no more see no more yes I must to make an end a few more old words find a few more not quite so old as when Pim part two those are done never were but old too vast stretch of time this voice these voices as if borne on all the winds but not a breath another antiquity a little more recent stop panting let it stop ten seconds fifteen seconds a few old words on and off string them together make phrases

a few old images always the same no more blue the blue is done never was the sack the arms the body the mud the dark living hair and nails all that my voice no objection back at last a voice back at last in my mouth my mouth no objection a voice at last in the dark the mud unimaginable tracts of time

this breath hold this breath be it held once twice per day and night the time that means to those under whom and all above and all about the earth turns and all turns who hasten so from one goal to the next that but for this breath I would fancy I hear their hastening feet hold it be it held ten seconds fifteen seconds try and hear

of this old tale quaqua on all sides then in me bits and scraps try and hear a few scraps two or three each time per day and night string them together make phrases more phrases the last how it was after Pim how it is something wrong there end of part three and last

this voice these voices no knowing not meaning a choir no no only one but quaqua meaning on all sides megaphones possibly technique something wrong there

wrong for never twice the same unless time vast tracts aged out of recognition no for often fresher stronger after than before unless sickness sorrow they sometimes pass one feels better less wretched after than before

unless recordings on ebonite or suchlike a whole life generations on ebonite one can imagine it nothing to prevent one mix it all up change the natural order play about with that

unless unchanging after all the voice we're talking of the voice and all my fault lack of attention want of memory the various times mixed up in my head all the various times before during after vast tracts of time

and always the same old thing the same old things possible and impossible or me my fault who can find nothing else when the panting stops hear nothing else the same old things four or five a few adornments life above little scenes

things said to me said of me to whom else of whom else clench the eyes try and see another to whom of whom to whom of me of whom to me or even a third clench the eyes try and see a third mix up all that

quaqua the voice of us all who all all those here before me and to come alone in this wallow or glued together all the Pims tormentors promoted victims past if it ever passes and to come that's sure more than ever by the earth undone its light all those

from it I learn from it I learnt what little remained learn what little remains of how it was before Pim with Pim after Pim and how it is for that too it found words

for how it would be when I had it no more before I had mine that vast pit and when I had it at last that vast stretch how it would be then when I had mine at last and when I had it no more mine no more how it would be then

the moment when I would need to say and could not mamma papa hear those sounds slake my thirst for labials and could not from then on words for that moment and following vast stretch of time

movements for nothing of the lower face no sound no word and then not even that no further point no more reliance to be placed on that when it's the last hope look for something else how it would be then words for that

from it all that of that so little what little remains I've named myself the panting stops and I am an instant that old ever dwindling little that I think I hear of an ancient voice quaqua on all sides the voice of us all as many as we are as many as we'll end if we ever end by having been something wrong there

namely days of great gaiety thicker than on earth since the age of gold above in the light the leaves fallen dead

some on the bough flutter on to the reawakening black dead flaunting in the green shit yes some in this condition manage two springs a summer and half three-quarters

before Pim the journey part one right leg right arm push pull ten yards fifteen yards halt nap a sardine or suchlike tongue in the mud an image or two little scenes mute words hang on off again push pull all that part one but before that again

another story leave it dark no the same story not two stories leave it dark all the same like the rest a little darker a few words all the same a few old words like for the rest stop panting let it stop

How It Is belongs to the third period in everything but its length (that of a standard novel). Thereafter Beckett's fictional texts have tended to be short, sometimes only a few pages boiled down from a long manuscript. One of the most evocative of these is *Imagination Dead Imagine*, which describes an enclosed space where two naked bodies are huddled, their knees drawn up to their chins, where the temperature rises and falls and the light with it, the whole perhaps hurtling through space, a metaphor not only for spaceship Earth, from which there is no escape, but more poignantly for an embodied mind that is helpless to do more than describe its environment. Others of these short texts are more anecdotal, brief episodes recounted, but always in a claustrophobic manner, suggesting that all is imaginary and contained inside the cavity of the skull (as all imaginative writing is until it is set down on the page). The memories themselves and the anecdotes lighten the texts for the reader so that he or she does not have to lose himself entirely in a world of geometrical description and introspection; there is always a human presence containing the mind that contains the voice, and we eventually reach the relative equanimity of the *Fizzles*, written at different times between 1960 and 1975, and the tranquillity of the work written around or after his seventieth birthday. Beckett's plays have always had an extraordinary visual impact; this is certainly true of the later ones, where the point of departure for the stage picture may have been some everyday sight that caught his eye and held his attention (as for instance a chef's head on a cardboard urn), or a painting where the light or the formal pattern for some reason attracted him as something he could use. In other cases he has produced parables: in *Lessness*, six narrators from six tribes try to describe a disaster that overtook them, their voices mingling together, but later separated by the author for a reading in a BBC radio broadcast; in *The Lost Ones* he pictures a hollow cylinder standing on its end with little people imprisoned inside, endlessly trying to climb ladders to reach the top or to escape, and burrowing into tunnels on the inside of the cylinder. They can be seen as parables of human existence, or, in the case of *Lessness*, a title that well depicts Mr Beckett's world, as a prophecy of a natural or a man-made Armageddon.

Samuel Beckett is thought of by some as an off-putting author because of the pessimism of his outlook, his concentration on the darker side of life, and the little attention given to life's pleasures, felicities, and, not least, to romantic love. In addition the grotesque or bizarre quality of his imagery, whether in creating stage pictures or conjuring up similar visions in the minds of his readers, puzzles the public, which is not accustomed to such a strong visual element in literature – plasticity is perhaps as important as music in his work. The answer to the first objection, that his vision is entirely black, is that the accusation is not true. Beckett does depict all aspects of life, although usually in a stylised and unconventional way, often puncturing the surface gaiety with a caustic aside, or lightening a grim scene with a flash of humour. His work is by no means lacking in erotic interest, indeed some of it has been considered pornographic in the past. (The odd four-letter word occurs, used selectively and usually unexpectedly for maximum effect.) The humour is legendary, whether in such asides as 'Thanks I suppose said the urchin as I picked up his marble', or 'The sun shone, having no alternative, on the nothing new', or 'Adulterers, take warning, never admit', or in such an early passage as this where the student Belacqua Shuah, walking through Dublin, meets another:

Painfully then under the College ramparts, past the smart taxis, he set off, clearing his mind for its song. The Fire Station worked without a hitch and all was going as well as could be expected considering what the evening held in pickle for him when the blow fell. He was run plump into by one Chas, a highbrow bromide of French nationality with a diabolical countenance compound of Skeat's and Paganini's and a mind like a tattered concordance. It was Chas who would not or could not leave well alone, Belacqua being rapt in his burning feet and the line of the song in his head.

'Halte-là' piped the pirate, 'whither so gay?'

In the lee of the Monumental Showroom Belacqua was obliged to pause and face this machine. It carried butter and eggs from the Hibernian Dairy. Belacqua however was not to be drawn.

'Ramble' he said vaguely 'in the twilight.'

'Just a song' said Chas 'at twilight. No?'

Belacqua tormented his hands in the gloom. Had he been blocked on his way and violated in the murmur of his mind to listen to this clockwork Bartlett? Apparently.

'How's the world' he said nevertheless, in spite of everything, 'and what's the news of the great world?'

'Fair' said Chas, cautiously, 'fair to meedling. The poem moves, eppure.'

If he mentions ars longa, Belacqua made this covenant with himself, he will have occasion to regret it.

'Limae labor' said Chas 'et mora.'

'Well' said Belacqua, casting off with clean hands, 'see you again.'

'But shortly, I thrrust' cried Chas, 'casa Frica, dis collied night. No?'

'Alas' said Belacqua, well adrift.

Behold the Frica, she visits talent in the Service Flats. In she lands, singing Havelock Ellis in a deep voice, frankly itching to work that which is not seemly. Open upon her concave breast as on a lectern lies Portigliotti's Penombre Claustrali, bound in tawed caul. In her talons earnestly she grasps Sade's 120 Days and the Anterotica of Aliosha G. Brignole-Sale, unopened, bound in shagreened caul. A septic pudding hoodwinks her, a stodgy turban of pain it laps her horse face. The eyehole is clogged with the bulbus, the round pale globe goggles exposed. Solitary meditation has furnished her with nostrils of generous bore. The mouth clamps an invisible bit, foam gathers at the bitter commissures. The crateriform brisket, lipped with sills of paunch, cowers ironically behind a maternity tunic. Keyholes have wrung the unfriendly withers, the osseous rump screams behind the hobble-skirt. Wastes of woad worsted advertise the pasterns. Aïe!

This in its absinthe whinny had bidden Belacqua and, what is more, the Alba, to backstairs, claret cup and the intelligentsia. The Alba, Belacqua's current one and only, had much pleasure in accepting for her scarlet gown and broad pale bored face. The belle of the ball. Aïe!

But seldom one without two and scarcely had Chas been shed than lo from out the Grosvenor sprang the homespun Poet wiping his mouth and a little saprophile of an anonymous politico-ploughboy setting him off. The Poet sucked his teeth over this unexpected pleasure. The golden eastern lay of his bullet head was muted by no covering. Beneath the Wally Whitmaneen of his Donegal tweeds a body was to be presumed. He gave the impression of having lost a harrow and found a figure of speech. Belacqua was numbed.

'Drink' decreed the Poet in a voice of thunder.

Belacqua slunk at his heels into the Grosvenor, the gimlet eyes of the saprophile probed his loins.

'Now' exulted the Poet, as though he had just brought an army across the Beresina, 'give it a name and knock it back.'

'Pardon me' stuttered Belacqua 'just a moment, will you be so kind.' He waddled out of the bar and into the street and up it at all speed and into the lowly public through the groceries door like a bit of dirt into a Hoover. This was a rude thing to do. When intimidated he was rude beyond measure, not timidly insolent like Stendhal's Comte de Thaler, but finally rude on the sly. Timidly insolent when, as by Chas, exasperated; finally rude on the sly when intimidated, outrageously rude behind the back of his oppressor. This was one of his little peculiarities.

'A Wet Night'

As for the Beckett imagery, it is most extraordinarily effective. Molloy, severly crippled, gets around on a bicycle with the help of crutches. Pozzo, in *Waiting for Godot*, is pulled along in the first act by a slave carrying his belongings (including a suitcase full of sand) by a rope around his neck, perhaps a wartime symbolic image of France. On stage it looks very striking. By the second act he has gone blind and Lucky the slave, capable in the first act of giving an erudite theological sermon on orders from his master, has unaccountably gone dumb. He was being taken to market to be sold in the first act, but Pozzo is totally dependent on him by the second. The master–slave relationship in all its aspects is cleverly portrayed, but Beckett sees no reason to explain to his audience the cause of the double misfortune, because life is full of such incidents which we take for granted, while to complain that life is unjust is a useless waste of breath. In a famous passage, Pozzo breaks into a tirade. Vladimir asks when he went blind and when Lucky went dumb.

POZZO: (*suddenly furious*). Have you not done tormenting me with your accursed time? It's abominable. When! When! One day, is that

37

not enough for you, one day like any other day, one day he went dumb, one day I went blind, one day we'll go deaf, one day we were born, one day we'll die, the same day, the same second, is that not enough for you? (*Calmer.*) They give birth astride of a grave, the light gleams an instant, then it's night once more.

Beckett always emphasises the shortness of life, often visualising birth and death as simultaneous events. Later in *Godot*, Vladimir picks up an image from Pozzo's speech in a soliloquy: 'Astride of a grave and a difficult birth. Down in the hole, lingeringly, the grave-digger puts on the forceps.' In one of his most poignant poems Beckett talks of

when I may cease from treading these long shifting thresholds
and live the space of a door
that opens and shuts

In the later work, however, this concept tends to disappear, and instead of shortening a lifetime into a second (or thirty seconds in the case of his short play *Breath*, where an amplified breath is drawn in and then exhaled while the lights go from black to bright and back again; a cry of birth is heard at full light and a death rattle at final blackout), he has instead lengthened the seconds after death to considerable length by giving voice to all the possibilities of thought continuing beyond death, portrayed most vividly in *The Unnamable* and the *Residua* (shorter texts of the third period), where physical life may well be extinguished but thought goes on. Much publicity was given in France in the 1950s to the question of how long cerebral life can outlast the stopping of the heart and clinical death. This followed experiments with the heads of guillotined murderers, who were often able to exhibit signs of consciousness through the eyes and control of the eyelids for several minutes after decapitation. Such a macabre discovery would have attracted the attention of Samuel Beckett and given an interesting new framework both to those of his monologues which continue beyond the point of death and to such stage works as *Play* where three heads set in jars are talking simultaneously and apparently endlessly, the voices weaker each time, but heard by the audience only when a light makes audible what is also seen. The light switches from face to face releasing fragments of three monologues concerning a not unusual but very comic situation between a man, his wife, and his mistress. For instance:

w2 (mistress): One morning as I was sitting stitching by the open window she burst in and flew at me. Give him up, she screamed, he's mine. Her photographs were kind to her. Seeing her now for the first time full length in the flesh I understood why he preferred me.

Or, after the reconciliation:

WI (wife): So he was mine again. All mine. I was happy again. I went
about singing. The world—
Spot from WI to M.
M (husband): At home all heart to heart, new leaf and bygones bygones.
I ran into your ex-doxy, she said one night, on the pillow, you're well
out of that. Rather uncalled for, I thought. I am indeed, sweetheart,
I said, I am indeed. God what vermin women. Thanks to you, angel,
I said.

Three heads perched on jars looking at the audience, a light flash-
ing on and off their faces, are without question a strange but
striking stage picture, perhaps derived from those French res-
taurants that show a chef's head perched on a cardboard urn. In
Endgame two of the characters, Hamm's parents, live in dustbins;
this is because they both lost their legs in a bicycling accident and
they are stuck on top of sawdust enabling them to talk to each
other and perform natural functions with the minimum of help. In
dramatic terms, it also means that they do not have to interrupt
the great concentration this play requires by making exits and
entrances. It is enough for Clov, Hamm's servant, to lift off the
dustbin lid to bring them into the conversational action or remove
them from it. In *Happy Days*, Winnie is embedded up to her waist
in a mound in the first act and up to her neck in the second, with
the obvious inference that she will be underground if the curtain
should rise a third time. Throughout the play she ignores her
predicament, of which she must be well aware, except for little
moments when her fear breaks through the keeping-up-appear-
ances cheerfulness. In *That Time*, a dying man is suspended ten
feet above the stage in such a way that we look at his exhausted
face with white hair spread out as if seeing him from above;
Beckett's use of a cinema technique greatly increases the effec-
tiveness of a powerful, but for him conventional, short play. In his
prose texts he describes naked figures, knees drawn up to the
chin, sitting inside a skull-like shape, described in detail, just big
enough to hold the body in that position, sometimes in darkness,
sometimes in light, in freezing cold or great heat. We have already
talked of the cylinder of *The Lost Ones*. Such images, with their
connotations of punishment, owe a great deal to his studies of
Dante at Trinity College, but Beckett's metaphorical visual trans-
formations and after-life visions are based on the imaginative use
of images that have caught his eye for literary purposes, while
Dante gave his imaginative thrust to Christian teaching. The minds
of the Florentine and the Dublin poet work in similar ways, picking
up the grotesque in life and translating it into art.

The reader will become aware of a very individual use of language, of inverted words that he will have no difficulty in understanding. Archaic word order, poetic conceits, echoes, and half-quotations abound, effectively adding life and colour to passages that apart from their content can be enjoyed as high style, although the author's intention has often been to abolish style because it gets in the way of the message and waters it down by giving the reader too many other things to distract him. But the magician is the slave of his own magic; Beckett can no more avoid giving pleasure through his use of words than he can write unoriginally, and all his attempts to avoid style have led him into new felicities.

Finally something must be said about Beckett the poet. All his work is poetry in a sense – literary poetry, visual poetry, and musical poetry – but he has also written enough in verse to be seen as an important poet in his own right. Here too he has written in English and in French, and he has made some astonishing translations and, in some cases, adaptations from French, Spanish, and German. He may well have translated work from other languages that no one has ever seen, because his drawers contain much work that he considers unfinished or unworthy of publication. His own self-criticism is justified in so far as work that he has reluctantly allowed to go into print because of the insistence of his friends and publishers usually falls considerably below the standard of his best, yet none of it is negligible or bad. A selection of poems is included in this volume, together with a few translations facing the originals to enable a comparison to be made. With the exception of the poems, which are arranged together in one section, this volume is organised as closely as possible in chronological order. The selections are representative, complete enough in themselves to be read and enjoyed as such, and to encourage wider reading. I hope the reader will discover through them the diversity of Beckett.

Earlier in this introduction I called the work of Samuel Beckett mannerist, and I sometimes describe him as a neo-mannerist. The best book I know on mannerist art, Arnold Hauser's *Mannerism*, contains the following definition.

A mannerist work of art is always a piece of bravura, a triumphant conjuring trick, a firework display with flying sparks and colours. The effect depends on the defiance of the obscure, the problematical, and the ambiguous, the incomplete nature of the manifest which points to its opposite, the latent, the missing link in the chain. Beauty too beautiful becomes unreal, strength too strong becomes acrobatics, too much content loses all meaning, form independent of content becomes an empty shell.

Hauser points out that mannerism belongs to periods of crisis and of transition; that we live in such an age is beyond dispute. Such a period produces a special kind of art to interpret the age, both to enable us to live in it with some resolution, whatever the nastiness we see about us, and, on occasion, to predict the dangers ahead in the hope that a warning will enable us to avoid or fend off some of them. Here is another remarkable insight of Hauser's:

Art may be altogether less an expression of inner peace, strength, and self-confidence, and of a direct, unproblematic relationship with life such as we meet in the fleeting moments of classical art, than a spontaneous, often wild and desperate, and sometimes barely articulate cry, the expression of an ungovernable urge to master reality, or of the feeling of being hopelessly and helplessly at its mercy.

Beckett's art, which this well describes, is perhaps not comfortable, and it is certainly not for the complacent or for those who cannot face reality.

The ability to think oneself out of and above the human condition separates the artist, the true philosopher, and the unfortunately few responsible scientists from the heedless, the selfish, and the ostrich-like. Beckett's work is at all times human, sometimes overpoweringly so, because every line is coloured with compassion, and if he is Promethean in his anger, it is not only because he is aware of the cruelty with which nature and natural selection create change and growth in Darwinian and Shavian terms, but even more because he well understands where man has outdone nature, in cruelty. Beckett feels for the world of animals as he does for the human world, because the capacity to suffer is universal. But once born we have to get through life. The power of Beckett's writing, the directness of his vision and understanding of human tragedy, and the dignity with which he, his characters, and by extension his readers are enabled to face that tragedy are an extraordinary phenomenon. Whatever horror life might produce, Beckett can help us to face it, and whatever the odds, Beckett never excludes hope.

There is a magic which is peculiar to art, by which suffering can be turned into joy, tragedy to laughter, and painful human experience into the kind of wisdom that makes life seem worth living after all. It is my contention that no one can read Beckett without undergoing a considerable change in outlook: observation is sharpened, awareness enhanced, and moral sense deepened, because this visionary, uncompromising writer makes it impossible for his public to avoid seeing the real world about us; he shames our baser instincts and admits us to that special circle of those enlightened enough to see what life lacks and what riches and pleasures are contained in his literature of lessness.

The Early
Work

More Pricks Than Kicks

These early short stories were first published in London in 1934, and for their time were considered decidedly odd; indeed, the title was too obscene for the book to be stocked by Irish booksellers. The author has made use of his very considerable erudition, his love of unusual and rarely used words, and gift for comic observation, to write what is really more a novel than a collection of linked short stories, concerning a young man in Dublin and the women in his life who either frighten, reject, humiliate him or in some other way blight his life. Certainly the author's description of Belacqua Shuah (see *Ding Dong* and the introduction) and his oddities resembles closely the splay-footed, handsome young aesthete described by people who knew Samuel Beckett as a young man. But resemblances should never be carried too far. 'Ding Dong' is one of the earlier stories and offers no difficulty to the reader. The deliberate pedantry of some of the style and vocabulary contrasts with unemotionally but touchingly described incidents like that of the little girl casually run down by a bus, and Belacqua's purchase of seats in heaven.

Ding Dong

My sometime friend Belacqua enlivened the last phase of his solipsism, before he toed the line and began to relish the world, with the belief that the best thing he had to do was to move constantly from place to place. He did not know how this conclusion had been gained, but that it was not thanks to his preferring one place to another he felt sure. He was pleased to think that he could give what he called the Furies the slip by merely setting himself in motion. But as for sites, one was as good as another, because they all disappeared as soon as he came to rest in them. The mere act of rising and going, irrespective of whence and whither, did him good. That was so. He was sorry that he did not enjoy the means to indulge this humour as he would have wished, on a large scale, on land and sea. Hither and thither on land and sea! He could not afford that, for he was poor. But in a small way he did what he could. From the ingle to the window, from the nursery to the bedroom, even from one quarter of the town to another, and back, these little acts of motion he was in a fair way of making, and they certainly did do him some good as a rule. It was the old story of the salad days, torment in the terms and in the intervals a measure of ease.

Being by nature however sinfully indolent, bogged in indolence, asking nothing better than to stay put at the good pleasure of what he called the Furies, he was at times tempted to wonder whether the remedy were not rather more disagreeable than the complaint. But he could only suppose that it was not, seeing that he continued to have recourse to it, in a small way it is true, but nevertheless for years he continued to have recourse to it, and to return thanks for the little good it did him.

The simplest form of this exercise was boomerang, out and back; nay, it was the only one that he could afford for many years. Thus it is clear that his contrivance did not proceed from any discrimination between different points in space, since he returned directly, if we except an occasional pause for refreshment, to his point of departure, and truly no less recruited in spirit than if the interval had been whiled away abroad in the most highly-reputed cities.

I know all this because he told me. We were Pylades and Orestes for a period, flattened down to something very genteel; but the relation abode and was highly confidential while it lasted. I have witnessed every stage of the exercise. I have been there when he set out, springing up and hastening away without as much as by your leave, impelled by some force that he did not care to gainsay. I have had glimpses of him enjoying his little trajectory. I have been there again when he returned, transfigured and transformed. It was very nearly the reverse of the author of the Imitation's 'glad out and sad coming in'.

He was at pains to make it clear to me, and to all those to whom he exposed his manoeuvre, that it was in no way cognate with the popular act of brute labour, digging and such like, exploited to disperse the dumps, an antidote depending for its efficaciousness on mere physical exhaustion, and for which he expressed the greatest contempt. He did not fatigue himself, he said; on the contrary. He lived a Beethoven pause, he said, whatever he meant by that. In his anxiety to explain himself, he was liable to come to grief. Nay, this anxiety in itself, or so at least it seemed to me, constituted a break-down in the self-sufficiency which he never wearied of arrogating to himself, a sorry collapse of my little internus homo, and alone sufficient to give him away as inept ape of his own shadow. But he wriggled out of everything by pleading that he had been drunk at the time, or that he was an incoherent person and content to remain so, and so on. He was an impossible person in the end. I gave him up in the end because he was not serious.

One day, in a positive geyser of confidence, he gave me an account of one of these 'moving pauses'. He had a strong weakness for oxymoron. In the same way he overindulged in gin and tonic-water.

Not the least charm of this pure blank movement, this 'gress' or 'gression', was its aptness to receive, with or without the approval of the subject, in all their integrity the faint inscriptions of the outer world. Exempt from destination, it had not to shun the unforeseen nor turn aside from the agreeable odds and ends of vaudeville that are liable to crop up. This sensitiveness was not the least charm of this roaming that began by being blank, not the least charm of this pure act the alacrity with which it welcomed defilement. But very nearly the least.

Emerging, on the particular evening in question, from the underground convenience in the maw of College Street, with a vague impression that he had come from following the sunset up the Liffey till all the colour had been harried from the sky, all the tulips and aerugo expunged, he squatted, not that he had too much drink taken but simply that for the moment there were no grounds for his favouring one direction rather than another, against Tommy Moore's plinth. Yet he durst not dally. Was it not from brooding shill I, shall I, dilly, dally, that he had come out? Now the summons to move on was a subpoena. Yet he found he could not, any more than Buridan's ass, move to right or left, backward or forward. Why this was he could not make out at all. Nor was it the moment for self-examination. He had experienced little or no trouble coming back from the Park Gate along the north quay, he had taken the Bridge and Westmoreland Street in his stride, and now he suddenly found himself good for nothing but to loll against the plinth of this bull-necked bard, and wait for a sign.

There were signs on all hands. There was the big Bovril sign to begin with, flaring beyond the Green. But it was useless. Faith, Hope and – what was it? – Love, Eden missed, every ebb derided, all the tides ebbing from the shingle of Ego Maximus, little me. Itself it went nowhere, only round and round, like the spheres, but mutely. It could not dislodge him now, it could only put ideas into his head. Was it not from sitting still among his ideas, other people's ideas, that he had come away? What would he not give now to get on the move again! Away from ideas!

Turning aside from this and other no less futile emblems, his attention was arrested by a wheel-chair being pushed rapidly under the arcade of the Bank, in the direction of Dame Street. It moved in and out of sight behind the bars of the columns. This was the blind paralytic was sat all day near to the corner of Fleet Street, and in bad weather under the shelter of the arcade, the same being wheeled home to his home in the Coombe. It was past his time and there was a bitter look on his face. He would give his chairman a piece of his mind when he got him to himself. This chairman, hireling or poor relation, came every evening a little before the dark, unfastened from the beggar's neck and breast the placard announcing his distress, tucked him up snugly in his coverings and wheeled him home to his supper. He was well advised to be assiduous, for this beggar was a power in the Coombe. In the morning it was his duty to shave his man and wheel him, according to the weather, to one or other of his pitches. So it went, day after day.

This was a star the horizon adorning if you like, and Belacqua made off at all speed in the opposite direction. Down Pearse Street, that is to say, long straight Pearse Street, its vast Barrack of Glencullen granite, its home of tragedy restored and enlarged, its coal merchants and Florentine Fire Brigade Station, its two Cervi saloons, ice-cream and fried fish, its dairies, garages and monumental sculptors, and implicit behind the whole length of its southern frontage the College. Perpetuis futuris temporibus duraturum. It was to be hoped so, indeed.

It was a most pleasant street, despite its name, to be abroad in, full as it always was with shabby substance and honest-to-God coming and going. All day the roadway was a tumult of buses, red and blue and silver. By one of these a little girl was run down, just as Belacqua drew near to the railway viaduct. She had been to the Hibernian Dairies for milk and bread and then she had plunged out into the roadway, she was in such a childish fever to get back in record time with her treasure to the tenement in Mark Street where she lived. The good milk was all over the road and the loaf, which had sustained no injury, was sitting up against the kerb, for all the world as though a pair of hands had taken it up and set it down there. The queue standing for the Palace Cinema was torn between conflicting desires: to keep their places and to see the excitement. They craned their necks and called out to know the worst, but they stood firm. Only one girl, debauched in appearance and swathed in a black blanket, fell out near the sting of the queue and secured the loaf. With the loaf under her blanket she sidled unchallenged down Mark Street and turned into Mark Lane. When she got back to the queue her place had been taken of course. But her sally had not cost her more than a couple of yards.

Belacqua turned left into Lombard Street, the street of the sanitary engineers, and entered a public-house. Here he was known, in the sense that his grotesque exterior had long ceased to alienate the curates and made them giggle, and to the extent that he was served with his drink without having to call for it. This did not always seem a privilege. He was tolerated, what was more, and let alone by the rough but kindly habitués of the house, recruited for the most part from among dockers, railwaymen and vague joxers on the dole. Here also art and love, scrabbling in dispute or staggering home, were barred, or, perhaps better, unknown. The aesthetes and the impotent were far away.

These circumstances combined to make of this place a very grateful refuge for Belacqua, who never omitted, when he found himself in its neighbourhood with the price of a drink about him, to pay it a visit.

When I enquired how he squared such visits with his anxiety to keep on the move and his distress at finding himself brought to a standstill, as when he had come out of the underground in the mouth of College Street, he replied that he did not. 'Surely' he said 'my resolution has the right to break down.' I supposed so indeed. 'Or' he said 'if you prefer, I make the raid in two hops instead of non-stop. From what' he cried 'does that disqualify me, I should very much like to know.' I hastened to assure him that he had a perfect right to suit himself in what, after all, was a manoeuvre of his own contriving, and that the raid, to adopt his own term, lost nothing by being made in easy stages. 'Easy!' he exclaimed, 'how easy?'

But notice the double response, like two holes to a burrow.

Sitting in this crapulent den, drinking his drink, he gradually ceased to see its furnishings with pleasure, the bottles, representing centuries of loving research, the stools, the counter, the powerful screws, the shining phalanx of the pulls of the beer-engines, all cunningly devised and elaborated to further the relations between purveyor and consumer in this domain. The bottles drawn and emptied in a twinkling, the casks responding to the slightest pressure on their joysticks, the weary proletarians at rest on arse and elbow, the cash-register that never complains, the graceful curates flying from customer to customer, all this made up a spectacle in which Belacqua was used to take delight and chose to see a pleasant instance of machinery decently subservient to appetite. A great major symphony of supply and demand, effect and cause, fulcrate on the middle C of the counter and waxing, as it proceeded, in the charming harmonies of blasphemy and broken glass and all the aliquots of fatigue and ebriety. So that he would say that the only place where he could come to anchor and be happy was a low public-house and that all the wearisome tactics of gress and dud Beethoven would be done away with if only he could spend his life in such a place. But as they closed at ten, and as residence and good faith were viewed as incompatible, and as in any case he had not the means to consecrate his life to stasis, even in the meanest bar, he supposed he must be content to indulge this whim from time to time, and return thanks for such sporadic mercy.

All this and much more he laboured to make clear. He seemed to derive considerable satisfaction from his failure to do so.

But on this particular occasion the cat failed to jump, with the result that he became as despondent as though he were sitting at home in his own great armchair, as anxious to get on the move and quite as hard put to it to do so. Why this was he could not make out. Whether the trituration of the child in Pearse Street had upset him without his knowing it, or whether (and he put forward this alternative with a truly insufferable complacency) he had come to some parting of the ways, he did not know at all. All he could say was that the objects in which he was used to find such recreation and repose lost gradually their hold upon him, he became insensible to them little by little, the old itch and algos crept back into his mind. He had come briskly all the way from Tommy Moore, and now he suddenly found himself sitting paralysed and grieving in a pub of all places, good for nothing but to stare at his spoiling porter and wait for a sign.

To this day he does not know what caused him to look up, but look up he did. Feeling the impulse to do this strong upon him, he forced his eyes away from the glass of dying porter and was rewarded by seeing a hatless woman advancing slowly towards him up the body of the bar. No sooner had she come in than he must have become aware of her. That was surely very curious in the first instance. She seemed to be hawking some ware or other, but what it was he could not see, except that it was not studs or laces or matches or lavender or any of the usual articles. Not that it was unusual to find a woman in that public-house, for they came and went freely, slaking their thirst and beguiling their sorrows with no less freedom than their menfolk. Indeed it was always a pleasure to see them, their advances were always most friendly and honourable, Belacqua had many a delightful recollection of their commerce.

Hence there was no earthly reason why he should see in the advancing figure of this mysterious pedlar anything untoward, or in the nature of the sign in default of which he was clamped to his stool till closing-time. Yet the impulse to do so was so strong that he yielded to it, and as she drew nearer, having met with more rebuffs than pence in her endeavours to dispose of her wares, whatever they were, it became clear to him that his instinct had not played him false, in so far at least as she was a woman of very remarkable presence indeed.

Her speech was that of a woman of the people, but of a gentle-woman of the people. Her gown had served its time, but yet contrived to be respectable. He noticed with a pang that she sported about her neck the insidious little mock fur so prevalent in tony slumland. The one deplorable feature of her get up, as apprehended by Belacqua in his hasty survey, was the footwear – the cruel strait outsizes of the suffragette or welfare worker. But he did not doubt for a moment that they had been a gift, or picked up in the pop for a song. She was of more than average height and well in flesh. She might be past middle-age. But her face, ah her face, was what Belacqua had rather refer to as her countenance, it was so full of light. This she lifted up upon him and no error. Brimful of light and serene, serenissime, it bore no trace of suffering, and in this alone it might be said to be a notable face. Yet like tormented faces that he had seen, like the face in the National Gallery in Merrion Square by the Master of Tired Eyes, it seemed to have come a long way and subtend an infinitely narrow angle of affliction, as eyes focus a star. The features were null, only luminous, impassive and secure, petrified in radiance, or words to that effect, for the reader is requested to take notice that this sweet style is Belacqua's. An act of expression, he said, a wreathing or wrinkling, could only have had the effect of a dimmer on a headlight. The implications of this triumphant figure, the just and the unjust, etc., are better forgone.

At long last she addressed herself to Belacqua.

'Seats in heaven' she said in a white voice 'tuppence apiece, four fer a tanner.'

'No' said Belacqua. It was the first syllable to come to his lips. It had not been his intention to deny her.

'The best of seats' she said 'again I'm sold out. Tuppence apiece the best of seats, four fer a tanner.'

This was unforeseen with a vengeance, if not exactly vaudeville. Belacqua was embarrassed in the last degree, but transported also. He felt the sweat coming in the small of his back, above his Montrouge belt.

'Have you got them on you?' he mumbled.

'Heaven goes round' she said, whirling her arm, 'and round and round and round and round.'

'Yes' said Belacqua 'round and round.'

'Rowan' she said, dropping the d's and getting more of a spin into the slogan, 'rowan an' rowan an' rowan.'

Belacqua scarcely knew where to look. Unable to blush he came out in this beastly sweat. Nothing of the kind had ever happened to him before. He was altogether disarmed, unsaddled and miserable. The eyes of them all, the dockers, the railwaymen and, most terrible of all, the joxers, were upon him. His tail drooped. This female dog of a pixy with her tiresome Ptolemy, he was at her mercy.

'No' he said 'no thank you, no not this evening thank you.'

'Again I'm sold out' she said 'an' buked out, four fer a tanner.'

'On whose authority . . .' began Belacqua, like a Scholar.

'For yer frien' ' she said 'yer da, yer ma an' yer motte, four fer a tanner.' The voice ceased, but the face did not abate.

'How do I know' piped Belacqua 'you're not sellin' me a pup?'

'Heaven goes rowan an' rowan . . .'

'Rot you' said Belacqua 'I'll take two. How much is that?'

'Four dee' she said.

Belacqua gave her a sixpence.

'Gobbless yer honour' she said, in the same white voice from which she had not departed. She made to go.

'Here' cried Belacqua 'you owe me twopence.' He had not even the good grace to say tuppence.

'Arragowan' she said 'make it four cantcher, yer frien', yer da, yer ma an' yer motte.'

Belacqua could not bicker. He had not the strength of mind for that. He turned away.

'Jesus' she said distinctly 'and his sweet mother preserve yer honour.'

'Amen' said Belacqua, into his dead porter.

Now the woman went away and her countenance lighted her to her room in Townsend Street.

But Belacqua tarried a little to listen to the music. Then he also departed, but for Railway Street, beyond the river.

Murphy

Only Iris Murdoch is known to have commented favourably on
Murphy when it was first published in 1938, and, as most of the
first edition was destroyed during the London blitz, not many
people outside the author's immediate circle can have read it.
Harold Pinter discovered a mint unread copy in a public library in
the 1950s, decided that having been untouched that long it was
meant for him, and took it. But since then *Murphy* has become a
cult book, one of Samuel Beckett's most widely read novels, and
is often considered the best introduction to his work for beginners.
As with much of his early writing, the author has given a fictional
substance to a philosophical concept. Murphy is intent on achiev-
ing a separation of mind and body to enter the state of *nirvana*
known by Eastern mystics and perhaps some Christian saints. He
does this by binding his naked body tightly to a chair and rocking
himself into the desired state. Interestingly, rocking chairs play a
significant role in some of Mr Beckett's later work, in *Rockaby* for
instance, where an old woman rocks herself towards death.

An entire chapter of *Murphy* is a description of his mind, which
is described as split from his body, although 'They had intercourse
apparently, otherwise he could not have known that they had
anything in common. But he felt his mind to be bodytight.' The
description of Murphy's mind is very like the enclosed spaces in
some of Beckett's later imaginative creations:

Murphy's mind pictured itself as a large hollow sphere, hermetically
closed to the universe without. This was not an impoverishment, for it
excluded nothing that it did not itself contain. Nothing ever had been,
was or would be in the universe outside it but was already present as
virtual, or actual, or virtual rising into actual, or actual falling into virtual,
in the universe inside it.

(Chapter 6)

The two chapters which follow are from the beginning of the
novel and describe Murphy's relationship with Celia, a prostitute
on whom he is entirely dependent, written in a comic style that is
on occasion reminiscent of other comic writers of the period, such
as Evelyn Waugh. Celia, an orphan, lives with her paternal grand-

father, who, while dependent on her earnings, derives some voyeuristic satisfaction – and dissatisfaction – from her accounts of her activities. Murphy's death at the end of the novel is also comically described, when he is accidentally blown up by a gas heater in the Magdalen Mental Mercyseat. When his will is read out it contains the following:

With regard to the disposal of these my body, mind and soul, I desire that they be burnt and placed in a paper bag and brought to the Abbey Theatre, Lr. Abbey Street, Dublin, and without pause into what the great and good Lord Chesterfield calls the necessary house, where their happiest hours have been spent, on the right as one goes down into the pit, and I desire that the chain be there pulled upon them, if possible during the performance of a piece, the whole to be executed without ceremony or show of grief.

On the way to carry out the instructions of the will after the cremation, Murphy's friend Cooper

got away from the Mercyseat with the parcel of ash under his arm. It must have weighed well on four pounds. Various ways of getting rid of it suggested themselves to him on the way to the station. Finally he decided that the most convenient and inconspicuous was to drop it in the first considerable receptacle for refuse that he came to. In Dublin he need only have sat down on the nearest bench and waited. Soon one of the gloomy dustmen would have come, wheeling his cart marked, 'Post your litter here.' But London was less conscious of her garbage, she had not given her scavenging to aliens.

He was turning into the station, without having met any considerable receptacle for refuse, when a burst of music made him halt and turn. It was the pub across the way, opening for the evening session. The lights sprang up in the saloon, the doors burst open, the radio struck up. He crossed the street and stood on the threshold. The floor was palest ochre, the pin-tables shone like silver, the quoits board had a net, the stools the high rungs that he loved, the whiskey was in glass tanks, a slow cascando of pellucid yellows. A man brushed past him into the saloon, one of the millions that had been wanting a drink for the past two hours. Cooper followed slowly and sat down at the bar, for the first time in more than twenty years.

'What are you taking, friend?' said the man.

'The first is mine,' said Cooper, his voice trembling.

Some hours later Cooper took the packet of ash from his pocket, where earlier in the evening he had put it for greater security, and threw it angrily at a man who had given him great offence. It bounced, burst, off the wall on to the floor, where at once it became the object of much dribbling, passing, trapping, shooting, punching, heading and even some recognition from the gentleman's code. By closing time the body, mind and soul of Murphy were freely distributed over the floor of the saloon; and before another dayspring greyened the earth had been swept away with the sand, the beer, the butts, the glass, the matches, the spits, the vomit.

Here are the two opening chapters of *Murphy*.

I

The sun shone, having no alternative, on the nothing new. Murphy sat out of it, as though he were free, in a mew in West Brompton. Here for what might have been six months he had eaten, drunk, slept, and put his clothes on and off, in a medium-sized cage of north-western aspect commanding an unbroken view of medium-sized cages of south-eastern aspect. Soon he would have to make other arrangements, for the mew had been condemned. Soon he would have to buckle to and start eating, drinking, sleeping, and putting his clothes on and off, in quite alien surroundings.

He sat naked in his rocking-chair of undressed teak, guaranteed not to crack, warp, shrink, corrode, or creak at night. It was his own, it never left him. The corner in which he sat was curtained off from the sun, the poor old sun in the Virgin again for the billionth time. Seven scarves held him in position. Two fastened his shins to the rockers, one his thighs to the seat, two his breast and belly to the back, one his wrists to the strut behind. Only the most local movements were possible. Sweat poured off him, tightened the thongs. The breath was not perceptible. The eyes, cold and unwavering as a gull's, stared up at an iridescence splashed over the cornice moulding, shrinking and fading. Somewhere a cuckoo-clock, having struck between twenty and thirty, became the echo of a street-cry, which now entering the mew gave *Quid pro quo! Quid pro quo!* directly.

These were sights and sounds that he did not like. They detained him in the world to which they belonged, but not he, as he fondly hoped. He wondered dimly what was breaking up his sunlight, what wares were being cried. Dimly, very dimly.

He sat in his chair in this way because it gave him pleasure! First it gave his body pleasure, it appeased his body. Then it set him free in his mind. For it was not until his body was appeased that he could come alive in his mind, as described in section six. And life in his mind gave him pleasure, such pleasure that pleasure was not the word.

Murphy had lately studied under a man in Cork called Neary. This man, at that time, could stop his heart more or less whenever he liked and keep it stopped, within reasonable limits, for as long as he liked. This rare faculty, acquired after years of application somewhere north of the Nerbudda, he exercised frugally, reserving it for situations irksome beyond endurance, as when he wanted a drink and could not get one, or fell among Gaels and could not escape, or felt the pangs of hopeless sexual inclination.

Murphy's purpose in going to sit at Neary's feet was not to develop the Neary heart, which he thought would quickly prove fatal to a man of his temper, but simply to invest his own with a little of what Neary, at that time a Pythagorean, called the Apmonia. For Murphy had such an irrational heart that no physician could get to the root of it. Inspected, palpated, auscultated, percussed, radiographed and cardiographed, it was all that a heart should be. Buttoned up and left to perform, it was like Petrushka in his box. One moment in such labour that it seemed on the point of seizing, the next in such ebullition that it seemed on the point of bursting. It was the mediation between these extremes that Neary called the Apmonia. When he got tired of calling it the Apmonia he called it the Isonomy. When he got sick of the sound of Isonomy he called it the Attunement. But he might call it what he liked, into Murphy's heart it would not enter. Neary could not blend the opposites in Murphy's heart.

Their farewell was memorable. Neary came out of one of his dead sleeps and said:

'Murphy, all life is figure and ground.'

'But a wandering to find home,' said Murphy.

'The face,' said Neary, 'or system of faces, against the big blooming buzzing confusion. I think of Miss Dwyer.'

Murphy could have thought of a Miss Counihan. Neary clenched his fists and raised them before his face.

'To gain the affections of Miss Dwyer,' he said, 'even for one short hour, would benefit me no end.'

The knuckles stood out white under the skin in the usual way – that was the position. The hands then opened quite correctly to the utmost limit of their compass – that was the negation. It now seemed to Murphy that there were two equally legitimate ways in which the gesture might be concluded, and the sublation effected. The hands might be clapped to the head in a smart gesture of despair, or let fall limply to the seams of the trousers, supposing that to have been their point of departure. Judge then of his annoyance when Neary clenched them again more violently than before and dashed them against his breast-bone.

'Half an hour,' he said, 'fifteen minutes.'

'And then?' said Murphy. 'Back to Teneriffe and the apes?'

'You may sneer,' said Neary, 'and you may scoff, but the fact remains that all is dross, for the moment at any rate, that is not Miss Dwyer. The one closed figure in the waste without form, and void! My tetrakyt!'

Of such was Neary's love for Miss Dwyer, who loved a Flight-Lieutenant Elliman, who loved a Miss Farren of Ringsakiddy, who loved a Father Fitt of Ballinclashet, who in all sincerity was bound to acknowledge a certain vocation for a Mrs West of Passage, who loved Neary.

'Love requited,' said Neary, 'is a short circuit,' a ball that gave rise to a sparkling rally.

'The love that lifts up its eyes,' said Neary, 'being in torment; that craves for the tip of her little finger, dipped in lacquer, to cool its tongue – is foreign to you, Murphy, I take it.'

'Greek,' said Murphy.

'Or put it another way,' said Neary; 'the single, brilliant, organized, compact blotch in the tumult of heterogeneous stimulation.'

'Blotch is the word,' said Murphy.

'Just so,' said Neary. 'Now pay attention to this. For whatever reason you cannot love— But there is a Miss Counihan, Murphy, is there not?'

There was indeed a Miss Counihan.

'Now say you were invited to define let us say your commerce with this Miss Counihan, Murphy,' said Neary. 'Come now, Murphy.'

'Precordial,' said Murphy, 'rather than cordial. Tired. Cork County. Depraved.'

'Just so,' said Neary. 'Now then. For whatever reason you cannot love in my way, and believe me there is no other, for that same reason, whatever it may be, your heart is as it is. And again for that same reason—'

'Whatever it may be,' said Murphy.

'I can do nothing for you,' said Neary.

'God bless my soul,' said Murphy.

'Just so,' said Neary. 'I should say your conarium has shrunk to nothing.'

He worked up the chair to its maximum rock, then relaxed. Slowly the world died down, the big world where *Quid pro quo* was cried as wares and the light never waned the same way twice; in favour of the little, as described in section six, where he could love himself.

A foot from his ear the telephone burst into its rail. He had neglected to take down the receiver. If he did not answer it at once his landlady would come running to do so, or some other lodger. Then he would be discovered, for his door was not locked. There was no means of locking his door. It was a strange room, the door hanging off its hinges, and yet a telephone. But its last occupant had been a harlot, long past her best, which had been scarlet. The telephone that she had found useful in her prime, in her decline she found indispensable. For the only money she made was when a client from the old days rang her up. Then she was indemnified for having been put to unnecessary inconvenience.

Murphy could not free his hand. Every moment he expected to hear the urgent step of his landlady on the stairs, or of some other lodger. The loud calm crake of the telephone mocked him. At last he freed a hand and seized the receiver, which in his agitation he clapped to his head instead of dashing to the ground.

'God blast you,' he said.

'He is doing so,' she replied. Celia.

He laid the receiver hastily in his lap. The part of him that he hated craved for Celia, the part that he loved shrivelled up at the thought of her. The voice lamented faintly against his flesh. He bore it for a little, then took up the receiver and said:

'Are you never coming back?'

'I have it,' she said.

'Don't I know,' said Murphy.

'I don't mean that,' she said, 'I mean what you told me—'

'I know what you mean,' said Murphy.

'Meet me at the usual at the usual,' she said. 'I'll have it with me.'

'That is not possible,' said Murphy. 'I expect a friend.'

'You have no friends,' said Celia.

'Well,' said Murphy, 'not exactly a friend, a funny old chap I ran into.'

'You can get rid of him before then,' said Celia.

'That is not possible,' said Murphy.

'Then I'll bring it round,' said Celia.

'You mustn't do that,' said Murphy.

'Why don't you want to see me?' said Celia.

'How often have I to tell you,' said Murphy, 'I—'

'Listen to me,' said Celia. 'I don't believe in your funny old chap. There isn't any such animal.'

Murphy said nothing. The self that he tried to love was tired.

'I'll be with you at nine,' said Celia, 'and I'll have it with me. If you're not there—'

'Yes,' said Murphy. 'Suppose I have to go out?'

'Goodbye.'

He listened for a little to the dead line, he dropped the receiver on the floor, he fastened his hand back to the strut, he worked up the chair. Slowly he felt better, astir in his mind, in the freedom of that light and dark that did not clash, nor alternate, nor fade nor lighten except to their communion, as described in section six. The rock got faster and faster, shorter and shorter, the iridescence was gone, the cry in the mew was gone, soon his body would be quiet. Most things under the moon got slower and slower and then stopped, a rock got faster and faster and then stopped. Soon his body would be quiet, soon he would be free.

II

Age	Unimportant
Head	Small and round
Eyes	Green
Complexion	White
Hair	Yellow
Features	Mobile
Neck	$13^3/_4''$
Upper arm	$11''$
Forearm	$9^1/_2''$
Wrist	$6''$
Bust	$34''$
Waist	$27''$
Hips, etc	$35''$
Thigh	$21^3/_4''$
Knee	$13^3/_4''$
Calf	$13''$
Ankle	$8^1/_4''$
Instep	Unimportant
Height	$5'\ 4''$
Weight	123 lb

She stormed away from the callbox, accompanied delightedly by her hips, etc. The fiery darts encompassing her about of the amorously disposed were quenched as tow. She entered the saloon bar of a Chef and Brewer and had a sandwich of prawn and tomato and a dock glass of white port off the zinc. She then made her way rapidly on foot, followed by four football pool collectors at four shillings in the pound commission, to the apartment in Tyburnia of her paternal grandfather, Mr Willoughby Kelly. She kept nothing from Mr Kelly except what she thought might give him pain, ie, next to nothing.

She had left Ireland at the age of four.

Mr Kelly's face was narrow and profoundly seamed with a lifetime of dingy, stingy repose. Just as all hope seemed lost it burst into a fine bulb of skull, unobscured by hair. Yet a little while and his brain–body ratio would have sunk to that of a small bird. He lay back in bed, doing nothing, unless an occasional pluck at the counterpane be entered to his credit.

'You are all I have in the world,' said Celia.

Mr Kelly nestled.

'You,' said Celia, 'and possibly Murphy.'

Mr Kelly started up in the bed. His eyes could not very well protrude, so deeply were they imbedded, but they could open, and this they did.

'I have not spoken to you of Murphy,' said Celia, 'because I thought it might give you pain.'

'Pain my rump,' said Mr Kelly.

Mr Kelly fell back in the bed, which closed his eyes, as though he were a doll. He desired Celia to sit down, but she preferred to pace to and fro, clasping and unclasping her hands, in the usual manner. The friendship of a pair of hands.

Celia's account, expurgated, accelerated, improved and reduced, of how she came to have to speak of Murphy, gives the following.

When her parents, Mr and Mrs Quentin Kelly died, which they did clinging warmly to their respective partners in the ill-fated *Morro Castle*, Celia, being an only child, went on the street. While this was a step to which Mr Willoughby Kelly could not wholeheartedly subscribe, yet he did not attempt to dissuade her. She was a good girl, she would do well.

It was on the street, the previous midsummer's night, the sun being then in the Crab, that she met Murphy. She had turned out of Edith Grove into Cremorne Road, intending to refresh herself with a smell of the Reach and then return by Lot's Road, when chancing to glance to her right she saw, motionless in the mouth of Stadium Street, considering alternately the sky and a sheet of paper, a man. Murphy.

'But I beseech you,' said Mr Kelly, 'be less beastly circumstantial. The junction for example of Edith Grove, Cremorne Road and Stadium Street, is indifferent to me. Get up to your man.'

She halted— 'Get away!' said Mr Kelly – set herself off in the line that his eyes must take on their next declension and waited. When his head moved at last, it was to fall with such abandon on his breast that he caught and lost sight of her simultaneously. He did not immediately hoist it back to the level at which she could be assessed in comfort, but occupied himself with his sheet. If on his eyes' way back to the eternities she were still in position, he would bid them stay and assess her.

'How do you know all this?' said Mr Kelly.

'What?' said Celia.

'All these demented particulars,' said Mr Kelly.

'He tells me everything,' said Celia.

'Lay off them,' said Mr Kelly. 'Get up to your man.'

When Murphy had found what he sought on the sheet he dispatched his head on its upward journey. Clearly the effort was considerable. A little short of halfway, grateful for the breather, he arrested the movement and gazed at Celia. For perhaps two minutes she suffered this gladly, then with outstretched arms began slowly to rotate – 'Brava!' said Mr Kelly – like the Roussel dummy in Regent Street. When she came full circle she found, as she had fully expected, the eyes of Murphy still open and upon her. But almost at once they closed, as for a supreme exertion, the jaws clenched, the chin jutted, the knees sagged, the hypogastrium came forward, the mouth opened, the head tilted slowly back. Murphy was returning to the brightness of the firmament.

Celia's course was clear: the water. The temptation to enter it was strong, but she set it aside. There would be time for that. She walked to a point about halfway between the Battersea and Albert Bridges and sat down on a bench between a Chelsea pensioner and an Eldorado hokey-pokey man, who had dismounted from his cruel machine and was enjoying a short interlude in paradise. Artists of every kind, writers, underwriters, devils, ghosts, columnists, musicians, lyricists, organists, painters and decorators, sculptors and statuaries, critics and reviewers, major and minor, drunk and sober, laughing and crying, in schools and singly, passed up and down. A flotilla of barges, heaped high with waste paper of many colours, riding at anchor or aground on the mud, waved to her from across the water. A funnel vailed to Battersea Bridge. A tug and barge, coupled abreast, foamed happily out of the Reach. The Eldorado man slept in a heap, the Chelsea pensioner tore at his scarlet tunic, exclaiming: 'Hell roast this weather, I shill niver fergit it.' The clock of Chelsea Old Church ground out grudgingly the hour of ten. Celia rose and walked back the way she had come. But instead of keeping straight on into Lot's Road, as she had hoped, she found herself dragged to the right into Cremorne Road. He was still in the mouth of Stadium Street, in a modified attitude.

'Hell roast this story,' said Mr Kelly, 'I shall never remember it.'

Murphy had crossed his legs, pocketed his hands, dropped the sheet and was staring straight before him. Celia now accosted him in form— 'Wretched girl!' said Kelly – whereupon they walked off happily arm-in-arm, leaving the star chart for June lying in the gutter.

'This is where we put on the light,' said Mr Kelly.

Celia put on the light and turned Mr Kelly's pillows.

From that time forward they were indispensable the one to the other.

'Hey!' exclaimed Mr Kelly, 'don't skip about like that, will you? You walked away happily arm-in-arm. What happened then?'

Celia loved Murphy, Murphy loved Celia, it was a striking case of love requited. It dated from that first long lingering look exchanged in the mouth of Stadium Street, not from their walking away arm-in-arm nor any subsequent accident. It was the condition of their walking away, etc, as Murphy had shown her many times in Barbara, Baccardi and Baroko, though never in Bramantip. Every moment that Celia spent away from Murphy seemed an eternity devoid of significance, and Murphy for his part expressed the same thought if possible more strongly in the words: 'What is my life now but Celia?'

On the following Sunday, the moon being at conjunction, he proposed to her in the Battersea Park sub-tropical garden, immediately following the ringing of the bell.

Mr Kelly groaned.

Celia accepted.

'Wretched girl,' said Mr Kelly, 'most wretched.'

Resting on Campanella's *City of the Sun*, Murphy said they must get married by hook or by crook before the moon came into opposition. Now it was September, the sun was back in the Virgin, and their relationship had not yet been regularized.

Mr Kelly saw no reason why he should contain himself any longer. He started up in the bed, which opened his eyes, as he knew perfectly well it would, and wanted to know the who, what, where, by what means, why, in what way and when. Scratch an old man and find a Quintilian.

'Who is this Murphy,' he cried, 'for whom you have been neglecting your work, as I presume? What is he? Where does he come from? What is his family? What does he do? Has he any money? Has he any prospects? Has he any retrospects? Is he, has he, anything at all?'

Taking the first point first, Celia replied that Murphy was Murphy. Continuing then in an orderly manner she revealed that he belonged to no profession or trade; came from Dublin— 'My God!' said Mr Kelly – knew of one uncle, a Mr Quigley, a well-to-do ne'er-do-well, resident in Holland, with whom he strove to correspond; did nothing that she could discern; sometimes had the price of a concert; believed that the future held great things in store for him; and never ripped up old stories. He was Murphy. He had Celia.

Mr Kelly mustered all his hormones.

'What does he live on?' he shrieked.

'Small charitable sums,' said Celia.

Mr Kelly fell back. His bolt was shot. The heavens were free to fall.

Celia now came to that part of her relation which she rather despaired of explaining to Mr Kelly, because she did not properly understand it herself. She knew that if by any means she could insert the problem into that immense cerebrum, the solution would be returned as though by clockwork. Pacing to and fro at a slightly faster rate, racking her brain which was not very large for the best way to say it, she felt she had come to an even more crucial junction in her affairs than that composed by Edith Grove, Cremorne Road and Stadium Street.

'You are all I have in the world,' she said.

'I,' said Mr Kelly, 'and possibly Murphy.'

'There is no one else in the world,' said Celia, 'least of all Murphy, that I could speak to of this.'

'You mollify me,' said Mr Kelly.

Celia halted, raised her clasped hands though she knew his eyes were closed and said:

'Will you please pay attention to this, tell me what it means and what I am to do?'

'Stop!' said Mr Kelly. His attention could not be mobilized like that at a moment's notice. His attention was dispersed. Part was with his caecum, which was wagging its tail again; part with his extremities, which were dragging anchor; part with his boyhood; and so on. All this would have to be called in. When he felt enough had been scraped together he said:

'Go!'

Celia spent every penny she earned and Murphy earned no pennies. His honourable independence was based on an understanding with his landlady, in pursuance of which she sent exquisitely cooked accounts to Mr Quigley and handed over the difference, less a reasonable commission, to Murphy. This superb arrangement enabled him to consume away at pretty well his own gait, but was inadequate for a domestic establishment, no matter how frugal. The position was further complicated by the shadows of a clearance area having fallen, not so much on Murphy's abode as on Murphy's landlady. And it was certain that the least appeal to Mr Quigley would be severely punished. 'Shall I bite the hand that starves me,' said Murphy, 'to have it throttle me?'

Surely between them they could contrive to earn a little. Murphy thought so, with a look of such filthy intelligence as left her, self-aghast, needing him still. Murphy's respect for the imponderables of personality was profound, he took the miscarriage of his tribute very nicely. If she felt she could not, why then she could not, and that was all. Liberal to a fault, that was Murphy.

'So far I keep abreast,' said Mr Kelly. 'There is just this tribute—'

'I have tried so hard to understand that,' said Celia.

'But what makes you think a tribute was intended?' said Mr Kelly.

'I tell you he keeps nothing from me,' said Celia.

'Did it go something like this?' said Mr Kelly. ' "I pay you the highest tribute that a man can pay a woman, and you throw a scene." '

'Hark to the wind,' said Celia.

'Damn your eyes,' said Mr Kelly, 'did he or didn't he?'

66

'It's not a bad guess,' said Celia.

'Guess my rump,' said Mr Kelly. 'It is the formula.'

'So long as one of us understands,' said Celia.

In respecting what he called the Archeus, Murphy did no more than as he would be done by. He was consequently aggrieved when Celia suggested that he might try his hand at something more remunerative than apperceiving himself into a glorious grave and checking the starry concave, and would not take the anguish on his face for an answer. 'Did I press you?' he said. 'No. Do you press me? Yes. Is that equitable? My sweet.'

'Will you conclude now as rapidly as possible,' said Mr Kelly. 'I weary of Murphy.'

He begged her to believe him when he said he could not earn. Had he not already sunk a small fortune in attempts to do so? He begged her to believe that he was a chronic emeritus. But it was not altogether a question of economy. There were metaphysical considerations, in whose gloom it appeared that the night had come in which no Murphy could work. Was Ixion under any contract to keep his wheel in nice running order? Had any provision been made for Tantalus to eat salt? Not that Murphy had ever heard of.

'But we cannot go on without any money,' said Celia.

'Providence will provide,' said Murphy.

The imperturbable negligence of Providence to provide goaded them to such transports as West Brompton had not know since the Earl's Court Exhibition. They said little. Sometimes Murphy would begin to make a point, sometimes he may have even finished making one, it was hard to say. For example, early one morning he said: 'The hireling fleeth because he is an hireling.' Was that a point? And again: 'What shall a man give in exchange for Celia?' Was that a point?

'Those were points undoubtedly,' said Mr Kelly.

When there was no money left and no bill to be cooked for another week, Celia said that either Murphy got work or she left him and went back to hers. Murphy said work would be the end of them both.

'Points one and two,' said Mr Kelly.

Celia had not been long back on the street when Murphy wrote imploring her to return. She telephoned to say that she would return if he undertook to look for work. Otherwise it was useless. He rang off while she was still speaking. Then he wrote again saying he was starved out and would do as she wished. But as there was no possibility of his finding in himself any reason for work taking one form rather than another, would she kindly procure a corpus of incentives based on the only system outside his own in which he felt the least confidence, that of the heavenly bodies. In Berwick Market there was a swami who cast excellent nativities for sixpence. She knew the year and date of the unhappy event, the time did not matter. The science that had got over Jacob and Esau would not insist on the precise moment of vagitus. He would attend to the matter himself, were it not that he was down to fourpence.

'And now I ring him up,' concluded Celia, 'to tell him I have it, and he tries to choke me off.'

'It?' said Mr Kelly.

'What he told me to get,' said Celia.

'Are you afraid to call it by its name?' said Mr Kelly.

'That is all,' said Celia. 'Now tell me what to do, because I have to go.'

Drawing himself up for the third time in the bed Mr Kelly said: 'Approach, my child.'

Celia sat down on the edge of the bed, their four hands mingled on the counterpane, they gazed at one another in silence.

'You are crying, my child,' said Mr Kelly. Not a thing escaped him.

'How can a person love you and go on like that?' said Celia. 'Tell me how it is possible.'

'He is saying the same about you,' said Mr Kelly.

'To his funny old chap,' said Celia.

'I beg your pardon,' said Mr Kelly.

'No matter,' said Celia. 'Hurry up and tell me what to do.'

'Approach, my child,' said Mr Kelly, slipping away a little from his surroundings.

'Damn it, I am approached,' said Celia. 'Do you want me to get in beside you?'

The blue glitter of Mr Kelly's eyes in the uttermost depths of their orbits became fixed, then veiled by the classical pythonic glaze. He raised his left hand, where Celia's tears had not yet dried, and seated it pronate on the crown of his skull – that was the position. In vain. He raised his right hand and laid the forefinger along his nose. He then returned both hands to their point of departure with Celia's on the counterpane, the glitter came back into his eye and he pronounced:

'Chuck him.'

Celia made to rise, Mr Kelly pinioned her wrists.

'Sever your connexion with this Murphy,' he said, 'before it is too late.'

'Let me go,' said Celia.

'Terminate an intercourse that must prove fatal,' he said, 'while there is yet time.'

'Let me go,' said Celia.

He let her go and she stood up. They gazed at each other in silence. Mr Kelly missed nothing, his seams began to work.

'I bow to passion,' he said.

Celia went to the door.

'Before you go,' said Mr Kelly, 'you might hand me the tail of my kite. Some tassels have come adrift.'

Celia went to the cupboard where he kept his kite, took out the tail and loose tassels and brought them over to the bed.

'As you say,' said Mr Kelly, 'hark to the wind. I shall fly her out of sight tomorrow.'

He fumbled vaguely at the coils of tail. Already he was in position, straining his eyes for the speck that was he, digging in his heels against the immense pull skyward. Celia kissed him and left him.

'God willing,' said Mr Kelly, 'right out of sight.'

Now I have no one, thought Celia, except possibly Murphy.

Watt

Written mostly during and finished after the war, *Watt* is similar
to *Murphy* in that it is a novel used as a framework to test out a
number of philosophical ideas given concrete form. Watt wanders
through the novel, finding himself in various situations which he
tries to reconcile with his own particular inability to believe anything from hearsay or even observed evidence. A Joycean influence is evident in the work, as in what might be considered a
reinterpretation of the surrealist scepticism of reality. Beckett
spreads himself over a larger canvas than in his earlier work and
he uses such quirky eccentricities as incorporating a group of
addenda at the end of *Watt* with phrases that he liked enough to
want to use but did not because 'fatigue and disgust prevented its
incorporation'. Watt is already one of Beckett's wandering heroes
moving in and out of various predicaments for reasons not clear
to the reader, more abstract as a personality than Murphy, a system of philosophical principles rather more than a human being,
and already showing some of the characteristics that would distinguish Molloy. The following extract recounts Watt's experiences
when he goes to work for Mr Knott, as a servant of sorts. Beckett
finds much comic opportunity for alliteration, comic rhyme and
wordplay. The incident of the Galls, father and son, destroys Watt's
faith in objective reality, and enables the author to engage in some
philosophical fun.

Mr Knott was a good master, in a way.

Watt had no direct dealings with Mr Knott, at this period. Not that Watt was ever to have any direct dealings with Mr Knott, for he was not. But he thought, at this period, that the time would come when he would have direct dealings with Mr Knott, on the first-floor. Yes, he thought that time would come for him, as he thought it had ended for Arsene, and for Erskine just begun.

For the moment all Watt's work was on the ground-floor. Even the first-floor slops that he emptied, it was Erskine who carried them down, every morning, in a pail. The first-floor slops could have been emptied, quite as conveniently, if not more conveniently, and the pail rinsed, on the first-floor, but they never were, for reasons that are not known. It is true that Watt had instructions to empty these slops, not in the way that slops are usually emptied, no, but in the garden, before sunrise, or after sunset, on the violet bed in violet time, and on the pansy bed in pansy time, and on the rose bed in rose time, and on the celery banks in celery time, and on the seakale pits in seakale time, and in the tomato house in tomato time, and so on, always in the garden, in the flower garden, and in the vegetable garden, and in the fruit garden, on some young growing thirsty thing at the moment of its most need, except of course in time of frost, or when the snow was on the ground, or when the water was on the ground. Then his instructions were to empty the slops on the dunghill.

But Watt was not so foolish as to suppose that this was the real reason why Mr Knott's slops were not emptied away on the first-floor, as they could so easily have been. This was merely the reason offered to the understanding.

It was remarkable that no such instructions existed touching the second-floor slops, that is to say, Watt's slops and Erskine's slops. These, when they had been carried down, Erskine's by Erskine, and Watt's by Watt, Watt was free to dispose of as he pleased.

But he was given nevertheless to understand that their commixture with those of the first-floor, if not formally forbidden, was not encouraged.

So Watt saw little of Mr Knott. For Mr Knott was seldom on the ground-floor, unless it was to eat a meal, in the dining-room, or to pass through it, on his way to and from the garden. And Watt was seldom on the first-floor, unless it was when he came down to begin his day, in the morning, and then again at evening, when he went up to begin his night.

Even in the dining-room Watt did not see Mr Knott, although Watt was responsible for the dining-room, and for the service there of Mr Knott's meals. The reasons for this may appear when the time comes to treat of that complex and delicate matter, Mr Knott's food.

This is not to say that Watt never saw Mr Knott at this period, for he did, to be sure. He saw him from time to time, passing through the ground-floor on his way to the garden from his quarters on the first-floor, and on his way back from the garden to his quarters, and he saw him also in the garden itself. But these rare appearances of Mr Knott, and the strange impression they made on Watt, will be described please God at greater length, at another time.

Callers were few. Tradesmen called, of course, and beggars, and hawkers. The postman, a charming man, called Severn, a great dancer and lover of greyhounds, seldom called. But he did sometimes, always in the evening, with his light eager step and his dog by his side, to deliver a bill, or a begging letter.

The telephone seldom rang, and when it did it was about some indifferent matter touching the plumbing, or the roof, or the food supplies, that Erskine could deal with, or even Watt, without troubling their master.

Mr Knott saw nobody, heard from nobody, as far as Watt could see. But Watt was not so foolish as to draw any conclusion from this.

But these fleeting acknowledgements of Mr Knott's establishment, like little splashes on it from the outer world and without which it would have been hard set to keep going, will it is to be hoped be considered in greater detail, later on, and how some were of moment to Watt, and how some were of none. In particular the appearance of the gardener, a Mr Graves, at the back door, twice and even three times every day, should be gone into with the utmost care, though there is little likelihood of its shedding any light on Mr Knott, or on Watt, or on Mr Graves.

But even there where there was no light for Watt, where there is none for his mouthpiece, there may be light for others. Or was there perhaps some light for Watt, on Mr Knott, on Watt, in such relations as those with Mr Graves, or with the fishwoman, that he left unspoken. That is by no means impossible.

Mr Knott never left the grounds, as far as Watt could judge. Watt thought it unlikely that Mr Knott could leave the grounds, without its coming to his notice. But he did not reject the possibility of Mr Knott's leaving the grounds, without his being any the wiser. But the unlikelihood, on the one hand of Mr Knott's leaving the grounds, and on the other of his doing so without exciting the general comment, seemed too very great, to Watt.

On only one occasion, during Watt's period of service on the ground-floor, was the threshold crossed by a stranger, by other feet that is than Mr Knott's, or Erskine's, or Watt's, for all were strangers to Mr Knott's establishment, as far as Watt could see, with the exception of Mr Knott himself, and his personnel at any given moment.

This fugitive penetration took place shortly after Watt's arrival. On his answering the door, as his habit was, when there was a knock at the door, he found standing before it, or so he realized later, arm in arm, an old man and a middle-aged man. The latter said:

We are the Galls, father and son, and we are come, what is more, all the way from town, to choon the piano.

They were two, and they stood, arm in arm, in this way, because the father was blind, like so many members of his profession. For if the father had not been blind, then he would not have needed his son to hold his arm, and guide him on his rounds, no, but he would have set his son free, to go about his own business. So Watt supposed, though there was nothing in the father's face to show that he was blind, nor in his attitude either, except that he leaned on his son in a way expressive of a great need of support. But he might have done this, if he had been halt, or merely tired, on account of his great age. There was no family likeness between the two, as far as Watt could make out, and nevertheless he knew that he was in the presence of a father and son, for had he not just been told so. Or were they not perhaps merely stepfather and stepson. We are the Galls, stepfather and stepson – those were perhaps the words that should have been spoken. But it was natural to prefer the others. Not that they could not very well be a true father and son, without resembling each other in the very least, for they could.

How very fortunate for Mr Gall, said Watt, that he has his son at his command, whose manner is all devotion and whose mere presence, when he might obviously be earning an honest penny elsewhere, attests an affliction characteristic of the best tuners, and justifies emoluments rather higher than the usual.

When he had led them to the music-room, and left them there, Watt wondered if he had done right. He felt he had done right, but he was not sure. Should he not perhaps rather have sent them flying about their business? Watt's feeling was that anyone who demanded, with such tranquil assurance, to be admitted to Mr Knott's house, deserved to be admitted, in the absence of precise instructions to the contrary.

The music-room was a large bare white room. The piano was in the window. The head, and neck, in plaster, very white, of Buxtehude, was on the mantelpiece. A ravanastron hung, on the wall, from a nail, like a plover.

After a short time Watt returned to the music-room, with a tray, of refreshments.

Not Mr Gall Senior, but Mr Gall Junior, was tuning the piano, to Watt's great surprise. Mr Gall Senior was standing in the middle of the room, perhaps listening. Watt did not take this to mean that Mr Gall Junior was the true piano-tuner, and Mr Gall Senior simply a poor blind old man, hired for the occasion, no. But he took it rather to mean that Mr Gall Senior, feeling his end at hand, and anxious that his son should follow in his footsteps, was putting the finishing touches to a hasty instruction, before it was too late.

While Watt looked round, for a place to set down his tray, Mr Gall Junior brought his work to a close. He reassembled the piano case, put back his tools in their bag, and stood up.

The mice have returned, he said.

The elder said nothing. Watt wondered if he had heard.

Nine dampers remain, said the younger, and an equal number of hammers.

Not corresponding, I hope, said the elder.

In one case, said the younger.

The elder had nothing to say to this.

The strings are in flitters, said the younger.

The elder had nothing to say to this either.

The piano is doomed, in my opinion, said the younger.

The piano-tuner also, said the elder.

The pianist also, said the younger.

This was perhaps the principal incident of Watt's early days in Mr Knott's house.

In a sense it resembled all the incidents of note proposed to Watt during his stay in Mr Knott's house, and of which a certain number will be recorded in this place, without addition, or subtraction, and in a sense not.

It resembled them in the sense that it was not ended, when it was past, but continued to unfold, in Watt's head, from beginning to end, over and over again, the complex connexions of its lights and shadows, the passing from silence to sound and from sound to silence, the stillness before the movement and the stillness after, the quickenings and retardings, the approaches and the separations, all the shifting detail of its march and ordinance, according to the irrevocable caprice of its taking place. It resembled them in the vigour with which it developed a purely plastic content, and gradually lost, in the nice processes of its light, its sound, its impacts and its rhythm, all meaning, even the most literal.

Thus the scene in the music-room, with the two Galls, ceased very soon to signify for Watt a piano tuned, an obscure family and professional relation, an exchange of judgments more or less intelligible, and so on, if indeed it had ever signified such things, and became a mere example of light commenting bodies, and stillness motion, and silence sound, and comment comment.

This fragility of the outer meaning had a bad effect on Watt, for it caused him to seek for another, for some meaning of what had passed, in the image of how it had passed.

The most meagre, the least plausible, would have satisfied Watt, who had not seen a symbol, nor executed an interpretation, since the age of fourteen, or fifteen, and who had lived, miserably it is true, among face values all his adult life, face values at least for him. Some see the flesh before the bones, and some see the bones before the flesh, and some never see the bones at all, and some never see the flesh at all, never never see the flesh at all. But whatever it was Watt saw, with the first look, that was enough for Watt, that had always been enough for Watt, more than enough for Watt. And he had experienced literally nothing, since the age of fourteen, or fifteen, of which in retrospect he was not content to say, That is what happened then. He could recall, not indeed with any satisfaction, but as ordinary occasions, the time when his dead father appeared to him in a wood, with his trousers rolled up over his knees and his shoes and socks in his hand; or the time when in his surprise at hearing a voice urging him, in terms of unusual coarseness, to do away with himself, he narrowly escaped being knocked down, by a dray; or the time when alone in a rowing-boat, far from land, he suddenly smelt flowering currant; or the time when an old lady of delicate upbringing, and advantageous person, for she was amputated well above the knee, whom he had pursued with his assiduities on no fewer than three distinct occasions, unstrapped her wooden leg, and laid aside her crutch. Here no tendency appeared, on the part of his father's trousers, for example, to break up into an arrangement of appearances, grey, flaccid and probably fistular, or of his father's legs to vanish in the farce of their properties, no, but his father's legs and trousers, as then seen, in the wood, and subsequently brought to mind, remained legs and trousers, and not only legs and trousers, but his father's legs and trousers, that is to say quite different from any of the legs and trousers that Watt had ever seen, and he had seen a great quantity, both of legs and of trousers, in his time. The incident of the Galls, on the contrary, ceased so rapidly to have even the paltry significance of two men, come to tune a piano, and tuning it, and exchanging a few words, as men will do, and going, that this seemed rather to belong to some story heard long before, an instant in the life of another, ill-told, ill-heard, and more than half forgotten.

So Watt did not know what had happened. He did not care, to do him justice, what had happened. But he felt the need to think that such and such a thing had happened then, the need to be able to say, when the scene began to unroll its sequences, Yes, I remember, that is what happened then.

This need remained with Watt, this need not always satisfied, during the greater part of his stay in Mr Knott's house. For the incident of the Galls father and son was followed by others of a similar kind, incidents that is to say of great formal brilliance and indeterminable purport.

Watt's stay in Mr Knott's house was less agreeable, on this account, than it would have been, if such incidents had been unknown, or his attitude towards them less anxious, that is to say, if Mr Knott's house had been another house, or Watt another man. For outside Mr Knott's house, and of course grounds, such incidents were unknown, or so Watt supposed. And Watt could not accept them for what they perhaps were, the simple games that time plays with space, now with these toys, and now with those, but was obliged, because of his peculiar character, to enquire into what they meant, oh not into what they really meant, his character was not so peculiar as all that, but into what they might be induced to mean, with the help of a little patience, a little ingenuity.

But what was this pursuit of meaning, in this indifference to meaning? And to what did it tend? These are delicate questions. For when Watt at last spoke of this time, it was a time long past, and of which his recollections were, in a sense, perhaps less clear than he would have wished, though too clear for his liking, in another. Add to this the notorious difficulty of recapturing, at will, modes of feeling peculiar to a certain time, and to a certain place, and perhaps also to a certain state of the health, when the time is past, and the place left, and the body struggling with quite a new situation. Add to this the obscurity of Watt's communications, the rapidity of his utterance and the eccentricities of his syntax, as elsewhere recorded. Add to this the material conditions in which these communications were made. Add to this the scant aptitude to receive of him to whom they were proposed. Add to this the scant aptitude to give of him to whom they were committed. And some idea will perhaps be obtained of the difficulties experienced in formulating, not only such matters as those here in question, but the entire body of Watt's experience, from the moment of his entering Mr Knott's establishment to the moment of his leaving.

But before passing from the Galls father and son to matters less litigious, or less tediously litigious, it seems advisable that the little that is known, on this subject, should be said. For the incident of the Galls father and son was the first and type of many. And the little that is known about it had not yet all been said. Much has been said, but not all.

Not that many things remain to be said, on the subject of the Galls father and son, for they do not. For only three or four things remain to be said, in this connexion. And three or four things are not really many, in comparison with the number of things that might have been known, and said, on this subject, and now never shall.

What distressed Watt in this incident of the Galls father and son, and in subsequent similar incidents, was not so much that he did not know what had happened, for he did not care what had happened, as that nothing had happened, that a thing that was nothing had happened, with the utmost formal distinctness, and that it continued to happen, in his mind, he supposed, though he did not know exactly what that meant, and though it seemed to be outside him, before him, about him, and so on, inexorably to unroll its phases, beginning with the first (the knock that was not a knock) and ending with the last (the door closing that was not a door closing), and omitting none, uninvoked, at the most unexpected moments, and the most inopportune. Yes, Watt could not accept, as no doubt Erskine could not accept, and as no doubt Arsene and Walter and Vincent and the others had been unable to accept, that nothing had happened, with all the charity and solidity of something, and that it revisited him in such a way that he was forced to submit to it all over again, to hear the same sounds, see the same lights, touch the same surfaces, and so on, as when they had first involved him in their unintelligible intricacies. If he had been able to accept it, then perhaps it would not have revisited him, and this would have been a great saving of vexation, to put it mildly. But he could not accept it, could not bear it. One wonders sometimes where Watt thought he was. In a culture-park?

But if he could say, when the knock came, the knock become a knock, on the door become a door, in his mind, presumably in his mind, whatever that might mean, Yes, I remember, that is what happened then, if then he could say that, then he thought that then the scene would end, and trouble him no more, as the appearance of his father with his trousers rolled up and his shoes and socks in his hands troubled him no more, because he could say, when it began, Yes, yes, I remember, that was when my father appeared to me, in the wood, dressed for wading. But to elicit something from nothing requires a certain skill and Watt was not always successful, in his efforts to do so. Not that he was always unsuccessful either, for he was not. For if he had been always unsuccessful, how would it have been possible for him to speak of the Galls father and son, and of the piano they had come all the way from town to tune, and of their tuning it, and of their passing the remarks they had passed, the one to the other, in the way he did? No, he could never have spoken at all of these things, if all had continued to mean nothing, as some continued to mean nothing, that is to say, right up to the end. For the only way one can speak of nothing is to speak of it as though it were something, just as the only way one can speak of God is to speak of him as though he were a man, which to be sure he was, in a sense, for a time, and as the only way one can speak of man, even our anthropologists have realized that, is to speak of him as though he were a termite. But if Watt was sometimes unsuccessful, and sometimes successful, as in the affair of the Galls father and son, in foisting a meaning there where no meaning appeared, he was most often neither the one, nor the other. For Watt considered, with reason, that he was successful, in this enterprise, when he could evolve, from the meticulous phantoms that beset him, a hypothesis proper to disperse them, as often as this might be found necessary. There was nothing, in this operation, at variance with Watt's habits of mind. For to explain had always been to exorcize, for Watt. And he considered that he was unsuccessful, when he failed to do so. And he considered that he was neither wholly successful, nor wholly unsuccessful, when the hypothesis evolved lost its virtue, after one or two applications, and had to be replaced by another, which in its turn had to be replaced by another, which in due course ceased to be of the least assistance, and so on. And that is what happened, in the majority of cases. Now to give examples of Watt's failures, and of Watt's successes, and of Watt's partial successes, in this connexion, is so to speak impossible. For when he speaks, for example, of the incident of the Galls father and son, does he speak of it in terms of the unique hypothesis that was required, to deal with it, and render it innocuous, or in terms of the latest, or in terms of some other of the series? For when Watt spoke of an incident of this kind, he did not necessarily do so in terms of the unique hypothesis, or of the latest, though this at first sight seems the only possible alternative, and the reason why he did not, why it is not, is this, that when one of the series of hypotheses, with which Watt laboured to preserve his peace of mind, lost its virtue, and had to be laid aside, and another set up in its place, then it sometimes happened that the hypothesis in question, after a sufficient period of rest, recovered its virtue and could be made to serve again, in the place of another, whose usefulness had come to an end, for the time being at least. To such an extent is this true, that one is sometimes tempted to wonder, with reference to two or even three incidents related by Watt as separate and distinct, if they are not in reality the same incident, variously interpreted. As to giving an example of the second event, namely the failure, that is clearly quite out of the question. For there we have to do with events that resisted all Watt's efforts to saddle them with meaning, and a formula, so that he could neither think of them, nor speak of them, but only suffer them, when they recurred, though it seems probable that they recurred no more, at the period of Watt's revelation, to me, but were as though they had never been.

Finally, to return to the incident of the Galls father and son, as related by Watt, did it have that meaning for Watt at the time of its taking place, and then lose that meaning, and then recover it? Or did it have some quite different meaning for Watt at the time of its taking place, and then lose that meaning, and then receive that, alone or among others, which it exhibited, in Watt's relation? Or did it have no meaning whatever for Watt at the moment of its taking place, were there neither Galls nor piano then, but only an unintelligible succession of changes, from which Watt finally extracted the Galls and the piano, in self-defence? These are most delicate questions. Watt spoke of it as involving, in the original, the Galls and the piano, but he was obliged to do this, even if the original had nothing to do with the Galls and the piano. For even if the Galls and the piano were long posterior to the phenomena destined to become them, Watt was obliged to think, and speak, of the incident, even at the moment of its taking place, as the incident of the Galls and the piano, if he was to think and speak of it at all, and it may be assumed that Watt would never have thought or spoken of such incidents, if he had not been under the absolute necessity of doing so. But generally speaking it seems probable that the meaning attributed to this particular type of incident, by Watt, in his relations, was now the initial meaning that had been lost and then recovered, and now a meaning quite distinct from the initial meaning, and now a meaning evolved, after a delay of varying length, and with greater or less pains, from the initial absence of meaning.

One more word on this subject.

Watt learned towards the end of his stay in Mr Knott's house to accept that nothing had happened, that a nothing had happened, learned to bear it and even, in a shy way, to like it. But then it was too late.

That then is that in which the incident of the Galls father and son resembled other incidents, of which it was merely the first in time, other incidents of note. But to say, as has been said, that the incident of the Galls father and son had this aspect in common with all the subsequent incidents of note, is perhaps to go a little too far. For not all the subsequent incidents of note, with which Watt was called upon to deal, during his stay in Mr Knott's house, and of course grounds, presented this aspect, no, but some meant something from the very beginning, and continued to mean it, with all the tenacity of, for example, the flowering currant in the rowing-boat, or the capitulation of the one-legged Mrs Watson, right up to the end.

As to that in which the incident of the Galls father and son differed from the subsequent incidents of its category, that is no longer clear, and cannot therefore be stated, with profit. But it may be taken that the difference was so nice as with advantage to be neglected, in a synopsis of this kind.

Watt thought sometimes of Arsene. He wondered what Arsene had meant, nay, he wondered what Arsene had said, on the evening of his departure. For his declaration had entered Watt's ears only by fits, and his understanding, like all that enters the ears only by fits, hardly at all. He had realized, to be sure, that Arsene was speaking, and in a sense to him, but something had prevented him, perhaps his fatigue, from paying attention to what was being said and from enquiring into what was being meant. Watt was now inclined to regret this, for from Erskine no information was to be obtained. Not that Watt desired information, for he did not. But he desired words to be applied to his situation, to Mr Knott, to the house, to the grounds, to his duties, to the stairs, to his bedroom, to the kitchen, and in a general way to the conditions of being in which he found himself. For Watt now found himself in the midst of things which, if they consented to be named, did so as it were with reluctance. And the state in which Watt found himself resisted formulation in a way no state had ever done, in which Watt had ever found himself, and Watt had found himself in a great many states, in his day. Looking at a pot, for example, or thinking of a pot, at one of Mr Knott's pots, of one of Mr Knott's pots, it was in vain that Watt said, Pot, pot. Well, perhaps not quite in vain, but very nearly. For it was not a pot, the more he looked, the more he reflected, the more he felt sure of that, that it was not a pot at all. It resembled a pot, it was almost a pot, but it was not a pot of which one could say, Pot, pot, and be comforted. It was in vain that it answered, with unexceptionable adequacy, all the purposes, and performed all the offices, of a pot, it was not a pot. And it was just this hairbreadth departure from the nature of a true pot that so excruciated Watt. For if the approximation had been less close, then Watt would have been less anguished. For then he would not have said, This is a pot, and yet not a pot, no, but then he would have said, This is something of which I do not know the name. And Watt preferred on the whole having to do with things of which he did not know the name, though this too was painful to Watt, to having to do with things of which the known name, the proven name, was not the name, any more, for him. For he could always hope, of a thing of which he had never known the name, that he would learn the name, some day, and so be tranquillized. But he could not look forward to this in the case of a thing of which the true name had ceased, suddenly, or gradually, to be the true name for Watt. For the pot remained a pot, Watt felt sure of that, for everyone but Watt. For Watt alone it was not a pot, any more.

Then, when he turned for reassurance to himself, who was not Mr Knott's, in the sense that the pot was, who had come from without and whom the without would take again,* he made the distressing discovery that of himself too he could no longer affirm anything that did not seem as false as if he had affirmed it of a stone. Not that Watt was in the habit of affirming things of himself, for he was not, but he found it a help, from time to time, to be able to say, with some appearance of reason, Watt is a man, all the same, Watt is a man, or, Watt is in the street, with thousands of fellow-creatures within call. And Watt was greatly troubled by this tiny little thing, more troubled perhaps than he had ever been by anything, and Watt had been frequently and exceedingly troubled, in his time, by this imperceptible, no, hardly imperceptible, since he perceived it, by this indefinable thing that prevented him from saying, with conviction, and to his relief, of the object

*Watt, unlike Arsene, had never supposed that Mr Knott's house would be his last refuge. Was it his first? In a sense it was, but it was not the kind of first refuge that promised to be the last. It occurred to him, of course, towards the end of his stay, that it might have been, that he might have made it, this transitory refuge, the last, if he had been more adroit, or less in need of rest. But Watt was very subject to fancies, towards the end of his stay under Mr Knott's roof. And it was also under the pressure of a similar eleventh hour vision, of what might have been, that Arsene expressed himself on this subject, in the way he did, on the night of his departure. For it is scarcely credible that a man of Arsene's experience could have supposed, in advance, of any given halt, that it was to be the last halt.

that was so like a pot, that it was a pot, and of the creature that still in spite of everything presented a large number of exclusively human characteristics, that it was a man. And Watt's need of semantic succour was at times so great that he would set to trying names on things, and on himself, almost as a woman hats. Thus of the pseudo-pot he would say, after reflexion, It is a shield, or, growing bolder, It is a raven, and so on. But the pot proved as little a shield, or a raven, or any other of the things that Watt called it, as a pot. As for himself, though he could no longer call it a man, as he had used to do, with the intuition that he was perhaps not talking nonsense, yet he could not imagine what else to call it, if not a man. But Watt's imagination had never been a lively one. So he continued to think of himself as a man, as his mother had taught him, when she said, There's a good little man, or, There's a bonny little man, or, There's a clever little man. But for all the relief that this afforded him, he might just as well have thought of himself as a box, or an urn.

It was principally for these reasons that Watt would have been glad to hear Erskine's voice, wrapping up safe in words the kitchen space, the extraordinary newel-lamp, the stairs that were never the same and of which even the number of steps seemed to vary, from day to day, and from night to morning, and many other things in the house, and the bushes without and other garden growths, that so often prevented Watt from taking the air, even on the finest day, so that he grew pale, and constipated, and even the light as it came and went and the clouds that climbed the sky, now slow, now rapid, and generally from west to east, or sank down towards the earth on the other side, for the clouds seen from Mr Knott's premises were not quite the clouds that Watt was used to, and Watt had a great experience of clouds, and could distinguish the various sorts, the cirrhus, the stratus, the tumulus and the various other sorts, at a glance. Not that the fact of Erskine's naming the pot, or of his saying to Watt, My dear fellow, or, My good man, or, God damn you, would have changed the pot into a pot, or Watt into a man, for Watt, for it would not. But it would have shown that at least for Erskine the pot was a pot, and Watt a man. Not that the fact of the pot's being a pot, or Watt's being a man, for Erskine, would have caused the pot to be a pot, or Watt to be a man, for Watt, for it would not. But it would perhaps have lent a little colour to the hope, sometimes entertained by Watt, that he was in poor health, owing to the efforts of his body to adjust itself to an unfamiliar milieu, and that these would be successful, in the end, and his health restored, and things appear, and himself appear, in their ancient guise, and consent to be named, with the time-honoured names, and forgotten. Not that Watt longed at all times for this restoration, of things, of himself, to their comparative innocuousness, for he did not. For there were times when he felt a feeling closely resembling the feeling of satisfaction, at his being so abandoned, by the last rats. For after these there would be no more rats, not a rat left, and there were times when Watt almost welcomed this prospect, of being rid of his last rats, at last. It would be lonely, to be sure, at first, and silent, after the gnawing, the scurrying, the little cries. Things and himself, they had gone with him now for so long, in the foul weather, and in the less foul. Things in the ordinary sense, and then the emptinesses between them, and the light high up before it reached them, and then the other thing, the high heavy hollow jointed unstable thing, that trampled down the grasses, and scattered the sand, in its pursuits. But if there were times when Watt envisaged this dereliction with something like satisfaction, these were rare, particularly in the early stages of Watt's stay in Mr Knott's house. And most often he found himself longing for a voice, for Erskine's, since he was alone with Erskine, to speak of the little world of Mr Knott's establishment, with the old words, the old credentials.

First Love

When Beckett started to write in French after the war, he was at first still close to the style of his earlier writing, although a new economy is evident in his style and the Irishness much less evident. Of the four novellas and one novel which can be considered a bridge between *Watt* and the *Trilogy*, *First Love* is the most straightforward and direct, an account of a brief love affair from which the narrator finally flees rather than face marital responsibilities. Comically semi-tragic, but more naturalistic than almost any other Beckett text, it is perhaps for its directness that publication was suppressed until 1970, when it first appeared in France, and 1973 in Britain.

I associate, rightly or wrongly, my marriage with the death of my father, in time. That other links exist, on other levels, between these two affairs, is not impossible. I have enough trouble as it is in trying to say what I think I know.

I visited, not so long ago, my father's grave, that I do know, and noted the date of his death, of his death alone, for that of his birth had no interest for me, on that particular day. I set out in the morning and was back by night, having lunched lightly in the graveyard. But some days later, wishing to know his age at death, I had to return to the grave, to note the date of his birth. These two limiting dates I then jotted down on a piece of paper, which I now carry about with me. I am thus in a position to affirm that I must have been about twenty-five at the time of my marriage. For the date of my own birth, I repeat, my own birth, I have never forgotten, I never had to note it down, it remains graven in my memory, the year at least, in figures that life will not easily erase. The day itself comes back to me, when I put my mind to it, and I often celebrate it, after my fashion, I don't say each time it comes back, for it comes back too often, but often.

Personally I have no bone to pick with graveyards, I take the air there willingly, perhaps more willingly than elsewhere, when take the air I must. The smell of corpses, distinctly perceptible under those of grass and humus mingled, I do not find unpleasant, a trifle on the sweet side perhaps, a trifle heady, but how infinitely preferable to what the living emit, their feet, teeth, armpits, arses, sticky foreskins and frustrated ovules. And when my father's remains join in, however modestly, I can almost shed a tear. The living wash in vain, in vain perfume themselves, they stink. Yes, as a place for an outing, when out I must, leave me my graveyards and keep – you – to your public parks and beauty-spots. My sandwich, my banana, taste sweeter when I'm sitting on a tomb, and when the time comes to piss again, as it so often does, I have my pick. Or I wander, hands clasped behind my back, among the slabs, the flat, the leaning and the upright, culling the inscriptions. Of these I never weary, there are always three or four of such drollery that I have to hold on to the cross, or the stele, or the angel, so as not to fall. Mine I composed long since and am still pleased with it, tolerably pleased. My other writings are no sooner dry than they revolt me, but my epitaph still meets with my approval. There is little chance unfortunately of its ever being reared above the skull that conceived it, unless the State takes up the matter. But to be unearthed I must first be found, and I greatly fear those gentlemen will have as much trouble finding me dead as alive. So I hasten to record it here and now, while there is yet time:

Hereunder lies the above who up below
So hourly died that he lived on till now.

The second and last or rather latter line limps a little perhaps, but that is no great matter, I'll be forgiven more than that when I'm forgotten. Then with a little luck you hit on a genuine interment, with real live mourners and the odd relict trying to throw herself into the pit. And nearly always that charming business with the dust, though in my experience there is nothing less dusty than holes of this type, verging on muck for the most part, nor anything particularly powdery about the deceased, unless he happed to have died, or she, by fire. No matter, their little gimmick with the dust is charming. But my father's yard was not among my favourite. To begin with it was too remote, way out in the wilds of the country on the side of a hill, and too small, far too small, to go on with. Indeed it was almost full, a few more widows and they'd be turning them away. I infinitely preferred Ohlsdorf, particularly the Linne section, on Prussian soil, with its nine hundred acres of corpses packed tight, though I knew no one there, except by reputation the wild animal collector Hagenbeck. A lion, if I remember right, is carved on his monument, death must have had for Hagenbeck the countenance of a lion. Coaches ply to and fro, crammed with widows, widowers, orphans and the like. Groves, grottoes, artificial lakes with swans, offer consolation to the inconsolable. It was December, I have never felt so cold, the eel soup lay heavy on my stomach, I was afraid I'd die, I turned aside to vomit, I envied them.

But to pass on to less melancholy matters, on my father's death I had to leave the house. It was he who wanted me in the house.

He was a strange man. One day he said, Leave him alone, he's not disturbing anyone. He didn't know I was listening. This was a view he must have often voiced, but the other times I wasn't by. They would never let me see his will, they simply said he had left me such a sum. I believed then and still believe he had stipulated in his will that I be left the room I had occupied in his lifetime and food brought me there, as hitherto. He may even have given this the force of condition precedent. Presumably he liked to feel me under his roof, otherwise he would not have opposed my eviction. Perhaps he merely pitied me. But somehow I think not. He should have left me the entire house, then I'd have been all right, the others too for that matter, I'd have summoned them and said, Stay, stay by all means, your home is here. Yes, he was properly had, my poor father, if his purpose was really to go on protecting me from beyond the tomb. With regard to the money it is only fair to say they gave it to me without delay, on the very day following the inhumation. Perhaps they were legally bound to. I said to them, Keep this money and let me live on here, in my room, as in Papa's lifetime. I added, God rest his soul, in the hope of melting them. But they refused. I offered to place myself at their disposal, a few hours every day, for the little odd maintenance jobs every dwelling requires, if it is not to crumble away. Pottering is still just possible, I don't know why. I proposed in particular to look after the hothouse. There I would have gladly whiled away the hours, in the heat, tending the tomatoes, hyacinths, pinks and seedlings. My father and I alone, in that household, understood tomatoes. But they refused. One day, on my return from stool, I found my room locked and my belongings in a heap before the door. This will give you some idea how constipated I was, at that juncture. It was, I am now convinced, anxiety constipation. But was I genuinely constipated? Somehow I think not. Softly, softly. And yet I must have been, for how otherwise account for those long, those cruel sessions in the necessary house? At such times I never read, any more than at other times, never gave way to revery or meditation, just gazed dully at the almanac hanging from a nail before my eyes, with its chromo of a bearded stripling in the midst of sheep, Jesus no doubt, parted the cheeks with both hands and strained, heave! ho! heave! ho!, with the motions of one tugging at the oar, and only one thought in my mind, to be back in my room and flat on my back again. What can that have been but constipation? Or am I confusing it with the diarrhoea? It's all a muddle in my head, graves and nuptials and the different varieties of motion. Of my scanty belongings they had made a little heap, on the floor, against the door. I can still see that little heap, in the kind of recess full of shadow between the landing and my room. It was in this narrow space, guarded on three sides only, that I had to change, I mean exchange my dressing-gown and nightgown for my travelling costume, I mean shoes, socks, trousers, shirt, coat, greatcoat and hat, I can think of nothing else. I tried other doors, turning the knobs and pushing, or pulling, before I left the house, but none yielded. I think if I'd found one open I'd have barricaded myself in the room, nothing less than gas would have dislodged me. I felt the house crammed as usual, the usual pack, but saw no one. I imagined them in their various rooms, all bolts drawn, every sense on the alert. Then the rush to the window, each holding back a little, hidden by the curtain, at the sound of the street door closing behind me, I should have left it open. Then the doors fly open and out they pour, men, women and children, and the voices, the sighs, the smiles, the hands, the keys in the hands, the blessed relief, the precautions rehearsed, if this then that, but if that then this, all clear and joy in every heart, come let's eat, the fumigation can wait. All imagination to be sure, I was already on my way, things may have passed quite differently, but who cares how things pass, provided they pass. All those lips that had kissed me, those hearts that had loved me (it is with the heart one loves, is it not, or am I confusing it with something else?), those hands that had played with mine and those minds that had almost made their own of me! Humans are truly strange. Poor Papa, a nice mug he must have felt that day if he could see me, see us, a nice mug on my account I mean. Unless in his great disembodied wisdom he saw further than his son whose corpse was not yet quite up to scratch.

But to pass on to less melancholy matters, the name of the woman with whom I was soon to be united was Lulu. So at least she assured me and I can't see what interest she could have had in lying to me, on this score. Of course one can never tell. She also disclosed her family name, but I've forgotten it. I should have made a note of it, on a piece of paper, I hate to forget a proper name. I met her on a bench, on the bank of the canal, one of the canals, for our town boasts two, though I never knew which was which. It was a well situated bench, backed by a mound of solid earth and garbage, so that my rear was covered. My flanks too, partially, thanks to a pair of venerable trees, more than venerable, dead, at either end of the bench. It was no doubt these trees one fine day, aripple with all their foliage, that had sown the idea of a bench, in someone's fancy. To the fore, a few yards away, flowed the canal, if canals flow, don't ask me, so that from that quarter too the risk of surprise was small. And yet she surprised me. I lay stretched out, the night being warm, gazing up through the bare boughs interlocking high above me, where the trees clung together for support, and through the drifting cloud, at a patch of starry sky as it came and went. Shove up, she said. My first movement was to go, but my fatigue, and my having nowhere to go, dissuaded me from acting on it. So I drew back my feet a little way and she sat. Nothing more passed between us that evening and she soon took herself off, without another word. All she had done was sing, beneath her breath, as to herself, and without the words fortunately, some old folk songs, and so disjointedly, skipping from one to another and finishing none, that even I found it strange. The voice, though out of tune, was not unpleasant. It breathed of a soul too soon wearied ever to conclude, that perhaps least arse-aching soul of all. The bench itself was soon more than she could bear and as for me, one look had been enough for her. Whereas in reality she was a most tenacious woman. She came back next day and the day after and all went off more or less as before. Perhaps a few words were exchanged. The next day it was raining and I felt in security. Wrong again. I asked her if she was resolved to disturb me every evening. I disturb you? she said. I felt her eyes on me. They can't have seen much, two eyelids at the most, with a hint of nose and brow, darkly, because of the dark. I thought we were easy, she said. You disturb me, I said, I can't stretch out with you there. The collar of my greatcoat was over my mouth and yet she heard me. Must you stretch out? she said. The mistake one makes is to speak to people. You have only to put your feet on my knees, she said. I didn't wait to be asked twice, under my miserable calves I felt her fat thighs. She began stroking my ankles. I considered kicking her in the cunt. You speak to people about stretching out and they immediately see a body at full length. What mattered to me in my dispeopled kingdom, that in regard to which the disposition of my carcass was the merest and most futile of accidents, was supineness in the mind, the dulling of the self and of that residue of execrable frippery known as the non-self and even the world, for short. But man is still today, at the age of twenty-five, at the mercy of an erection, physically too, from time to time, it's the common lot, even I was not immune, if that may be called an erection. It did not escape her naturally, women smell a rigid phallus ten miles away and wonder, How on earth did he spot me from there? One is no longer oneself, on such occasions, and it is painful to be no longer oneself, even more painful if possible than when one is. For when one is one knows what to do to be less so, whereas when one is not one is any old one irredeemably. What goes by the name of love is banishment, with now and then a postcard from the homeland, such is my considered opinion, this evening. When she had finished and my self been resumed, mine own, the mitigable, with the help of a brief torpor, it was alone. I sometimes wonder if that is not all invention, if in reality things did not take quite a different course, one I had no choice but to forget. And yet her image remains bound, for me, to that of the bench, not the bench by day, nor yet the bench by night, but the bench at evening, in such sort that to speak of the bench, as it appeared to me at evening, is to speak of her, for me. That proves nothing, but there is nothing I wish to prove. On the subject of the bench by day no words need be wasted, it never knew me, gone before morning and never back till dusk. Yes, in the daytime I foraged for food and marked down likely cover. Were you to inquire, as undoubtedly you itch, what I had done with the money my father had left me, the answer would be I had done nothing with it but leave it lie in my pocket. For I knew I would not be always young, and that summer does not last for ever either, not even autumn, my mean soul told me so. In the end I told her I'd had enough. She disturbed me exceedingly, even absent. Indeed she still disturbs me, but no worse now than the rest. And it matters nothing to me now, to be disturbed, or so little, what does it mean, disturbed, and what would I do with myself if I wasn't? Yes, I've changed my system, it's the winning one at last, for the ninth or tenth time, not to mention not long now, not long till curtain down, on disturbers and disturbed, no more tattle about that, all that, her and the others, the shitball and heaven's high halls. So you don't want me to come any more, she said. It's incredible the way they repeat what you've just said to them, as if they risked faggot and fire in believing their ears. I told her to come just the odd time. I didn't understand women at that period. I still don't for that matter. Nor men either. Nor animals either. What I understand best, which is not saying much, are my pains. I think them through daily, it doesn't take long, thought moves so fast, but they are not only in my thought, not all. Yes, there are moments, particularly in the afternoon, when I go all syncretist, à la Reinhold. What equilibrium! But even them, my pains, I understand ill. That must come from my not being all pain and nothing else. There's the rub. Then they recede, or I, till they fill me with amaze and wonder, seen from a better planet. Not often, but I ask no more. Catch-cony life! To be nothing but pain, how that would simplify matters! Omnidolent! Impious dream. I'll tell them to you some day none the less, if I think of it, if I can, my strange pains, in detail, distinguishing between the different kinds, for the sake of clarity, those of the mind, those of the heart or emotional conative, those of the soul (none prettier than these) and finally those of the frame proper, first the inner or latent, then those affecting the surface, beginning with the hair and scalp and moving methodically down, without haste, all the way down to the feet beloved of the corn, the cramp, the kibe, the bunion, the hammer toe, the nail ingrown, the fallen arch, the common blain, the club foot, duck foot, goose foot, pigeon foot, flat foot, trench foot and other curiosities. And I'll tell by the same token, for those kind enough to listen, in accordance with a system whose inventor I forget, of those instants when, neither drugged, nor drunk, nor in ecstasy, one feels nothing. Next of course she desired to know what I meant by the odd time, that's what you get for opening your mouth. Once a week? Once in ten days? Once a fortnight? I replied less often, far less often, less often to the point of no more if she could, and if she could not the least often possible. And the next day (what is more) I abandoned the bench, less I must confess on her account that on its, for the site no longer answered my requirements, modest though they were, now that the air was beginning to strike chill, and for other reasons better not wasted on cunts like you, and took refuge in a deserted cowshed marked on one of my forays. It stood in the corner of a field richer on the surface in nettles than in grass and in mud than in nettles, but whose subsoil was perhaps possessed of exceptional qualities. It was in this byre, littered with dry and hollow cowclaps subsiding with a sigh at the poke of my finger, that for the first time in my life, and I would not hesitate to say the last if I had not to husband my cyanide, I had to contend with a feeling which gradually assumed, to my dismay, the dread name of love. What constitutes the charm of our country, apart of course from its scant population, and this without help of the meanest contraceptive, is that all is derelict, with the sole exception of history's ancient faeces. These are ardently sought after, stuffed and carried in procession. Wherever nauseated time has dropped a nice fat turd you will find our patriots, sniffing it up on all fours, their faces on fire. Elysium of the roofless. Hence my happiness at last. Lie down, all seems to say, lie down and stay down. I see no connexion between these remarks. But that one exists, and even more than one, I have little doubt, for my part. But what? Which? Yes, I loved her, it's the name I gave, still give alas, to what I was doing then. I had nothing to go by, having never loved before, but of course had heard of the thing, at home, in school, in brothel and at church, and read romances, in prose and verse, under the guidance of my tutor, in six or seven languages, both dead and living, in which it was handled at length. I was therefore in a position, in spite of all, to put a label on what I was about when I found myself inscribing the letters of Lulu in an old heifer pat or flat on my face in the mud under the moon trying to tear up the nettles by the roots. They were giant nettles, some full three foot high, to tear them up assuaged my pain, and yet it's not like me to do that to weeds, on the contrary, I'd smother them in manure if I had any. Flowers are a different matter. Love brings out the worst in man and no error. But what kind of love was this, exactly? Love-passion? Somehow I think not. That's the priapic one, is it not? Or is this a different variety? There are so many, are there not? All equally if not more delicious, are they not? Platonic love, for example, there's another just occurs to me. It's disinterested. Perhaps I loved her with a platonic love? But somehow I think not. Would I have been tracing her name in old cowshit if my love had been pure and disinterested? And with my devil's finger into the bargain, when I then sucked. Come now! My thoughts were all of Lulu, if that doesn't give you some idea nothing will. Anyhow I'm sick and tired of this name Lulu, I'll give her another, more like her, Anna for example, it's not more like her but no matter. I thought of Anna then, I who had learnt to think of nothing, nothing except my pains, a quick think through, and of what steps to take not to perish off-hand of hunger; or cold, or shame, but never on any account of living beings as such (I wonder what that means) whatever I may have said, or may still say, to the contrary or otherwise, on this subject. But I have always spoken, no doubt always shall, of things that never existed, or that existed if you insist, no doubt always will, but not with the existence I ascribe to them. Kepis, for example, exist beyond a doubt, indeed there is little hope of their ever disappearing, but personally I never wore a kepi. I wrote somewhere, They gave me . . . a hat. Now the truth is they never gave me a hat, I have always had my own hat, the one my father gave me, and I have never had any other hat than that hat. I may add it has followed me to the grave. I thought of Anna then, long long sessions, twenty minutes, twenty-five minutes and even as long as half an hour daily. I obtain these figures by the addition of other, lesser figures. That must have been my way of loving. Are we to infer from this I loved her with that intellectual love which drew from me such drivel, in another place? Somehow I think not. For had my love been of this kind would I have stooped to inscribe the letters of Anna in time's forgotten cowplats? To divellicate urtica *plenis manibus*? And felt, under my tossing head, her thighs to bounce like so many demon bolsters? Come now! In order to put an end, to try and put an end, to this plight, I returned one evening to the bench, at the hour she had used to join me there. There was no sign of her and I waited in vain. It was December already, if not January, and the cold was seasonable, that is to say reasonable, like all that is seasonable. But one is the hour of the dial, and another that of changing air and sky, and another yet again the heart's. To this thought, once back in the straw, I owed an excellent night. The next day I was earlier to the bench, much earlier, night having barely fallen, winter night, and yet too late, for she was there already, on the bench, under the boughs tinkling with rime, her back to the frosted mound, facing the icy water. I told you she was a highly tenacious woman. I felt nothing. What interest could she have in pursuing me thus? I asked her, without sitting down, stumping to and fro. The cold had embossed the path. She replied she didn't know. What could she see in me, would she kindly tell me that at least, if she could. She replied she couldn't. She seemed warmly clad, her hands buried in a muff. As I looked at this muff, I remember, tears came to my eyes. And yet I forget what colour it was. The state I was in then! I have always wept freely, without the least benefit to myself, till recently. If I had to weep this minute I could squeeze till I was blue, I'm convinced not a drop would fall. The state I am in now! It was things made me weep. And yet I felt no sorrow. When I found myself in tears for no apparent reason it meant I had caught sight of something unbeknownst. So I wonder if it was really the muff that evening, if it was not rather the path, so iron hard and bossy as perhaps to feel like cobbles to my tread, or some other thing, some chance thing glimpsed below the threshold, that so unmanned me. As for her, I might as well never have laid eyes on her before. She sat all huddled and muffled up, her head sunk, the muff with her hands in her lap, her legs pressed tight together, her heels clear of the ground. Shapeless, ageless, almost lifeless, it might have been anything or anyone, an old woman or a little girl. And the way she kept on saying, I don't know, I can't. I alone did not know and could not. Is it on my account you came? I said. She managed yes to that. Well here I am, I said. And I? Had I not come on hers? Here we are, I said. I sat down beside her but sprang up again immediately as though scalded. I longed to be gone, to know if it was over. But before going, to be on the safe side, I asked her to sing me a song. I thought at first she was going to refuse, I mean simply not sing, but no, after a moment she began to sing and sang for some time, all the time the same song it seemed to me, without change of attitude. I did not know the song, I had never heard it before and shall never hear it again. It had something to do with lemon trees, or orange trees, I forget, that is all I remember, and for me that is no mean feat, to remember it had something to do with lemon trees, or orange trees, I forget, for of all the other songs I have ever heard in my life, and I have heard plenty, it being apparently impossible, physically impossible short of being deaf, to get through this world, even my way, without hearing singing, I have retained nothing, not a word, not a note, or so few words, so few notes, that, that what, that nothing, this sentence has gone on long enough. Then I started to go and as I went I heard her singing another song, or perhaps more verses of the same, fainter and fainter the further I went, then no more, either because she had come to an end or because I was gone too far to hear her. To have to harbour such a doubt was something I preferred to avoid, at that period. I lived of course in doubt, on doubt, but such trivial doubts as this, purely somatic as some say, were best cleared up without delay, they could nag at me like gnats for weeks on end. So I retraced my steps a little way and stopped. At first I heard nothing, then the voice again, but only just, so faintly did it carry. First I didn't hear it, then I did, I must therefore have begun hearing it, at a certain point, but no, there was no beginning, the sound emerged so softly from the silence and so resembled it. When the voice ceased at last I approached a little nearer, to make sure it had really ceased and not merely been lowered. Then in despair, saying, No knowing, no knowing, short of being beside her, bent over her, I turned on my heel and went, for good, full of doubt. But some weeks later, even more dead than alive than usual, I returned to the bench, for the fourth or fifth time since I had abandoned it, at roughly the same hour, I mean roughly the same sky, no, I don't mean that either, for it's always the same sky and never the same sky, what words are there for that, none I know, period. She wasn't there, then suddenly she was, I don't know how, I didn't see her come, nor hear her, all ears and eyes though I was. Let us say it was raining, nothing like a change, if only of weather. She had her umbrella up, naturally, what an outfit. I asked if she came every evening. No, she said, just the odd time. The bench was soaking wet, we paced up and down, not daring to sit. I took her arm, out of curiosity, to see if it would give me pleasure, it gave me none, I let it go. But why these particulars. To put off the evil hour. I saw her face a little clearer, it seemed normal to me, a face like millions of others. The eyes were crooked, but I didn't know that till later. It looked neither young nor old, the face, as though stranded between the vernal and the sere. Such ambiguity I found difficult to bear, at that period. As to whether it was beautiful, the face, or had once been beautiful, or could conceivably become beautiful, I confess I could form no opinion. I had seen faces in photographs I might have found beautiful had I known even vaguely in what beauty was supposed to consist. And my father's face, on his death-bolster, had seemed to hint at some form of aesthetics relevant to man. But the faces of the living, all grimace and flush, can they be described as objects? I admired in spite of the dark, in spite of my fluster, the way still or scarcely flowing water reaches up, as though athirst, to that falling from the sky. She asked if I would like her to sing something. I replied no, I would like her to say something. I thought she would say she had nothing to say, it would have been like her, and so was agreeably surprised when she said she had a room, most agreeably surprised, though I suspected as much. Who has not a room? Ah I hear the clamour. I have two rooms, she said. Just how many rooms do you have? I said. She said she had two rooms and a kitchen. The premises were expanding steadily, given time she would remember a bathroom. Is it two rooms

I heard you say? I said. Yes, she said. Adjacent? I said. At last conversation worthy of the name. Separated by the kitchen, she said. I asked her why she had not told me before. I must have been beside myself, at this period. I did not feel easy when I was with her, but at least free to think of something else than her, of the old trusty things, and so little by little, as down steps towards a deep, of nothing. And I knew that away from her I would forfeit this freedom.

There were in fact two rooms, separated by a kitchen, she had not lied to me. She said I should have fetched my things. I explained I had no things. It was at the top of an old house, with a view of the mountains for those who cared. She lit an oil-lamp. You have no current? I said. No, she said, but I have running water and gas. Ha, I said, you have gas. She began to undress. When at their wit's end they undress, no doubt the wisest course. She took off everything, with a slowness fit to enflame an elephant, except her stockings, calculated presumably to bring my concupiscence to the boil. It was then I noticed the squint. Fortunately she was not the first naked woman to have crossed my path, so I could stay, I knew she would not explode. I asked to see the other room which I had not yet seen. If I had seen it already I would have asked to see it again. Will you not undress? she said. Oh you know, I said, I seldom undress. It was the truth, I was never one to undress indiscriminately. I often took off my boots when I went to bed, I mean when I composed myself (composed!) to sleep, not to mention this or that outer garment according to the outer temperature. She was therefore obliged, out of common savoir faire, to throw on a wrap and light me the way. We went via the kitchen. We could just as well have gone via the corridor, as I realized later, but we went via the kitchen, I don't know why, perhaps it was the shorter way. I surveyed the room with horror. Such density of furniture defeats imagination. Not a doubt, I must have seen that room somewhere. What's this? I cried. The parlour, she said. The parlour! I began putting out the furniture through the door to the corridor. She watched, in sorrow I suppose, but not necessarily. She asked me what I was doing. She can't have expected an answer. I put it out piece by piece, and even two at a time, and stacked it all up in the corridor, against the outer wall. They were hundreds of pieces, large and small, in the end they blocked the door, making egress impossible, and *a fortiori* ingress, to and from the corridor. The door could be opened and closed, since it opened inwards, but had become impassable. To put it wildly. At least take off your hat, she said. I'll treat of my hat some other time perhaps. Finally the room was empty but for a sofa and some shelves fixed to the wall. The former I dragged to the back of the room, near the door, and next day took down the latter and put them out, in the corridor, with the rest. As I was taking them down, strange memory, I heard the word fibrome, or brone, I don't know which, never knew, never knew what it meant and never had the curiosity to find out. The things one recalls! And records! When all was in order at last I dropped on the sofa. She had not raised her little finger to help me. I'll get sheets and blankets, she said. But I wouldn't hear of sheets. You couldn't draw the curtain? I said. The window was frosted over. The effect was not white, because of the night, but faintly luminous none the less. This faint cold sheen, though I lay with my feet towards the door, was more than I could bear. I suddenly rose and changed the position of the sofa, that is to say turned it round so that the back, hitherto against the wall, was now on the outside and consequently the front, or way in, on the inside. Then I climbed back, like a dog into its basket. I'll leave you the lamp, she said, but I begged her to take it with her. And suppose you need something in the night, she said. She was going to start quibbling again, I could feel it. Do you know where the convenience is? she said. She was right, I was forgetting. To relieve oneself in bed is enjoyable at the time, but soon a source of discomfort. Give me a chamber-pot, I said. But she did not possess one. I have a close-stool of sorts, she said. I saw the grandmother on it, sitting up very stiff and grand, having just purchased it, pardon, picked it up, at a charity sale, or perhaps won it in a raffle, a period piece, and now trying it out, doing her best rather, almost wishing someone could see her. That's the idea, procrastinate. Any old recipient, I said, I don't have the flux. She came back with a kind of saucepan, not a true saucepan for it had no handle, it was oval in shape with two lugs and a lid. My stewpan, she said. I don't need the lid, I said. You don't need the lid? she said. If I had said I needed the lid she would have said, You need the lid? I drew this utensil down under the blanket, I like something in my hand when sleeping, it reassures me, and my hat was still wringing. I turned to the wall. She caught up the lamp off the mantelpiece where she had set it down, that's the idea every particular, it flung her waving shadowing over me, I thought she was off, but no, she came stooping down towards me over the sofa back. All family possessions, she said. I in her shoes would have tiptoed away, but not she, not a stir. Already my love was waning, that was all that mattered. Yes, already I felt better, soon I'd be up to the slow descents again, the long submersions, so long denied me through her fault. And I had only just moved in! Try and put me out now, I said. I seemed not to grasp the meaning of these words, nor even hear the brief sound they made, till some seconds after having uttered them. I was so unused to speech that my mouth would sometimes open, of its own accord, and vent some phrase or phrases, grammatically unexceptionable but entirely devoid if not of meaning, for on close inspection they would reveal one, and even several, at least of foundation. But I heard each word no sooner spoken. Never had my voice taken so long to reach me as on this occasion. I turned over on my back to see what was going on. She was smiling. A little later she went away, taking the lamp with her. I heard her steps in the kitchen and then the door of her room close behind her. Why behind her? I was alone at last, in the dark at last. Enough about that. I thought I was all set for a good night, in spite of the strange surroundings, but no, my night was most agitated. I woke next morning quite worn out, my clothes in disorder, the blanket likewise, and Anna beside me, naked naturally. One shudders to think of her exertions. I still had the stewpan in my grasp. It had not served. I looked at my member. If only it could have spoken! Enough about that. It was my night of love.

Gradually I settled down, in this house. She brought my meals at the appointed hours, looked in now and then to see if all was well and make sure I needed nothing, emptied the stewpan once a day and did out the room once a month. She could not always resist the temptation to speak to me, but on the whole gave me no cause to complain. Sometimes I heard her singing in her room, the song traversed her door, then the kitchen, then my door, and in this way won to me, faint but indisputable. Unless it travelled by the corridor. This did not greatly incommode me, this occasional sound of singing. One day I asked her to bring me a hyacinth, live, in a pot. She brought it and put it on the mantelpiece, now the only place in my room to put things, unless you put them on the floor. Not a day passed without my looking at it. At first all went well, it even put forth a bloom or two, then it gave up and was soon no more than a limp stem hung with limp leaves.

The bulb, half clear of the clay as though in search of oxygen, smelt foul. She wanted to remove it, but I told her to leave it. She wanted to get me another, but I told her I didn't want another. I was more seriously disturbed by other sounds, stifled giggles and groans, which filled the dwelling at certain hours of the night, and even of the day. I had given up thinking of her, quite given up, but still I needed silence, to live my life. In vain I tried to listen to such reasonings as that air is made to carry the clamours of the world, including inevitably much groan and giggle, I obtained no relief. I couldn't make out if it was always the same gent or more than one. Lovers' groans are so alike, and lovers' giggles. I had such horror then of these paltry perplexities that I always fell into the same error, that of seeking to clear them up. It took me a long time, my lifetime so to speak, to realize that the colour of an eye half seen, or the source of some distant sound, are closer to Giudecca in the hell of unknowing than the existence of God, or the origins of protoplasm, or the existence of self, and even less worthy than these to occupy the wise. It's a bit much, a lifetime, to achieve this consoling conclusion, it doesn't leave you much time to profit by it. So a fat lot of help it was when, having put the question to her, I was told they were clients she received in rotation. I could obviously have got up and gone to look through the keyhole. But what can you see, I ask you, through holes the likes of those? So you live by prostitution, I said. We live by prostitution, she said. You couldn't ask them to make less noise? I said, as if I believed her. I added, Or a different kind of noise. They can't help but yap and yelp, she said. I'll have to leave, I said. She found some old hangings in the family junk and hung them before our doors, hers and mine. I asked her if it would not be possible, now and then, to have a parsnip. A parsnip! she cried, as if I had asked for a dish of sucking Jew. I reminded her that the parsnip season was fast drawing to a close and that if, before it finally got there, she could feed me nothing but parsnips I'd be grateful. I like parsnips because they taste like violets and violets because they smell like parsnips. Were there no parsnips on earth violets would leave me cold and if violets did not exist I would care as little for parsnips as I do for turnips, or radishes. And even in the present state of their flora, I mean on this planet where parsnips and violets contrive to coexist, I could do without both with the utmost ease, the uttermost ease. One day she had the impudence to announce she was with child, and four or five months gone into the bargain, by me of all people! She offered me a side view of her belly. She even undressed, no doubt to prove she wasn't hiding a cushion under her skirt, and then of course for the pure pleasure of undressing. Perhaps it's just wind, I said, by way of consolation. She gazed at me with her big eyes whose colour I forget, with one big eye rather, for the other seemed riveted on the remains of the hyacinth. The more naked she was the more cross-eyed. Look, she said, stooping over her breasts, the haloes are darkening already. I summoned up my remaining strength and said, Abort, abort, and they'll blush like new. She had drawn back the curtain for a clear view of all her rotundities. I saw the mountain, impassible, cavernous, secret, where from morning to night I'd hear nothing but the wind, the curlews, the clink like distant silver of the stone-cutters' hammers. I'd come out in the daytime to the heather and gorse, all warmth and scent, and watch at night the distant city lights, if I chose, and the other lights, the lighthouses and lightships my father had named for me, when I was small, and whose names I could find again, in my memory, if I chose, that I knew. From that day forth things went from bad to worse, to worse and worse. Not that she neglected me, she could never have neglected me enough, but the way she kept plaguing me with *our* child, exhibiting her belly and breasts and saying it was due any moment, she could feel it lepping already. If it's lepping, I said, it's not mine. I might have been worse off than I was, in that house, that was certain, it fell short of my ideal naturally, but I wasn't blind to its advantages. I hesitated to leave, the leaves were falling already, I dreaded the winter. One should not dread the winter, it too has its bounties, the snow gives warmth and deadens the tumult and its pale days are soon over. But I did not yet know, at that time, how tender the earth can be for those who have only her and how many graves in her giving, for the living. What finished me was the birth. It woke me up. What that infant must have been going through! I fancy she had a woman with her, I seemed to hear steps in the kitchen, on and off. It went to my heart to leave a house without being put out. I crawled out over the back of the sofa, put on my coat, greatcoat and hat, I can think of nothing else, laced up my boots and opened the door to the corridor. A mass of junk barred my way, but I scrabbled and barged my way through it in the end, regardless of the clatter. I used the word marriage, it was a kind of union in spite of all. Precautions would have been superfluous, there was no competing with those cries. It must have been her first. They pursued me down the stairs and out into the street. I stopped before the house door and listened. I could still hear them. If I had not known there was crying in the house I might not have heard them. But knowing it I did. I was not sure where I was. I looked among the stars and constellations for the Wains, but could not find them. And yet they must have been there. My father was the first to show them to me. He had shown me others, but alone, without him beside me, I could never find any but the Wains. I began playing with the cries, a little in the same way as I had played with the song, on, back, on, back, if that may be called playing. As long as I kept walking I didn't hear them, because of the footsteps. But as soon as I halted I heard them again, a little fainter each time, admittedly, but what does it matter, faint or loud, cry is cry, all that matters is that it should cease. For years I thought they would cease. Now I don't think so any more. I could have done with other loves perhaps. But there it is, either you love or you don't.

Mercier and Camier

Mercier and Camier, Beckett's first full-length French novel, is very close to *Watt* in style and humour. Mercier and Camier have an arrangement to meet but by a series of extraordinary coincidences keep on just missing each other, until luck changes and they finally get together, situations that in a grimmer light Beckett often encountered during the war. Comic incidents happen to them, and their experiences and attitudes can be seen as illustrations of philosophical observations; each chapter is amusingly analysed at the end by a brief one-page summary.

The following is the third chapter of the book and it opens with the monologue of another traveller whom Mercier and Camier are unable to avoid on their train; they then continue on their way until they get drunkenly unconscious at an inn; the chapter is followed by a synopsis. This is a good illustration of the high comedy resulting from wordplay, vividly comic incidents and characters, and the writer's attempt to reconcile his own jaundiced view of the world with the fruits of much reading and study. Unknown and unpublished when he wrote this, his pre-war work long out of print, his wartime experiences fresh in his mind, Beckett had not yet found the voice with which he was soon to conquer the literary world. Although he has always depicted himself as doing very little, the evidence points to constant starting and stopping, the artist constantly reworking texts with which he is never entirely satisfied and moving away from whatever new form of literature he has last invented; retrospectively each step can be seen as extraordinary for its time and moving towards a new development for which the stylistic framework has still to be forged. *Mercier and Camier* was suppressed by the author for many years, apparently because he was unwilling, after publication of the *Trilogy*, to release work in an earlier style.

I trust an only child, I was born at P—. My parents came from Q—. It was from them I received, together with the treponema pallidum, the huge nose whose remains you have before you. They were severe with me, but just. For the least peccadillo my father beat me till I bled, with his solid razor-strop. But he never failed to notify my mother that she might dress my wounds, with tincture of iodine or permanganate of potash. Here lies no doubt the explanation of my unconfiding character and general surliness. Unfitted for the pursuit of knowledge I was taken away from school at the age of thirteen and placed with farmers near by. Heaven, as they put it, having denied them offspring of their own, they fell back on me with very natural virulence. And when my parents perished, in a providential railway smash, they adopted me with all the forms and observances required by the law. But no less feeble of body than of mind I was for them a constant source of disappointment. To follow the plough, ply the scythe, flounder in the mangel-wurzels, and so on, were labours so far beyond my strength that I literally collapsed whenever forced to undertake them. Even as shepherd, cowherd, goatherd, pigherd, it was in vain I strained every nerve, I could never give satisfaction. For the animals strayed, unnoticed by me, into the neighbouring properties and there ate their bellyful of vegetables, fruit and flowers. I pass over in silence the combats between rutting males, when I fled in terror to take shelter in the nearest outhouse. Add to this that the flock or herd, because of my inability to count beyond ten, seldom came home at full muster, and with this too I was deservedly reproached. The only branches in which I may boast of having, if not excelled, at least succeeded, were the slaughter of little lambs, calves, kids and porklings and the emasculation of little bullocks, rams, billy goats and piglets, on condition of course they were still unspoiled, all innocence and trustingness. It was therefore to these specialities I confined myself, from the age of fifteen. I have still at home some charming little – well, comparatively little – ram's testes dating from that happy time. In the fowl-yard too I was a terror of accuracy and elegance. I had a way of smothering geese that was the admiration and envy of all. Oh I know you are listening with only half an ear, and that half unwilling, but that is nothing to me. For my life is behind me and my only pleasure left to summon up, out loud, the good old days happily gone for ever. At the age of twenty, or possibly nineteen, having been awkward enough to fecundate a milkmaid, I ran away, under cover of night, for I was closely watched. I improved this occasion by setting light to the barns, granaries and stables. But the flames were scarcely under way when they were doused by a downfall none could have foreseen, so starry was the sky at the moment of ignition. That was fifty years ago, feels like five hundred. He brandished his stick and brought it down with a thump on the seat which emitted instantaneously a cloud of fine ephemeral dust. Five hundred! he bellowed.

The train slowed down. Mercier and Camier exchanged a look. The train stopped.

Woe is us, said Mercier, we're in the slow and easy.

The train moved on.

We might have alit, said Mercier, now it's too late.

Next stop, said the old man, you alight with me.

This puts a fresh complexion on it, said Mercier.

Butcher's boy, said the old man, poulterer's boy, knacker's boy, undertaker's man, sexton, one corpse on top of another, there's my life for you. Gab was my salvation, every day a little more, a little better. The truth is I had that too in my bleeding blood, my father having sprung, with what alacrity you may imagine, from the loins of a parish priest, it was common knowledge. I infested the outlying whoreshops and saloons. Comrades, I said, having never learnt to write, comrades, Homer tells us, Iliad Book 3, lines 85 and following, in what consists happiness here below, that is to say happiness. Oh I gave it to them! *Potopompos scroton evohe*! Like that, hot and strong! Picked up at nightschool – he burst into a wild raucous laugh – free nightschool for glimmer-thirsty wrecks. Potopompos scroton evohe, the soft cock and buckets of the hard. Step out of here, I said, with a stout heart and your bollocks in your boots and come again tomorrow, tell the missus to go chase apes in hell. There were delicate moments. Then up I'd get, covered with blood and my rags in ribbons, and at 'em again. Brats the offscourings of fornication and God Almighty a cheap scent in a jakes. I cleaned myself up and crashed their weddings, funerals, balls, wakes and christenings. They made me welcome, another ten years and I'd be popular. I let them have it on the lot, hymen, vaseline, the evil day from dawn to dark. Till I came in for the farm, or better still the farms, for there were two. The creatures bless their hearts, they loved me to the end. A good job for me they did, for my snout was starting to crumble. People love you less when your snout starts to crumble.

The train slowed down. Mercier and Camier drew in their legs to let him pass. The train stopped.

Not alighting? said the old man. You're right, only the damned alight here.

He wore gaiters, a yellow block-hat and a rusty frock-coat reaching down to his knees. He lowered himself stiffly to the platform, turned, slammed the door and raised towards them his hideous face.

The train moved on.

Adieu adieu, cried Mr Madden, they loved me to the end, they loved—.

Mercier, whose back was to the engine, saw him as he stood there, dead to the passengers hastening towards the exit, bow down his head till it lay on his hands at rest on the knob of his stick.

With what relief the eyes from this clutter to the empty sky, with what relief back again.

A fresh complexion, said Mercier, a totally fresh complexion.

Camier wiped the pane with the cuff of his sleeve caught between the palm and four crooked fingers.

It's the end, said Mercier, that just about—. He paused for thought. That just about finishes me, he said.

Visibility nil, said Camier.

You remain strangely calm, said Mercier. Am I right in thinking you took advantage of my condition to substitute this hearse for the express we agreed on?

Camier mumbled something about burnt bridges and indecent haste.

I knew it, said Mercier. I've been shamefully abused. I'd throw myself out of the window if I wasn't afraid I might sprain my ankle.

I'll explain everything, said Camier.

You'll explain nothing, said Mercier. You took advantage of my weakness to cod me I was getting on an express when in fact—. His face fell apart. More readily than Mercier's few faces fell apart. Words fail me, he said, to disguise what I feel.

But your weakness it was precisely, said Camier, that prompted this little subterfuge.

Explain yourself, said Mercier.

Seeing the state you were in, said Camier, it was imperative to go, and yet at the same time stay.

You are cheap, said Mercier.

We'll get down at the next stop, said Camier, and consider how to proceed. If we see fit to go on we'll go on. We'll have lost two hours. What are two hours?

I wouldn't like to say, said Mercier.

If on the other hand, said Camier, we see fitter to return to town—.

To town! cried Mercier.

To town, said Camier, to town we shall return.

But we have just come from town, said Mercier, and now you speak of returning there.

When we left town, said Camier, it was necessary to leave town. So we very properly left it. But we are not children and necessity has her whims. If having elected to drive us forth she now elects to drive us back shall we balk? I trust not.

The only necessity I know, said Mercier, is to get away from that hell as fast and as far as possible.

That remains to be seen, said Camier. Never trust the wind that swells your sails, it is always obsolete.

Mercier controlled himself.

A third and last possibility, said Camier, since none are to be neglected, is that we form the heroic resolution to stay where we are. In which case I have all we need.

A village just one long street, everything lined up in a row, dwellings, shops, bars, the two stations, railway and petrol, the two churches, graveyard and so on. A strait.

Take the raincoat, said Camier.

Pah I won't melt, said Mercier.

They entered an inn.

Wrong address, said the man. This is Messrs Clappe and Sons, Wholesale Fruit and Vegetable Suppliers.

And what leads you to suppose, said Camier, that we have not business with father Clappe or one of his waste products?

They regained the street.

Is this an inn, said Camier, or is it the fish market?

This time the man made way, all of a flutter.

Come in, gentlemen, he said, step right in. It's not the Savoy, but it's . . . how shall I say? He took their measure with a quick furtive look. How shall I say? he said.

Say it, said Camier, and put us out of our pain.

It's . . . snug, said the man, there is no other word. Patrick! he cried. But there was another word, for he added, in a tone of tentative complicity, whatever that sounds like, it's . . . *gemütlich.*

He takes us for globe-trotters, said Mercier.

Ah, said the man, rubbing his hands, physiognomies – pronouncing as was his right the *g* – have no secrets for me. It's not every day that I have the honour . . . He hesitated. That I have the honour, he said. Patrick!

Speaking for myself, said Mercier, I am happy to meet you at last, you have been haunting me this long time.

Ah, said the man.

Yes sir, said Mercier. You appear to me most often on a threshold, or at a window. Behind you torrents of light and joy which should normally annihilate your features, but do not. You smile. Presumably you do not see me, across the alley from where you stand and plunged in deepest shadow. I too smile – and pass on. Do you see me, in my dreams, Mr Gall?

Let me relieve you, said the man.

In any case it is a happiness to meet you again, said Mercier, in such happier circumstances.

Relieve us of what? said Camier.

Why, said the man, of your coats, your hats, how shall I say? Patrick!

But will you look at us, said Camier. Do we appear to be hatted? Are we wearing gloves, without our knowledge? Come sir!

A porter for our trunks, said Mercier, what are you waiting for?

Patrick! cried the man.

Vengeance! cried Mercier, taking a step forward.

It was fair day. The saloon was crowded with farmers, cattle-dealers and the like. The beasts proper were far on their way already, straggling along the miry backland roads, to the cries of the herds. Some would come at night to their familiar byres, others to others they knew not of. Bringing up the rear, behind the sodden ewes, a train of clattering carts. The herds held their pricks through the stuff of their pockets.

Mercier propped his elbows on the bar. Camier, on the contrary, leaned his back against it.

They guzzle with their hats on, he said.

Where is he now? said Mercier.

By the door, said Camier, observing us without appearing to do so.

Can one see his teeth? said Mercier.

His mouth is hidden behind his hand, said Camier.

I do not ask if his mouth is hidden, said Camier, I ask if one can see his teeth.

One cannot see his teeth from here, said Camier, owing to the hand that hides them.

What are we doing here? said Mercier.

First eat, said Camier. Barman, what are your titbits today?

The barman rattled off a list.

Mine will be a button-fish salad, said Camier, with Dutch dressing.

Not on today, said the barman.

Then make it a hopper sandwich, said Camier.

Just finished the last, said the barman. He had heard it was better to humour them.

You keep a civil tongue in your head, said Mercier. He turned to Camier. What kind of a kip is this? he said. What kind of a trip is this?

At this point the journey of Mercier and Camier seemed likely indeed to founder. That it did not was doubtless due to Camier, mirror of magnanimity and ingenuity.

Mercier, he said, leave it to me.

Do something for God's sake, said Mercier, do something? Why must I always be the one to lead the way?

Call your employer, said Camier.

The barman seemed reluctant.

Call him, my good fellow, said Mercier, call him when you're told. Make the little sound he can tell from every other and would not fail to hear even in a howling gale. Or the little beck that is lost on all but him and would bring him running though the heavens were to fall.

But he whom Mercier had called Mr Gall was already by their side.

Have I the honour of addressing the proprietor? said Camier.

I am the manager, said the manager, since he was the manager.

It appears there is no more hopper, said Mercier. You have a curious way of managing, for a manager. What have you done with your teeth? Is this what you call *gemütlich*?

The manager wore the air of one in thought. He had no taste for trouble. The extremities of his drooping grey moustache seemed bent on meeting. The barman watched him closely. Mercier was struck by the scant grey strands, fine as a babe's, trained forward with pitiable coquetry from the back of the head across the crown. Mr Gall had never appeared to him thus, but always erect and smiling and radiant.

Ah well, said Mercier, no more about it, such shortage is understandable, after all.

Would you have a room by any chance, said Camier, where my friend might take a moment's rest? He is dropping with fatigue. He leaned towards the manager and whispered in his ear.

His mother? said the manager.

My mother is it? said Mercier. She died perpetrating me, the slut. Rather than meet my eye. What's all this? he said to Camier. Have you no respect for my family?

I could manage a room, said the manager, but of course—.

A moment's rest, said Camier, he is out on his feet.

Come on, nightmare pal, said Mercier, you can't refuse me that.

Of course at the full day rate, said the manager.

On an upper floor as far as possible, said Mercier, where I can throw myself out of the window without misgiving, should occasion arise.

You'll stick by him? said the manager.

To the last, said Camier.

Patrick! cried the manager. Where's Patrick? he said to the barman.

Out sick, said the barman.

What do you mean out sick? said the manager. I saw him last night. I even thought I saw him just now.

Out sick, said the barman. No hope they say. Sinking fast.

How aggravating, said the manager. What's the matter with him?

I do not know, said the barman.

And why was I not informed? said the manager.

We must have thought you knew, said the barman.

And who says it's serious? said the manager.

It's a rumour going the rounds, said the barman.

And where is he? said the manager. At home or—.

A pox on your Patrick! cried Mercier. Do you want to finish me?

Show the gentlemen up, said the manager. Take their order and hurry back.

Six? said the barman.

Or seven, said the manager. As the gentlemen prefer.

He watched them go. He poured himself a glass and tossed it off.

Ah Mr Graves, he said, good day, what are you taking?

Nice pair, said Mr Graves.

Oh that's nothing, said the manager, I'm used to it.

And where might I ask did you get used to it? said Mr Graves in his incipient pastoral patriarch's thick bass. Not among us, I vow.

Where I got used to it? said the manager. He closed his eyes the better to see what was still in spite of all a little dear to him. Among my masters, he said.

I'm happy to hear you say so, said Mr Graves. I wish you good day.

The manager capped this.

His weary gaze strayed over the saloon where the honourable yokels were making to depart. Mr Graves had given the signal, they would not be slow to follow an example of such moment.

The barman reported back.

Mr Gast did not at once reply, intent on the scene as it faded and gave way, before his open eyes, to a little grey medieval square where silent shapes, muffled up to the eyes, passed slowly with laboured tread in the deep snow.

They took both, said the barman.

Mr Gast turned towards him.

They ordered a bottle of malt, said the barman.

Have they settled? said Mr Gast.

Yes, said the barman.

Nothing else matters, said Mr Gast.

I don't like the look of them at all, said the barman. Particular the long hank with the beard. The little fat one I wouldn't mind so much.

You keep out of it, said Mr Gast.

He went and stood by the door to take civil leave of his customers whose departure, in a body, was now clearly imminent. Most of them climbed aboard old high-slung Fords, others dispersed through the village in search of bargains. Others gathered talking in the rain which did not seem to incommode them. They were perhaps so pleased, who knows, for professional reasons, to see it fall, that they were pleased to feel it fall, wetting them through. Soon they would be on their several ways, scattered along the muddy roads shadowy already in the last gleams of niggard day. Each hastens towards his little kingdom, his waiting wife, his beasts snugly stalled, his dogs listening for the coming of their lord.

Mr Gast returned to the saloon.

Have you served them? he said.

Yes, said the barman.

They made no remark? said Mr Gast.

Only not to be disturbed, said the barman.

Where's Patrick? said Mr Gast. At home or in hospital?

I think he's at home, said the barman, but I wouldn't vouch for it.

You don't know a great deal, said Mr Gast.

I keep my mind on my work, said the barman. He fixed Mr Gast in the eye. On my duties and prerogatives, he said.

You couldn't do better, said Mr Gast, that way greatness lies. He went to the door. If I'm wanted, he said, I've gone out and won't be long.

He went out sure enough and sure enough was not long.

Dead, he said.

The barman wiped his hands in haste and crossed himself.

His last words, said Mr Gast, before yielding up the ghost, were unintelligible. Not so his second last, a gem of their kind, namely, A pint, for the love of Christ, a pint.

What ailed him exactly? said the barman.

How many days had he coming to him? said the barman.

He drew on Saturday like the rest, said the barman.

Negligible so, said Mr Gast. I'll send a sheaf.

A good pal as ever was, said the barman.

Mr Gast shrugged his shoulders.

Where's Teresa? he said. Don't tell me she's been taken too. Teresa! he cried.

In the toilet, said the barman.

Nothing escapes you, said Mr Gast.

Coming! cried Teresa.

A buxom wench appeared, a big tray under her arm and a clout in her hand.

Look at this sty, said Mr Gast.

A man entered the saloon. He wore a cap, a trenchcoat all tabs, flaps, pockets and leather buttons, riding-breeches and mountaineering boots. His still brawny back was bowed beneath a knapsack filled to bursting and he held a huge stick in his hand. He lurched across the saloon, dragging noisily his hobnailed soles.

Some are best limned at first sight, those liable to vanish and never reappear.

My parquet, said Mr Gast.

Water, said Mr Conaire (the name without delay).

Mr Gast did not budge, nor did the barman. Had Mr Gast budged, then doubtless the barman too had budged. But Mr Gast not budging the barman did not budge either.

Water first, said Mr Conaire, then floods of liquor. Thanks. Again. Thanks. Enough.

He shed his sack with convulsive contortions of shoulders and loins.

Gin, he said.

He took off his cap and shook it violently in all directions. Then he put it back on his shining sugarloaf.

You have before you, gentlemen, he said, a man. Make the most of it. I have footed it from the very core of the metropolitan gas-chamber without rest or pause except twice to—. He looked about him, saw Teresa (already seen, but now with ostentation), leaned across the bar and finished his phrase in a murmur. He looked from Mr Gast to George (as the barman now is called), from George to Mr Gast, as though to make sure his words had done their work. Then drawing himself up he declared in ringing tones, Little and often, little and often, and gently, gently, that's what I've come to. He leered at Teresa and broke into a strident laugh. Where's your convenience? he said, adding, Convenience! They call that a convenience!

Mr Gast described the way that led to it.

What complications, said Mr Conaire. Always the same abominable well-bred latency. In Frankfurt, when you get off the train, what is the first thing you see, in gigantic letters of fire? A single word: HIER. Gin.

Neat? said Mr Gast.

Mr Conaire stepped back and struck an attitude.

What age would you say I was? he said. He rotated slowly. Speak up, he said, don't spare me.

Mr Gast named a figure.

Damnation, said Mr Conaire, got it in one.

Tis the baldness is deceptive, said Mr Gast.

Not another word, said Mr Conaire. In the yard, did I hear you say?

At the back on the left, said Mr Gast.

And to win from here to there? said Mr Conaire.

Mr Gast renewed his directions.

Lest I be taken short, said Mr Conaire.

On his way out he paused for a brush with Teresa.

Hello sweety, he said.

Teresa eyed him.

Sir, she said.

What loveliness, said Mr Conaire. At the door he turned. And graciousness, he said, what graciousness. He went out.

Mr Gast and George exchanged a look. Get out your slate, said Mr Gast. His next words were for Teresa. You couldn't be a little more endearing? he said.

The old dirt, said Teresa.

No one is asking you to wallow on the floor, said Mr Gast. He began to pace up and down, then halted, his mind made up. Stop what you're doing, he said, and collect yourselves. I shall now treat of the guest, that wild lovable beast. A shame that Patrick is not here to hear me.

He threw back his head, clasped his hands behind him and treated of the guest. Even as he spoke he saw a little window opening on an empty place, a moor unbroken save for a single track, where no shade ever falls, winding out of sight its gentle alternate curves. Not a breath stirs that pale grey air. In the far distance here and there the seam of earth and sky exudes a sun-flooded beyond. It seems an autumn afternoon, late November say. The little black mass slowly approaching gradually takes shape, a tilted wagon drawn by a black horse, without effort, saunteringly. The wagoner walks ahead, flourishing his whip. He wears a heavy greatcoat, light in colour, its skirts trailing on the ground. It may even be he is happy, for he sings as he goes, in snatches. Now and then he turns, no doubt to look inside. As he draws near he seems young, he lifts his head and smiles.

That will be all for today, said Mr Gast. Impregnate yourselves with these considerations. They are the fruit of an eternity of public fawning and private snarls. I make you a present of them. If I'm wanted I'm out. Call me at six as usual.

There's something in what he says, said George.

There's men all over for you, said Teresa, no more ideal than a monkey.

Mr Conaire reappeared, enchanted to have got it over so fast.

I had my work cut out, he said, but I did it, I did it. He shivered. Nice north pole you have here, he said, what will you take. Jump at the chance, I feel the other hell calling me back.

George jumped.

Your health, sir, he said.

Pledge it, pledge it, said Mr Conaire, none deserves it more. And rosebud here, he said, would she deign to clink with us?

She's married, said George, and mother of three.

Fie upon you! cried Mr Conaire. How can one say such things!

You're being stood a port, said George.

Teresa moved behind the bar.

When I think what it means, said Mr Conaire. The torn flesh! The pretty crutch in tatters! The screams! The blood! The glair! The afterbirth! He put his hand before his eyes. The afterbirth! he groaned.

All the best, said Teresa.

Drink, drink, said Mr Conaire, pay no heed to me. What an abomination! What an abomination!

He took away his hand and saw them smiling at him, as at a child.

Forgive me, he said, when I think of women I think of maidens, I can't help it. They have no hairs, they pee not neither do they cack.

Mention it not, said George.

I took you for a maiden, said Mr Conaire, I give you my oath, no flattery intended. On the buxom side I grant you, nice and plump, plenty of bounce, a bosom in a thousand, a bottom in a million, thighs—. He broke off. No good, he said, not a stir out of him.

Teresa went back to her work.

I now come to the object of my visit, said Mr Conaire. Would you happen to know of a man by the name of Camier?

No, said George.

Strange, said Mr Conaire, seeing I was to meet him here, this very place, this very afternoon. Here's his card.

George read:

F. X. CAMIER
Private Investigator
Soul of Discretion

New one on me, said George.

Small and fat, said Mr Conaire, red face, scant hair, four chins, protruding paunch, bandy legs, beady pig eyes.

There's a couple above, said George, showed up there a short time back.

What's the other like? said Mr Conaire.

A big bony hank with a beard, said George, hardly able to stand, wicked expression.

That's him, cried Mr Conaire, those are them! Slip up now and give him the word. Tell him Mr Conaire is waiting in the lounge. Co-naire.

They left word not to be disturbed, said George. They'd turn on you like a shot, I tell you.

Listen, said Mr Conaire.

George listened.

Well I don't mind trying, he said.

He went out and a moment later came back.

They're snoring, he said.

Rouse them, said Mr Conaire.

The bottle is empty, said George, and there they are—.

What bottle? said Mr Conaire.

They ordered a bottle of malt in the room, said George.

Oh the hogs, said Mr Conaire.

There they are stretched out side by side in their clothes on the floor, said George. Snoring hand in hand.

Oh the hogs, said Mr Conaire.

Summary of the preceding chapter

The train.
Madden interlude I.
The slow train.
Madden interlude conclusion.
The village.
The inn.
Mr Gast.
The beasts on the roads.
The farmers.
Mercier's dream.
The journey in jeopardy.
Camier's presence of mind.
Patrick's illness.
Mercier and Camier mount.
Mr Graves.
Patrick's death.
His second-last words.
Conaire interlude I.
Mr Gast treats of the guest.
Mr Gast's vision.
Conaire interlude II.
Mercier and Camier sleep.

The Mature Artist

Molloy

Increasingly concerned with language, and with finding a more economical way of isolating the inner voice, Beckett started to write in French after the war in order to escape the rhetoric of the Irish idiom and to discipline himself in the use of words. *Molloy* is divided into two monologues. The first is that of Molloy, who at the beginning of the narrative is ill and old, lying in a bed which he believes to have previously belonged to his mother, who recounts a series of adventures and brushes with the law, his liaison with a woman called Lousse, who adopts him as a sort of replacement for her dog which he has run over on his bicycle, and from whom he escapes, ending up with a period of crawling through the forest, pulling himself along by his crutches, until he emerges at the end on to a great plain in sight of a town. We are not told how he gets from the ditch, where the narrative ends, into the comparative safety of his bed where we find him at the beginning, but these details are unimportant. It is the mind of Molloy that counts, telling itself stories, capable of considerable philosophical rumination, observing the human comedy with interest and resignation and abounding in the folk lore of the tramp. Comedy is closely allied to viciousness, and there can be few books written in any age that enable the reader to understand his own anti-social tendencies as well as this one. Molloy has great reserves in the midst of his misery, both of physical stamina and of mental fortitude. He is one of Beckett's survivors. Two extracts, from the beginning and end of Molloy's narrative, follow. The second monologue, by Moran, is in sharp contrast to Molloy's. Moran is a rather spinsterish, prim, self-assured private detective. Unlike Molloy he has normal ambition, a passion for orderliness and is very finicky on matters of personal behaviour and theological nicety. He is approached by Gaber bringing him instructions to go to look for Molloy. He sets out with his son on a journey during which a number of misfortunes befall him, and returns almost as weak and crippled as Molloy himself to find his house dilapidated, his bees reduced to dust, his hens killed or flown. Only the beginning of Moran's story is given here.

I Molloy

I am in my mother's room. It's I who live there now. I don't know
how I got there. Perhaps in an ambulance, certainly a vehicle of
some kind. I was helped. I'd never have got there alone. There's
this man who comes every week. Perhaps I got here thanks to
him. He says not. He gives me money and takes away the pages.
So many pages, so much money. Yes, I work now, a little like I
used to, except that I don't know how to work any more. That
doesn't matter apparently. What I'd like now is to speak of the
things that are left, say my good-byes, finish dying. They don't
want that. Yes, there is more than one, apparently. But it's always
the same one that comes. You'll do that later, he says. Good. The
truth is I haven't much will left. When he comes for the fresh
pages he brings back the previous week's. They are marked with
signs I don't understand. Anyway I don't read them. When I've
done nothing he gives me nothing, he scolds me. Yet I don't work
for money. For what then? I don't know. The truth is I don't
know much. For example my mother's death. Was she already
dead when I came? Or did she only die later? I mean enough to
bury. I don't know. Perhaps they haven't buried her yet. In any
case I have her room. I sleep in her bed. I piss and shit in her pot.
I have taken her place. I must resemble her more and more. All
I need now is a son. Perhaps I have one somewhere. But I think
not. He would be old now, nearly as old as myself. It was a little
chambermaid. It wasn't true love. The true love was in another.
We'll come to that. Her name? I've forgotten it again. It seems to
me sometimes that I even knew my son, that I helped him. Then
I tell myself it's impossible. It's impossible I could ever have
helped anyone. I've forgotten how to spell too, and half the words.
That doesn't matter apparently. Good. He's a queer one the one
who comes to see me. He comes every Sunday apparently. The
other days he isn't free. He's always thirsty. It was he told me I'd
begun all wrong, that I should have begun differently. He must
be right. I began at the beginning, like an old ballocks, can you
imagine that? Here's my beginning. Because they're keeping it
apparently. I took a lot of trouble with it. Here it is. It gave me
a lot of trouble. It was the beginning, do you understand? Whereas
now it's nearly the end. Is what I do now any better? I don't know.
That's beside the point. Here's my beginning. It must mean something, or they wouldn't keep it. Here it is.

This time, then once more I think, then perhaps a last time, then I think it'll be over, with that world too. Premonition of the last but one but one. All grows dim. A little more and you'll go blind. It's in the head. It doesn't work any more, it says, I don't work any more. You go dumb as well and sounds fade. The threshold scarcely crossed that's how it is. It's the head. It must have had enough. So that you say, I'll manage this time, then perhaps once more, then perhaps a last time, then nothing more. You are hard set to formulate this thought, for it is one, in a sense. Then you try to pay attention, to consider with attention all those dim things, saying to yourself, laboriously, It's my fault. Fault? That was the word. But what fault? It's not good-bye, and what magic in those dim things to which it will be time enough, when next they pass, to say good-bye. For you must say good-bye, it would be madness not to say good-bye, when the time comes. If you think of the form and light of other days is it without regret. But you seldom think of them, with what would you think of them? I don't know. People pass too, hard to distinguish from yourself. That is discouraging. So I saw A and C going slowly towards each other, unconscious of what they were doing. It was on a road remarkably bare, I mean without hedges or ditches or any kind of edge, in the country, for cows were chewing in enormous fields, lying and standing, in the evening silence. Perhaps I'm inventing a little, perhaps embellishing, but on the whole that's the way it was. They chew, swallow, then after a short pause effortlessly bring up the next mouthful. A neck muscle stirs and the jaws begin to grind again. But perhaps I'm remembering things. The road, hard and white, seared the tender pastures, rose and fell at the whim of hills and hollows. The town was not far. It was two men, unmistakably, one small and one tall. They had left the town, first one, then the other, and then the first, weary or remembering a duty, had retraced his steps. The air was sharp, for they wore greatcoats. They looked alike, but no more than others do. At first a wide space lay between them. They couldn't have seen each other, even had they raised their heads and looked about, because of this wide space, and then because of the undulating land, which caused the road to be in waves, not high, but high enough, high enough. But the moment came when together they went down into the same trough and in this trough finally met. To say they knew each other, no, nothing warrants it. But perhaps at the sound of their steps, or warned by some obscure instinct, they raised their heads and observed each other, for a good fifteen paces, before they stopped, breast to breast. Yes, they did not pass each other by, but halted, face to face, as in the country, of an evening, on a deserted road, two wayfaring strangers will, without there being anything extraordinary about it. But they knew each other perhaps. Now in any case they do, now I think they will know each other, greet each other, even in the depths of the town. They turned towards the sea which, far in the east, beyond the fields, loomed high in the waning sky, and exchanged a few words. Then each went on his way. Each went on his way, A back towards the town, C on by ways he seemed hardly to know, or not at all, for he went with uncertain step and often stopped to look about him, like someone trying to fix landmarks in his mind, for one day perhaps he may have to retrace his steps, you never know. The treacherous hills where fearfully he ventured were no doubt only known to him from afar, seen perhaps from his bedroom window or from the summit of a monument which, one black day, having nothing in particular to do and turning to height for solace, he had paid his few coppers to climb, slower and slower, up the winding stones. From there he must have seen it all, the plain, the sea, and then these selfsame hills that some call mountains, indigo in places in the evening light, their serried ranges crowding to the skyline, cloven with hidden valleys that the eye divines from sudden shifts of colour and then from other signs for which there are no words, nor even thoughts. But all are not divined, even from that height, and often where only one escarpment is discerned, and one crest, in reality there are two, two escarpments, two crests, riven by a valley. But now he knows these hills, that is to say he knows them better, and if ever again he sees them from afar it will be I think with other eyes, and not only that but the within, all that inner space one never sees, the brain and heart and other caverns where thought and feeling dance their sabbath, all that too quite differently disposed. He looks old and it is a sorry sight to see him solitary after so many years, so many days and nights unthinkingly given to that rumour rising at birth and even earlier, What shall I do? What shall I do? now low, a murmur, now precise as the headwaiter's And to follow? and often rising to a scream. And in the end, or almost, to be abroad alone, by unknown ways, in the gathering night, with a stick. It was a stout stick, he used it to thrust himself onward, or as a defence, when the time came, against dogs and marauders. Yes, night was gathering, but the man was innocent, greatly innocent, he had nothing to fear, though he went in fear, he had nothing to fear, there was nothing they could do to him, or very little. But he can't have known it. I wouldn't know it myself, if I thought about it. Yes, he saw himself threatened, his body threatened, his reason threatened, and perhaps he was, perhaps they were, in spite of his innocence. What business has innocence here? What relation to the innumerable spirits of darkness? It's not clear. It seemed to me he wore a cocked hat. I remember being struck by it, as I wouldn't have been for example by a cap or by a bowler. I watched him recede, overtaken (myself) by his anxiety, at least by an anxiety which was not necessarily his, but of which as it were he partook. Who knows if it wasn't my own anxiety overtaking him. He hadn't seen me. I was perched higher than the road's highest point and flattened what is more against a rock the same colour as myself, that is grey. The rock he probably saw. He gazed around as if to engrave the landmarks on his memory and must have seen the rock in the shadow of which I crouched like Belacqua, or Sordello, I forget. But a man, a fortiori myself, isn't exactly a landmark, because, I mean if by some strange chance he were to pass that way again, after a long lapse of time, vanquished, or to look for some lost thing, or to destroy something, his eyes would search out the rock, not the haphazard in its shadow of that unstable fugitive thing, still living flesh. No, he certainly didn't see me, for the reasons I've given and then because he was in no humour for that, that evening, no humour for the living, but rather for all that doesn't stir, or stirs so slowly that a child would scorn it, let alone an old man. However that may be, I mean whether he saw me or whether he didn't, I repeat I watched him recede, at grips (myself) with the temptation to get up and follow him, perhaps even to catch up with him one day, so as to know him better, be myself less lonely. But in spite of my soul's leap out to him, at the end of its elastic, I saw him only darkly, because of the dark and then because of the terrain, in the folds of which he disappeared from time to time, to re-emerge further on, but most of all I think because of other things calling me and towards which too one after the other my soul was straining, wildly. I mean of course the fields, whitening under the dew, and the animals, ceasing from wandering and settling for the night, and the sea, of which nothing, and the sharpening line of crests, and the sky where without seeing them I felt the first stars tremble, and my hand on my knee and above all the other wayfarer, A or C, I don't remember, going resignedly home. Yes, towards my hand also, which my knee felt tremble and of which my eyes saw the wrist only, the heavily veined back, the pallid rows of knuckles. But that is not, I mean my hand, what I wish to speak of now, everything in due course, but A or C returning to the town he had just left. But after all what was there particularly urban in his aspect? He was bare-headed, wore sand-shoes, smoked a cigar. He moved with a kind of loitering indolence which rightly or wrongly seemed to me expressive. But all that proved nothing, refuted nothing. Perhaps he had come from afar, from the other end of the island even, and was approaching the town for the first time or returning to it after a long absence. A little dog followed him, a pomeranian I think, but I don't think so. I wasn't sure at the time and I'm still not sure, though I've hardly thought about it. The little dog followed wretchedly, after the fashion of pomeranians, stopping, turning in slow circles, giving up and then, a little further on, beginning all over again. Constipation is a sign of good health in pomeranians. At a given moment, pre-established if you like, I don't much mind, the gentleman turned back, took the little creature in his arms, drew the cigar from his lips and buried his face in the orange fleece, for it was a gentleman, that was obvious. Yes, it was an orange pomeranian, the less I think of it the more certain I am. And yet. But would he have come from afar, bare-headed, in sand-shoes, smoking a cigar, followed by a pomeranian? Did he not seem rather to have issued from the ramparts, after a good dinner, to take his dog and himself for a walk, like so many citizens, dreaming and farting, when the weather is fine? But was not perhaps in reality the cigar a cutty, and were not the sand-shoes boots, hobnailed, dust-whitened, and what prevented the dog from being one of those stray dogs that you pick up and take in your arms, from compassion or because you have long been straying with no other company than the endless roads, sands, shingle, bogs and heather, than this nature answerable to another court, than at long intervals the fellow-convict you long to stop, embrace, suck, suckle and whom you pass by, with hostile eyes, for fear of his familiarities? Until the day when, your endurance gone, in this world for you without arms, you catch up in yours the first mangy cur you meet, carry it the time needed for it to love you and you it, then throw it away. Perhaps he had come to that, in spite of appearances. He disappeared, his head on his chest, the smoking object in his hand. Let me try and explain. From things about to disappear I turn away in time. To watch them out of sight, no, I can't do it. It was in this sense he disappeared. Looking away I thought of him, saying. He is dwindling, dwindling. I knew what I meant. I knew I could catch him, lame as I was. I had only to want to. And yet no, for I did want to. To get up, to get down on the road, to set off hobbling in pursuit of him, to hail him, what could be easier? He hears my cries, turns, waits for me. I am up against him, up against the dog, gasping, between my crutches. He is a little frightened of me, a little sorry for me, I disgust him not a little. I am not a pretty sight, I don't smell good. What is it I want? Ah that tone I know, compounded of pity, of fear, of disgust. I want to see the dog, see the man, at close quarters, know what smokes, inspect the shoes, find out other things. He is kind, tells me of this and that and other things, whence he comes, whither he goes. I believe him, I know it's my only chance to – my only chance, I believe all I'm told, I've disbelieved only too much in my long life, now I swallow everything, greedily. What I need now is stories, it took me a long time to know that, and I'm sure of it. There I am then, informed as to certain things, knowing certain things about him, things I didn't know, things I had craved to know, things I had never thought of. What rigmarole. I am even capable of having learnt what his profession is, I who am so interested in professions. And to think I try my best not to talk about myself. In a moment I shall talk about the cows, about the sky, if I can. There I am then, he leaves me, he's in a hurry. He didn't seem to be in a hurry, he was loitering, I've already said so, but after three minutes of me he is in a hurry, he has to hurry. I believe him. And once again I am, I will not say alone, no, that's not like me, but, how shall I say, I don't know, restored to myself, no, I never left myself, free, yes, I don't know what that means, but it's the word I mean to use, free to do what, to do nothing, to know, but what, the laws of the mind perhaps, of my mind, that for example water rises in proportion as it drowns you and that you would do better, at least no worse, to obliterate texts than to blacken margins, to fill in the holes of words till all is blank and flat and the whole ghastly business looks like what it is, senseless, speechless, issueless misery. So I doubtless did better, at least no worse, not to stir from my observation post. But instead of observing I had the weakness to return in spirit to the other, the man with the stick. Then the murmurs began again. To restore silence is the role of objects. I said, Who knows if he hasn't simply come out to take the air, relax, stretch his legs, cool his brain by stamping the blood down to his feet, so as to make sure of a good night, a joyous awakening, an enchanting morrow. Was he carrying so much as a scrip? But the way of walking, the anxious looks, the club, could these be reconciled with one's conception of what is called a little turn? But the hat, a town hat, an old-fashioned town hat, which the least gust would carry far away. Unless it was attached under the chin, by means of a string or an elastic. I took off my hat and looked at it. It is fastened, it has always been fastened, to my buttonhole, always the same buttonhole, at all seasons, by a long lace. I am still alive then. That may come in useful. The hand that held the hat I thrust as far as possible from me and moved in an arc, to and fro. As I did so, I watched the lapel of my greatcoat and saw it open and close. I understand now why I never wore a flower in my buttonhole, though it was large enough to hold a whole nosegay. My buttonhole was set aside for my hat. It was my hat that I beflowered. But it is neither of my hat nor of my greatcoat that I hope to speak at present, it would be premature. Doubtless I shall speak of them later, when the time comes to draw up the inventory of my goods and possessions. Unless I lose them between now and then. But even lost they will have their place, in the inventory of my possessions. But I am easy in my mind, I shall not lose them. Nor my crutches, I shall not lose my crutches either. But I shall perhaps one day throw them away. I must have been on the top, or on the slopes, of some considerable eminence, for otherwise how could I have seen, so far away, so near at hand, so far beneath, so many things, fixed and moving. But what was an eminence doing in this land with hardly a ripple? And I, what was I doing there, and why come? These are things that we shall try and discover. But these are things we must not take seriously. There is a little of everything, apparently, in nature, and freaks are common. And I am perhaps confusing several different occasions, and different times, deep down, and deep down is my dwelling, oh not deepest down, somewhere between the mud and the scum. And perhaps it was A one day at one place, then C another at another, then a third the rock and I, and so on for the other components, the cows, the sky, the sea, the mountains. I can't believe it. No, I will not lie, I can easily conceive it. No matter, no matter, let us go on, as if all arose from one and the same weariness, on and on heaping up and up, until there is no room, no light, for any more. What is certain is that the man with the stick did not pass by again that night, because I would have heard him, if he had. I don't say I would have seen him, I say I would have heard him. I sleep little and that little by day. Oh not systematically, in my life without end I have dabbled with every kind of sleep, but at the time now coming back to me I took my doze in the daytime and, what is more, in the morning. Let me hear nothing of the moon, in my night there is no moon, and if it happens that I speak of the stars it is by mistake. Now of all the noises that night not one was of those heavy uncertain steps, or of that club with which he sometimes smote the earth until it quaked. How agreeable it is to be confirmed, after a more or less long period of vacillation, in one's first impressions. Perhaps that is what tempers the pangs of death. Not that I was so conclusively, I mean confirmed, in my first impressions with regard to – wait – C. For the wagons and carts which a little before dawn went thundering by, on their way to market with fruit, eggs, butter and perhaps cheese, in one of these perhaps he would have been found, overcome by fatigue or discouragement, perhaps even dead. Or he might have gone back to the town by another way too far away for me to hear its sounds, or by little paths through the fields, crushing the silent grass, pounding the silent ground. And so at last I came out of that distant night, divided between the murmurs of my little world, its dutiful confusions, and those so different (so different?) of all that between two suns abides and passes away. Never once a human voice. But the cows, when the peasants passed, crying in vain to be milked. A and C I never saw again. But perhaps I shall see them again. But shall I be able to recognise them? And am I sure I never saw them again? And what do I mean by seeing and seeing again? An instant of silence, as when the conductor taps on his stand, raises his arms, before the unanswerable clamour. Smoke, sticks, flesh, hair, at evening, afar, flung about the craving for a fellow. I know how to summon these rags to cover my shame. I wonder what that means. But I shall not always be in need. But talking of the craving for a fellow let me observe that having waked between eleven o'clock and midday (I heard the angelus, recalling the incarnation, shortly after) I resolved to go and see my mother. I needed, before I could resolve to go and see that woman, reasons of an urgent nature, and with such reasons, since I did not know what to do, or where to go, it was child's play for me, the play of an only child, to fill my mind until it was rid of all other preoccupation and I seized with a trembling at the mere idea of being hindered from going there, I mean to my mother, there and then. So I got up, adjusted my crutches and went down to the road, where I found my bicycle (I didn't know I had one) in the same place I must have left it. Which enables me to remark that, crippled though I was, I was no mean cyclist, at that period. This is how I went about it. I fastened my crutches to the cross-bar, one on either side, I propped the foot of my stiff leg (I forget which, now they're both stiff) on the projecting front axle, and I pedalled with the other. It was a chainless bicycle, with a free-wheel, if such a bicycle exists. Dear bicycle, I shall not call you bike, you were green, like so many of your generation. I don't know why. It is a pleasure to meet it again. To describe it at length would be a pleasure. It had a little red horn instead of the bell fashionable in your days. To blow this horn was for me a real pleasure, almost a vice. I will go further and declare that if I were obliged to record, in a roll of honour, those activities which in the course of my interminable existence have given me only a mild pain in the balls, the blowing of a rubber horn – toot! – would figure among the first. And when I had to part from my bicycle I took off the horn and kept it about me. I believe I have it still, somewhere, and if I blow it no more it is because it has gone dumb. Even motor-cars have no horns nowadays, as I understand the thing, or rarely. When I see one, through the lowered window of a stationary car, I often stop and blow it. This should all be re-written in the pluperfect. What a rest to speak of bicycles and horns. Unfortunately it is not of them I have to speak, but of her who brought me into the world, through the hole in her arse if my memory is correct. First taste of the shit. So I shall only add that every hundred yards or so I stopped to rest my legs, the good one as well as the bad, and not only my legs, not only my legs. I didn't properly speaking get down off the machine, I remained astride it, my feet on the ground, my arms on the handle-bars, my head on my arms, and I waited until I felt better. But before I leave this earthly paradise, suspended between the mountains and the sea, sheltered from certain winds and exposed to all that Auster vents, in the way of scents and langours, on this accursed country, it would ill become me not to mention the awful cries of the corncrakes that run in the corn, in the meadows, all the short summer night long, dinning their rattles. And this enables me, what is more, to know when that unreal journey began, the second last but one of a form fading among fading forms, and which I here declare without further ado to have begun in the second or third week of June, at the moment that is to say most painful of all when over what is called our hemisphere the sun is at its pitilessmost and the arctic radiance comes pissing on our midnights. It is then the corncrakes are heard. My mother never refused to see me, that is she never refused to receive me, for it was many a long day since she had seen anything at all. I shall try and speak calmly. We were so old, she and I, she had had me so young, that we were like a couple of old cronies, sexless, unrelated, with the same memories, the same rancours, the same expectations. She never called me son, fortunately, I couldn't have borne it, but Dan, I don't know why, my name is not Dan. Dan was my father's name perhaps, yes, perhaps she took me for my father. I took her for my mother and she took me for my father. Dan, you remember the day I saved the swallow, Dan, you remember the day you buried the ring. I remembered, I remembered, I mean I knew more or less what she was talking about, and if I hadn't always taken part personally in the scenes she evoked, it was just as if I had. I called her Mag, when I had to call her something. And I called her Mag because for me, without my knowing why, the letter g abolished the syllable Ma, and as it were spat on it, better than any other letter would have done. And at the same time I satisfied a deep and doubtless unacknowledged need, the need to have a Ma, that is a mother, and to proclaim it, audibly. For before you say mag, you say ma, inevitably. And da, in my part of the world, means father. Besides, for me the question did not arise, at the period I'm worming into now, I mean the question of whether to call her Ma, Mag or the Countess Caca, she having for countless years been as deaf as a post. I think she was quite incontinent, both of faeces and water, but a kind of prudishness made us avoid the subject when we met, and I could never be certain of it. In any case it can't have amounted to much, a few niggardly wetted goat-droppings, every two or three days. The room smelt of ammonia, oh not merely of ammonia, but of ammonia, ammonia. She knew it was me, by my smell. Her shrunken, hairy old face lit up, she was happy to smell me. She jabbered away with a rattle of dentures and most of the time didn't realise what she was saying. Anyone but myself would have been lost in this clattering gabble, which can only have stopped during her brief instants of unconsciousness. In any case I didn't come to listen to her. I got into communication with her by knocking on her skull. One knock meant yes, two no, three I don't know, four money, five good-bye. I was hard put to ram this code into her ruined and frantic understanding, but I did it, in the end. That she should confuse yes, no, I don't know and good-bye, was all the same to me, I confused them myself. But that she should associate the four knocks with anything but money was something to be avoided at all costs. During the period of training therefore, at the same time as I administered the four knocks on her skull, I stuck a bank-note under her nose or in her mouth. In the innocence of my heart! For she seemed to have lost, if not absolutely all notion of mensuration, at least the faculty of counting beyond two. It was too far for her, yes, the distance was too great, from one to four. By the time she came to the fourth knock she imagined she was only at the second, the first two having been erased from her memory as completely as if they had never been felt, though I don't quite see how something never felt can be erased from the memory, and yet it is a common occurrence. She must have thought I was saying no to her all the time, whereas nothing was further from my purpose. Enlightened by these considerations I looked for and finally found a more effective means of putting the idea of money into her head. This consisted in replacing the four knocks of my index knuckle by one or more (according to my needs) thumps of the fist, on her skull. That she understood. In any case I didn't come for money. I took her money, but I didn't come for that. My mother. I don't think too harshly of her. I know she did all she could not to have me, except of course the one thing, and if she never succeeded in getting me unstuck, it was that fate had earmarked me for less compassionate sewers. But it was well-meant and that's enough for me. No it is not enough for me, but I give her credit, though she is my mother, for what she tried to do for me. And I forgive her for having jostled me a little in the first months and spoiled the only endurable, just endurable, period of my enormous history. And I also give her credit for not having done it again, thanks to me, or for having stopped in time, when she did. And if ever I'm reduced to looking for a meaning to my life, you never can tell, it's in that old mess I'll stick my nose to begin with, the mess of that poor old uniparous whore and myself the last of my foul brood, neither man nor beast. I should add, before I get down to the facts, you'd swear they were facts, of that distant summer afternoon, that with this deaf, blind, impotent, mad old woman, who called me Dan and whom I called Mag, and with her alone, I – no, I can't say it. That is to say, I could say it, but I won't say it, yes, I could say it easily, because it wouldn't be true. What did I see of her? A head always, the hands sometimes, the arms rarely. A head always. Veiled with hair, wrinkles, filth, slobber. A head that darkened the air. Not that seeing matters, but it's something to go on with. It was I who took the key from under the pillow, who took the money out of the drawer, who put the key back under the pillow. But I didn't come for money. I think there was a woman who came each week. Once I touched with my lips, vaguely, hastily, that little grey wizened pear. Pah. Did that please her? I don't know. Her babble stopped for a second, then began again. Perhaps she said to herself, Pah. I smelt a terrible smell. It must have come from the bowels. Odour of antiquity. Oh I'm not criticising her, I don't diffuse the perfumes of Araby myself. Shall I describe the room? No. I shall have occasion to do so later perhaps. When I seek refuge there, beat to the world, all shame drunk, my prick in my rectum, who knows. Good. Now that we know where we're going, let's go there. It's so nice to know where you're going, in the early stages. It almost rids you of the wish to go there. I was distraught, who am so seldom distraught, from what should I be distraught, and as to my motions even more uncertain than usual.

. . . But you'd think that once well clear of the town, and having turned round to look at it, what there was to see of it, you'd think that then I should have realised whether it was really my town or not. But no, I looked at it in vain, and perhaps unquestioningly, and simply to give the gods a chance, by turning round. Perhaps I only made a show of looking at it. I didn't feel I missed my bicycle, no, not really, I didn't mind going on my way I said, swinging low in the dark over the earth, along the little empty country roads. And I said there was little likelihood of my being molested and that it was more likely I should molest them, if they saw me. Morning is the time to hide. They wake up, hale and hearty, their tongues hanging out for order, beauty and justice, baying for their due. Yes, from eight or nine till noon is the dangerous time. But towards noon things quiet down, the most implacable are sated, they go home, it might have been better but they've done a good job, there have been a few survivors, but they'll give no more trouble, each man counts his rats. It may begin again in the early afternoon, after the banquet, the celebrations, the congratulations, the orations, but it's nothing compared to the morning, mere fun. Coming up to four or five of course there is the night-shift, the watchmen, beginning to bestir themselves. But already the day is over, the shadows lengthen, the walls multiply, you hug the walls, bowed down like a good boy, oozing with obsequiousness, having nothing to hide, hiding from mere terror, looking neither right nor left, hiding but not provocatively, ready to come out, to smile, to listen, to crawl, nauseating but not pestilent, less rat than toad. Then the true night, perilous too, but sweet to him who knows it, who can open it to like the flower to the sun, who himself is night, day and night. No there is not much to be said for the night either, but compared to the day there is much to be said for it, and notably compared to the morning there is everything to be said for it. For the night purge is in the hands of technicians, for the most part. They do nothing else, the bulk of the population have no part in it, preferring their warm beds, all things considered. Day is the time for lynching, for sleep is sacred, and especially the morning, between breakfast and lunch. My first care then, after a few miles in the desert dawn, was to look for a place to sleep, for sleep too is a kind of protection, strange as it may seem. For sleep, if it excites the lust to capture, seems to appease the lust to kill, there and then and bloodily, any hunter will tell you that. For the monster on the move, or on the watch, lurking in his lair, there is no mercy, whereas he if taken unawares, in his sleep, may sometimes get the benefit of milder feelings, which deflect the barrel, sheathe the kris. For the hunter is weak at heart and sentimental, overflowing with repressed treasures of gentleness and compassion. And it is thanks to this sweet sleep of terror or exhaustion that many a foul beast, and worthy of extermination, can live on till he dies in the peace and quiet of our zoological gardens, broken only by the innocent laughter, the knowing laughter, of children and their elders, on Sundays and Bank Holidays. And I for my part have always preferred slavery to death, I mean being put to death. For death is a condition I have never been able to conceive to my satisfaction and which therefore cannot go down in the ledger of weal and woe. Whereas my notions on being put to death inspired me with confidence, rightly or wrongly, and I felt I was entitled to act on them, in certain emergencies. Oh they weren't notions like yours, they were notions like mine, all spasm, sweat and trembling, without an atom of common sense or lucidity. But they were the best I had. Yes, the confusion of my ideas on the subject of death was such that I sometimes wondered, believe me or not, if it wasn't a state of being even worse than life. So I found it natural not to rush into it and, when I forgot myself to the point of trying, to stop in time. It's my only excuse. So I crawled into some hole somewhere I suppose and waited, half sleeping, half sighing, groaning and laughing, or feeling my body, to see if anything had changed, for the morning frenzy to abate. Then I resumed my spirals.

The fact is, and I deplore it, but it is too late now to do anything about it, that I have laid too much stress on my legs, throughout these wanderings, to the detriment of the rest. For I was no ordinary cripple, far from it, and there were days when my legs were the best part of me, with the exception of the brain capable of forming such a judgement. I was therefore obliged to stop more and more often, I shall never weary of repeating it, and to lie down, in defiance of the rules, now prone, now supine, now on one side, now on the other, and as much as possible with the feet higher than the head, to dislodge the clots. And to lie with the feet higher than the head, when your legs are stiff, is no easy matter. But don't worry, I did it. When my comfort was at stake there was no trouble I would not go to. The forest was all about me and the boughs, twining together at a prodigious height, compared to mine, sheltered me from the light and the elements. Some days I advanced no more than thirty or forty paces, I give you my oath. To say I stumbled in impenetrable darkness, no, I cannot. I stumbled, but the darkness was not impenetrable. For there reigned a kind of blue gloom, more than sufficient for my visual needs. I was astonished this gloom was not green, rather than blue, but I saw it blue and perhaps it was. The red of the sun, mingling with the green of the leaves, gave a blue result, that is how I reasoned. But from time to time. From time to time. What tenderness in these little words, what savagery. But from time to time I came on a kind of crossroads, you know, a star, or circus, of the kind to be found in even the most unexplored of forests. And turning then methodically to face the radiating paths in turn, hoping for I know not what, I described a complete circle, or less than a circle, or more than a circle, so great was the resemblance between them. Here the gloom was not so thick and I made haste to leave it. I don't like gloom to lighten, there's something shady about it. I had a certain number of encounters in this forest, naturally, where does one not, but nothing to signify. I notably encountered a charcoal-burner. I might have loved him, I think, if I had been seventy years younger. But it's not certain. For then he too would have been younger by as much, oh not quite as much, but much younger. I never really had much love to spare, but all the same I had my little quota, when I was small, and it went to the old men, when it could. And I even think I had time to love one or two, oh not with true love, no, nothing like the old woman, I've lost her name again, Rose, no, anyway you see who I mean, but all the same, how shall I say, tenderly, as those on the brink of a better earth. Ah I was a precocious child, and then I was a precocious man. Now they all give me the shits, the ripe, the unripe and the rotting from the bough. He was all over me, begging me to share his hut, believe it or not. A total stranger. Sick with solitude probably. I say charcoal-burner, but I really don't know. I see smoke somewhere. That's something that never escapes me, smoke. A long dialogue ensued, interspersed with groans. I could not ask him the way to my town, the name of which escaped me still. I asked him the way to the nearest town, I found the necessary words and accents. He did not know. He was born in the forest probably and had spent his whole life there. I asked him to show me the nearest way out of the forest. I grew eloquent. His reply was exceedingly confused. Either I didn't understand a word he said, or he didn't understand a word I said, or he knew nothing, or he wanted to keep me near him. It was towards this fourth hypothesis that in all modesty I leaned, for when I made to go, he held me back by the sleeve. So I smartly freed a crutch and dealt him a good dint on the skull. That calmed him. The dirty old brute. I got up and went on. But I hadn't gone more than a few paces, and for me at this time a few paces meant something, when I turned and went back to where he lay, to examine him. Seeing he had not ceased to breathe I contented myself with giving him a few warm kicks in the ribs, with my heels. This is how I went about it. I carefully chose the most favourable position, a few paces from the body, with my back of course turned to it. Then, nicely balanced on my crutches, I began to swing, backwards, forwards, feet pressed together, or rather legs pressed together, for how could I press my feet together, with my legs in the state they were? But how could I press my legs together, in the state they were? I pressed them together, that's all I can tell you. Take it or leave it. Or I didn't press them together. What can that possibly matter? I swung, that's all that matters, in an ever-widening arc, until I decided the moment had come and launched myself forward with all my strength and consequently, a moment later, backward, which gave the desired result. Where did I get this access of vigour? From my weakness perhaps. The shock knocked me down. Naturally. I came a cropper. You can't have everything, I've often noticed it. I rested a moment, then got up, picked up my crutches, took up my position on the other side of the body and applied myself with method to the same exercise. I always had a mania for symmetry. But I must have aimed a little low and one of my heels sank in something soft. However. For if I had missed the ribs, with that heel, I had no doubt landed in the kidney, oh not hard enough to burst it, no, I fancy not. People imagine, because you are old, poor, crippled, terrified, that you can't stand up for yourself, and generally speaking that is so. But given favourable conditions, a feeble and awkward assailant, in your own class what, and a lonely place, and you have a good chance of showing what stuff you are made of. And it is doubtless in order to revive interest in this possibility, too often forgotten, that I have delayed over an incident of no interest in itself, like all that has a moral. But did I at least eat, from time to time? Perforce, perforce, roots, berries, sometimes a little mulberry, a mushroom from time to time, trembling, knowing nothing about mushrooms. What else, ah yes, carobs, so dear to goats. In a word whatever I could find, forests abound in good things. And having heard, or more probably read somewhere, in the days when I thought I would be well advised to educate myself, or amuse myself, or stupefy myself, or kill time, that when a man in a forest thinks he is going forward in a straight line, in reality he is going in a circle, I did my best to go in a circle, hoping in this way to go in a straight line. For I stopped being half-witted and became sly, whenever I took the trouble. And my head was a storehouse of useful knowledge. And if I did not go in a rigorously straight line, with my system of going in a circle, at least I did not go in a circle, and that was something. And by going on doing this, day after day, and night after night, I looked forward to getting out of the forest, some day. For my region was not all forest, far from it.

But there were plains too, mountains and sea, and some towns and villages, connected by highways and byways. And I was all the more convinced that I would get out of the forest some day as I had already got out of it, more than once, and I knew how difficult it was not to do again what you have done before. But things had been rather different then. And yet I did not despair of seeing the light tremble, some day, through the still boughs, the strange light of the plain, its pale wild eddies, through the bronze-still boughs, which no breath ever stirred. But it was a day I dreaded too. So that I was sure it would come sooner or later. For it was not so bad being in the forest, I could imagine worse, and I could have stayed there till I died, unrepining, yes, without pining for the light and the plain and the other amenities of my region. For I knew them well, the amenities of my region, and I considered that the forest was no worse. And it was not only no worse, to my mind, but it was better, in this sense, that I was there. That is a strange way, is it not, of looking at things. Perhaps less strange than it seems. For being in the forest, a place neither worse nor better than the others, and being free to stay there, was it not natural I should think highly of it, not because of what it was, but because I was there. For I was there. And being there I did not have to go there, and that was not to be despised, seeing the state of my legs and my body in general. That is all I wished to say, and if I did not say it at the outset it is simply that something was against it. But I could not, stay in the forest I mean, I was not free to. That is to say I could have, physically nothing could have been easier, but I was not purely physical, I lacked something, and I would have had the feeling, if I had stayed in the forest, of going against an imperative, at least I had that impression. But perhaps I was mistaken, perhaps I would have been better advised to stay in the forest, perhaps I could have stayed there, without remorse, without the painful impression of committing a fault, almost a sin. For I have greatly sinned, at all times, greatly sinned against my prompters. And if I cannot decently be proud of this I see no reason either to be sorry. But imperatives are a little different, and I have always been inclined to submit to them, I don't know why. For they never led me anywhere, but tore me from places where, if all was not well, all was no worse than anywhere else, and then went silent, leaving me stranded. So I knew my imperatives well, and yet I submitted to them. It had become a habit. It is true they nearly all bore on the same question, that of my relations with my mother, and on the importance of bringing as soon as possible some light to bear on these and even on the kind of light that should be brought to bear and the most effective means of doing so. Yes, these imperatives were quite explicit and even detailed until, having set me in motion at last, they began to falter, then went silent, leaving me there like a fool who neither knows where he is going nor why he is going there. And they nearly all bore, as I may have said already, on the same painful and thorny question. And I do not think I could mention even one having a different purport. And the one enjoining me then to leave the forest without delay was in no way different from those I was used to, as to its meaning. For in its framing I thought I noticed something new. For after the usual blarney there followed this solemn warning. Perhaps it is already too late. It was in Latin, 'nimis sero', I think that's Latin. Charming things, hypothetical imperatives. But if I had never succeeded in liquidating this matter of my mother, the fault must not be imputed solely to that voice which deserted me, prematurely. It was partly to blame, that's all it can be reproached with. For the outer world opposed my succeeding too, with its wiles, I have given some examples. And even if the voice could have harried me to the very scene of action, even then I might well have succeeded no better, because of the other obstacles barring my way. And in this command which faltered, then died, it was hard not to hear the unspoken entreaty, Don't do it, Molloy. In forever reminding me thus of my duty was its purpose to show me the folly of it? Perhaps. Fortunately it did no more than stress, the better to mock if you like, an innate velleity. And of myself, all my life, I think I had been going to my mother, with the purpose of establishing our relations on a less precarious footing. And when I was with her, and I often succeeded, I left her without having done anything. And when I was no longer with her I was again on my way to her, hoping to do better the next time. And when I appeared to give up and to busy myself with something else, or with nothing at all any more, in reality I was hatching my plans and seeking the way to her house. This is taking a queer turn. So even without this so-called imperative I impugn, it would have been difficult for me to stay in the forest, since I was forced to assume my mother was not there. And yet it might have been better for me to try and stay. But I also said, Yet a little while, at the rate things are going, and I won't be able to move, but will have to stay, where I happen to be, unless someone comes and carries me. Oh I did not say it in such limpid language. And when I say I said, etc., all I mean is that I knew confusedly things were so, without knowing exactly what it was all about. And every time I say, I said this, or, I said that, or speak of a voice saying, far away inside me, Molloy, and then a fine phrase more or less clear and simple, or find myself compelled to attribute to others intelligible words, or hear my own voice uttering to others more or less articulate sounds, I am merely complying with the convention that demands you either lie or hold your peace. For what really happened was quite different. And I did not say, Yet a little while, at the rate things are going, etc., but that resembled perhaps what I would have said, if I had been able. In reality I said nothing at all, but I heard a murmur, something gone wrong with the silence, and I pricked up my ears, like an animal I imagine, which gives a start and pretends to be dead. And then sometimes there arose within me, confusedly, a kind of consciousness, which I express by saying, I said, etc., or, Don't do it Molloy, or, Is that your mother's name? said the sergeant, I quote from memory. Or which I express without sinking to the level of *oratio recta*, but by means of other figures quite as deceitful, as for example, It seemed to me that, etc., or, I had the impression that, etc., for it seemed to me nothing at all, and I had no impression of any kind, but simply somewhere something had changed, so that I too had to change, or the world too had to change, in order for nothing to be changed. And it was these little adjustments, as between Galileo's vessels, that I can only express by saying, I feared that, or, I hoped that, or, Is that your mother's name? said the sergeant, for example, and that I might doubtless have expressed otherwise and better, if I had gone to the trouble. And so I shall perhaps some day when I have less horror of trouble than today. But I think not. So I said, Yet a little while, at the rate things are going, and I won't be able to move, but will have to stay, where I happen to be, unless some kind person comes and carries me. For my marches got shorter and shorter and my halts in consequence more and more frequent and I may add prolonged. For the notion of the long halt does not necessarily follow from that of the short march, nor that of the frequent halt either, when you come to think of it, unless you give frequent a meaning it does not possess, and I could never bring myself to do a thing like that. And it seemed to me all the more important to get out of this forest with all possible speed as I would very soon be powerless to get out of anything whatsoever, were it but a bower. It was winter, it must have been winter, and not only many trees had lost their leaves, but these lost leaves had gone all black and spongy and my crutches sank into them, in places right up to the fork. Strange to say I felt no colder than usual. Perhaps it was only autumn. But I was never very sensitive to changes of temperature. And the gloom, if it seemed less blue than before, was as thick as ever. Which made me say in the end, It is less blue because there is less green, but it is no less thick thanks to the leaden winter sky. Then something about the black dripping from the black boughs, something in that line. The black slush of leaves slowed me down even more. But leaves or no leaves I would have abandoned erect motion, that of man. And I still remember the day when, flat on my face by way of rest, in defiance of the rules, I suddenly cried, striking my brow, Christ, there's crawling, I never thought of that. But could I crawl, with my legs in such a state, and my trunk? And my head. But before I go on, a word about the forest murmurs. It was in vain I listened, I could hear nothing of the kind. But rather, with much goodwill and a little imagination, at long intervals a distant gong. A horn goes well with the forest, you expect it. It is the huntsman. But a gong! Even a tom-tom, at a pinch, would not have shocked me. But a gong! It was mortifying, to have been looking forward to the celebrated murmurs if to nothing else, and to succeed only in hearing, at long intervals, in the far distance, a gong. For a moment I dared hope it was only my heart, still beating. But only for a moment. For it does not beat, not my heart, I'd have to refer you to hydraulics for the squelch that old pump makes. To the leaves too I listened, before their fall, attentively in vain. They made no sound, motionless and rigid, like brass, have I said that before? So much for the forest murmurs. From time to time I blew my horn, through the cloth of my pocket. Its hoot was fainter every time. I had taken it off my bicycle. When? I don't know. And now, let us have done. Flat on my belly, using my crutches like grapnels, I plunged them ahead of me into the undergrowth, and when I felt they had a hold, I pulled myself forward, with an effort of the wrists. For my wrists were still quite strong, fortunately, in spite of my decrepitude, though all swollen and racked by a kind of chronic arthritis probably. That then briefly is how I went about it. The advantage of this mode of locomotion compared to others, I mean those I have tried, is this, that when you want to rest you stop and rest, without further ado. For standing there is no rest, nor sitting either. And there are men who move about sitting, and even kneeling, hauling themselves to right and left, forward and backward, with the help of hooks. But he who moves in this way, crawling on his belly, like a reptile, no sooner comes to rest than he begins to rest, and even the very movement is a kind of rest, compared to other movements, I mean those that have worn me out. And in this way I moved onward in the forest, slowly, but with a certain regularity, and I covered my fifteen paces, day in, day out, without killing myself. And I even crawled on my back, plunging my crutches blindly behind me into the thickets, and with the black boughs for sky to my closing eyes. I was on my way to mother. And from time to time I said, Mother, to encourage me I suppose. I kept losing my hat, the lace had broken long ago, until in a fit of temper I banged it down on my skull with such violence that I couldn't get it off again. And if I had met any lady friends, if I had had any lady friends, I would have been powerless to salute them correctly. But there was always present to my mind, which was still working, if laboriously, the need to turn, to keep on turning, and every three or four jerks I altered course, which permitted me to describe, if not a circle, at least a great polygon, perfection is not of this world, and to hope that I was going forward in a straight line, in spite of everything, day and night, towards my mother. And true enough the day came when the forest ended and I saw the light, the light of the plain, exactly as I had foreseen. But I did not see it from afar, trembling beyond the harsh trunks, as I had foreseen, but suddenly I was in it, I opened my eyes and saw I had arrived. And the reason for that was probably this, that for some time past I had not opened my eyes, or seldom. And even my little changes of course were made blindly, in the dark. The forest ended in a ditch, I don't know why, and it was in this ditch that I became aware of what had happened to me. I suppose it was the fall into the ditch that opened my eyes, for why would they have opened otherwise? I looked at the plain rolling away as far as the eye could see. No, not quite so far as that. For my eyes having got used to the light I fancied I saw, faintly outlined against the horizon, the towers and steeples of a town, which of course I could not assume was mine, on such slight evidence. It is true the plain seemed familiar, but in my region all the plains looked alike, when you knew one you knew them all. In any case, whether it was my town or not, whether somewhere under that faint haze my mother panted on, or whether she poisoned the air a hundred miles away, were ludicrously idle questions for a man in my position, though of undeniable interest on the plane of pure knowledge. For how could I drag myself over that vast moor, where my crutches would fumble in vain. Rolling perhaps. And then? Would they let me roll on to my mother's door? Fortunately for me at this painful juncture, which I had vaguely foreseen, but not in all its bitterness, I heard a voice telling me not to fret, that help was coming. Literally. These words struck it is not too much to say as clearly on my ear, and on my understanding, as the urchin's thanks I suppose when I stooped and picked up his marble. Don't fret, Molloy, we're coming. Well, I suppose you have to try everything once, succour included, to get a complete picture of the resources of their planet. I lapsed down to the bottom of the ditch. It must have been spring, a morning in spring. I thought I heard birds, skylarks perhaps. I had not heard a bird for a long time. How was it I had not heard any in the forest? Nor seen any. It had not seemed strange to me. Had I heard any at the seaside? Mews? I could not remember. I remembered the corncrakes. The two travellers came back to my memory. One had a club. I had forgotten them. I saw the sheep again. Or so I say now. I did not fret, other scenes of my life came back to me. There seemed to be rain, then sunshine, turn about. Real spring weather. I longed to go back into the forest. Oh not a real longing. Molloy could stay, where he happened to be.

II   Moran

It is midnight. The rain is beating on the windows. I am calm. All is sleeping. Nevertheless I get up and go to my desk. I can't sleep. My lamp sheds a soft and steady light. I have trimmed it. It will last till morning. I hear the eagle-owl. What a terrible battlecry! Once I listened to it unmoved. My son is sleeping. Let him sleep. The night will come when he too, unable to sleep, will get up and go to his desk. I shall be forgotten.

My report will be long. Perhaps I shall not finish it. My name is Moran, Jacques. That is the name I am known by. I am done for. My son too. All unsuspecting. He must think he's on the threshold of life, of real life. He's right there. His name is Jacques, like mine. This cannot lead to confusion.

I remember the day I received the order to see about Molloy. It was a Sunday in summer. I was sitting in my little garden, in a wicker chair, a black book closed on my knees. It must have been about eleven o'clock, still too early to go to church. I was savouring the day of rest, while deploring the importance attached to it, in certain parishes. To work, even to play on Sunday, was not of necessity reprehensible, in my opinion. It all depended on the state of mind of him who worked, or played, and on the nature of his work, of his play, in my opinion. I was reflecting with satisfaction on this, that this slightly libertarian view was gaining ground, even among the clergy, more and more disposed to admit that the sabbath, so long as you go to mass and contribute to the collection, may be considered a day like any other, in certain respects. This did not affect me personally, I've always loved doing nothing. And I would gladly have rested on weekdays too, if I could have afforded it. Not that I was positively lazy. It was something else. Seeing something done which I could have done better myself, if I had wished, and which I did do better whenever I put my mind to it, I had the impression of discharging a function to which no form of activity could have exalted me. But this was a joy in which, during the week, I could seldom indulge.

The weather was fine. I watched absently the coming and going of my bees. I heard on the gravel the scampering steps of my son, caught up in I know not what fantasy of flight and pursuit. I called to him not to dirty himself. He did not answer.

All was still. Not a breath. From my neighbours' chimneys the smoke rose straight and blue. None but tranquil sounds, the clicking of mallet and ball, a rake on pebbles, a distant lawnmower, the bell of my beloved church. And birds of course, blackbird and thrush, their song sadly dying, vanquished by the heat, and leaving dawn's high boughs for the bushes' gloom. Contentedly I inhaled the scent of my lemon-verbena.

In such surroundings slipped away my last moments of peace and happiness.

A man came into the garden and walked swiftly towards me. I knew him well. Now I have no insuperable objection to a neighbour's dropping in, on a Sunday, to pay his respects, if he feels the need, though I much prefer to see nobody. But this man was not a neighbour. Our dealings were strictly of a business nature and he had journeyed from afar, on purpose to disturb me. So I was disposed to receive him frostily enough, all the more so as he had the impertinence to come straight to where I was sitting, under my Beauty of Bath. With people who took this liberty I had no patience. If they wished to speak to me they had only to ring at the door of my house. Martha had her instructions. I thought I was hidden from anybody coming into my grounds and following the short path which led from the garden-gate to the front door, and in fact I must have been. But at the noise of the gate being slammed I turned angrily and saw, blurred by the leaves, this high mass bearing down on me, across the lawn. I neither got up nor invited him to sit down. He stopped in front of me and we stared at each other in silence. He was dressed in his heavy, sombre Sunday best, and at this my displeasure knew no bounds. This gross external observance, while the soul exults in its rags, has always appeared to me an abomination. I watched the enormous feet crushing my daisies. I would gladly have driven him away, with a knout. Unfortunately it was not he who mattered. Sit down, I said, mollified by the reflection that after all he was only acting his part of go-between. Yes, suddenly I had pity on him, pity on myself. He sat down and mopped his forehead. I caught a glimpse of my son spying on us from behind a bush. My son was thirteen or fourteen at the time. He was big and strong for his age. His intelligence seemed at times a little short of average. My son, in fact. I called him and ordered him to go and fetch some beer. Peeping and prying were part of my profession. My son imitated me instinctively. He returned after a remarkably short interval with two glasses and a quart bottle of beer. He uncorked the bottle and served us. He was very fond of uncorking bottles. I told him to go and wash himself, to straighten his clothes, in a word, to get ready to appear in public, for it would soon be time for mass. He can stay, said Gaber. I don't wish him to stay, I said. And turning to my son I told him again to go and get ready. If there was one thing displeased me, at that time, it was being late for the last mass. Please yourself, said Gaber. Jacques went away grumbling with his finger in his mouth, a detestable and unhygienic habit, but preferable, all things considered, to that of the finger in the nose, in my opinion. If putting his finger in his mouth prevented my son from putting it in his nose, or elsewhere, he was right to do it, in a sense.

Here are your instructions, said Gaber. He took a notebook from his pocket and began to read. Every now and then he closed the notebook, taking care to leave his finger in it as a marker, and indulged in comments and observations of which I had no need, for I knew my business. When at last he had finished I told him the job did not interest me and that the chief would do better to call on another agent. He wants it to be you, God knows why, said Gaber. I presume he told you why, I said, scenting flattery, for which I had a weakness. He said, replied Gaber, that no one could do it but you. This was more or less what I wanted to hear. And yet, I said, the affair seems childishly simple. Gaber began bitterly to inveigh against our employer, who had made him get up in the middle of the night, just as he was getting into position to make love to his wife. For this kind of nonsense, he added. And he said he had confidence in no one but me? I said. He doesn't know what he says, said Gaber. He added, Nor what he does. He wiped the lining of his bowler, peering inside as if in search of something. In that case it's hard for me to refuse, I said, knowing perfectly well that in any case it was impossible for me to refuse. Refuse! But we agents often amused ourselves with grumbling among ourselves and giving ourselves the airs of free men. You leave today, said Gaber. Today! I cried, but he's out of his mind! Your son goes with you, said Gaber. I said no more. When it came to the point we said no more. Gaber buttoned his notebook and put it back in his pocket, which he also buttoned. He stood up, rubbing his hands over his chest. I could do with another beer, he said. Go to the kitchen, I said, the maid will serve you. Goodbye, Moran, he said.

It was too late for mass. I did not need to consult my watch to know, I could feel mass had begun without me. I who never missed mass, to have missed it on that Sunday of all Sundays! When I so needed it! To buck me up! I decided to ask for a private communion, in the course of the afternoon. I would go without lunch. Father Ambrose was always very kind and accommodating.

I called Jacques. Without result. I said, Seeing me still in conference he has gone to mass alone. This explanation turned out subsequently to be the correct one. But I added, He might have come and seen me before leaving. I liked thinking in monologue and then my lips moved visibly. But no doubt he was afraid of disturbing me and of being reprimanded. For I was sometimes inclined to go too far when I reprimanded my son, who was consequently a little afraid of me. I myself had never been sufficiently chastened. Oh I had not been spoiled either, merely neglected. Whence bad habits ingrained beyond remedy and of which even the most meticulous piety has never been able to break me. I hoped to spare my son this misfortune, by giving him a good clout from time to time, together with my reasons for doing so. Then I said, Is he barefaced enough to tell me, on his return, that he has been to mass if he has not, if for example he has merely run off to join his little friends, behind the slaughter-house? And I determined to get the truth out of Father Ambrose, on this subject. For it was imperative my son should not imagine he was capable of lying to me with impunity. And if Father Ambrose could not enlighten me. I would apply to the verger, whose vigilance it was inconceivable that the presence of my son at twelve o'clock mass had escaped. For I knew for a fact that the verger had a list of the faithful and that, from his place beside the font, he ticked us off when it came to the absolution. It is only fair to say that Father Ambrose knew nothing of these manoeuvres, yes, anything in the nature of surveillance was hateful to the good Father Ambrose. And he would have sent the verger flying about his business if he had suspected him of such a work of supererogation. It must have been for his own edification that the verger kept this register, with such assiduity. Admittedly I knew only what went on at the mass, having no experience personally of the other offices, for the good reason that I never went within a mile of them. But I had heard it said that they were the occasion of exactly the same supervision, at the hands either of the verger himself or, when his duties called him elsewhere, of one of his sons. A strange parish whose flock knew more than its pastor of a circumstance which seemed rather in his province than in theirs.

Such were my thoughts as I waited for my son to come back and Gaber, whom I had not yet heard leave, to go. And tonight I find it strange I could have thought of such things, I mean my son, my lack of breeding, Father Ambrose, Verger Joly with his register, at such a time. Had I not something better to do, after what I had just heard? The fact is I had not yet begun to take the matter seriously. And I am all the more surprised as such light-mindedness was not like me. Or was it in order to win a few more moments of peace that I instinctively avoided giving my mind to it? Even if, as set forth in Garber's report, the affair had seemed unworthy of me, the chief's insistence on having me, me Moran, rather than anybody else, ought to have warned me that it was no ordinary one. And instead of bringing to bear upon it without delay all the resources of my mind and of my experience, I sat dreaming of my breed's infirmities and the singularities of those about me. And yet the poison was already acting on me, the poison I had just been given. I stirred restlessly in my arm-chair, ran my hands over my face, crossed and uncrossed my legs, and so on. The colour and weight of the world was changing already, soon I would have to admit I was anxious.

I remembered with annoyance the lager I had just absorbed. Would I be granted the body of Christ after a pint of Wallenstein? And if I said nothing? Have you come fasting, my son? He would not ask. But God would know, sooner or later. Perhaps he would pardon me. But would the eucharist produce the same effect, taken on top of beer, however light? I could always try. What was the teaching of the Church on the matter? What if I were about to commit sacrilege? I decided to suck a few peppermints on the way to the presbytery.

I got up and went to the kitchen. I asked if Jacques was back. I haven't seen him, said Martha. She seemed in bad humour. And the man? I said. What man? she said. The man who came for a glass of beer, I said. No one came for anything, said Martha. By the way, I said, unperturbed apparently, I shall not eat lunch today. She asked if I were ill. For I was naturally a rather heavy eater. And my Sunday midday meal especially I always liked extremely copious. It smelt good in the kitchen. I shall lunch a little later today, that's all, I said. Martha looked at me furiously. Say four o'clock, I said. In that wizened, grey, skull what raging and rampaging then, I knew. You will not go out today, I said coldly, I regret. She flung herself at her pots and pans, dumb with anger. You will keep all that hot for me, I said, as best you can. And knowing her capable of poisoning me I added, You can have the whole day off tomorrow, if that is any good to you.

I left her and went out on the road. So Gaber had gone without his beer. And yet he had wanted it badly. It was a good brand, Wallenstein. I stood there on the watch for Jacques. Coming from church he would appear on my right, on my left if he came from the slaughter-house. A neighbour passed. A free-thinker. Well, well, he said, no worship today? He knew my habits, my Sunday habit I mean. Everyone knew them and the chief perhaps better than any, in spite of his remoteness. You look as if you had seen a ghost, said the neighbour. Worse than that, I said, you. I went in, at my back the dutifully hideous smile. I could see him running to his concubine with the news, You know that poor bastard

Moran, you should have heard me, I had him lepping! Couldn't speak! Took to his heels!

Jacques came back soon afterwards. No trace of frolic. He said he had been to church alone. I asked him a few pertinent questions concerning the march of the ceremony. His answers were plausible. I told him to wash his hands and sit down to his lunch. I went back to the kitchen. I did nothing but go to and fro. You may dish up, I said. She had wept. I peered into the pots. Irish stew. A nourishing and economical dish, if a little indigestible. All honour to the land it has brought before the world. I shall sit down at four o'clock, I said. I did not need to add sharp. I liked punctuality, all those whom my roof sheltered had to like it too. I went up to my room. And there, stretched on my bed, the curtains drawn, I made a first attempt to grasp the Molloy affair.

My concern at first was only with its immediate vexations and the preparations they demanded of me. The kernel of the affair I continued to shirk. I felt a great confusion coming over me.

Should I set out on my autocycle? This was the question with which I began. I had a methodical mind and never set out on a mission without prolonged reflection as to the best way of setting out. It was the first problem to solve, at the outset of each enquiry, and I never moved until I had solved it to my satisfaction. Sometimes I took my autocycle, sometimes the train, sometimes the motor-coach, just as sometimes too I left on foot, or on my bicycle, silently, in the night. For when you are beset with enemies, as I am, you cannot leave on your autocycle, even in the night, without being noticed, unless you employ it as an ordinary bicycle, which is absurd. But if I was in the habit of first settling this delicate question of transport, it was never without having, if not fully sifted, at least taken into account the factors on which it depended. For how can you decide on the way of setting out if you do not first know where you are going, or at least with what purpose you are going there? But in the present case I was tackling the problem of transport with no other preparation than the languid cognisance I had taken of Gaber's report. I would be able to recover the minutest details of this report when I wished. But I had not yet troubled to do so, I had avoided doing so, saying, The affair is banal. To try and solve the problem of transport under such conditions was madness. Yet that was what I was doing. I was losing my head already.

I liked leaving on my autocycle, I was partial to this way of getting about. And in my ignorance of the reasons against it I decided to leave on my autocycle. Thus was inscribed, on the threshold of the Molloy affair, the fatal pleasure principle.

The sun's beams shone through the rift in the curtains and made visible the sabbath of the motes. I concluded from this that the weather was still fine and rejoiced. When you leave on your autocycle fine weather is to be preferred. I was wrong, the weather was fine no longer, the sky was clouding over, soon it would rain. But for the moment the sun was still shining. It was on this that I went, with inconceivable levity, having nothing else to go on.

Next I attacked, according to my custom, the capital question of the effects to take with me. And on this subject too I should have come to a quite otiose decision but for my son, who burst in wanting to know if he might go out. I controlled myself. He was wiping his mouth with the back of his hand, a thing I do not like to see. But there are nastier gestures, I speak from experience.

Out? I said. Where? Out! Vagueness I abhor. I was beginning to feel hungry. To the Elms, he replied. So we call our little public park. And yet there is not an elm to be seen in it, I have been told. What for? I said. To go over my botany, he replied. There were times I suspected my son of deceit. This was one. I would almost have preferred him to say, For a walk, or, To look at the tarts. The trouble was he knew far more than I, about botany. Otherwise I could have set him a few teasers, on his return. Personally I just liked plants, in all innocence and simplicity. I even saw in them at times a superfetatory proof of the existence of God. Go, I said, but be back at half-past four, I want to talk to you. Yes papa, he said. Yes papa! Ah!

I slept a little. Faster, faster. Passing the church, something made me stop. I looked at the door, baroque, very fine. I found it hideous. I hastened on to the presbytery. The Father is sleeping, said the servant. I can wait, I said. Is it urgent? she said. Yes and no, I said. She showed me into the sitting-room, bare and bleak, dreadful. Father Ambrose came in, rubbing his eyes. I disturb you, Father, I said. He clicked his tongue against the roof of his mouth, protestingly. I shall not describe our attitudes, characteristic his of him, mine of me. He offered me a cigar which I accepted with good grace and put in my pocket, between my fountain-pen and my propelling-pencil. He flattered himself, Father Ambrose, with being a man of the world and knowing its ways, he who never smoked. And everyone said he was most broad. I asked him if he had noticed my son at the last mass. Certainly, he said, we even spoke together. I must have looked surprised. Yes, he said, not seeing you at your place, in the front row, I feared you were ill. So I called for the dear child, who reassured me. A most untimely visitor, I said, whom I could not shake off in time. So your son explained to me, he said. He added, But let us sit down, we have no train to catch. He laughed and sat down, hitching up his heavy cassock. May I offer you a little glass of something? he said. I was in a quandary. Had Jacques let slip an allusion to the lager. He was quite capable of it. I came to ask you a favour, I said. Granted, he said. We observed each other. It's this, I said, Sunday for me without the Body and Blood is like—. He raised his hand. Above all no profane comparisons, he said. Perhaps he was thinking of the kiss without a moustache or beef without mustard. I dislike being interrupted. I sulked. Say no more, he said, a wink is as good as a nod, you want communion. I bowed my head. It's a little unusual, he said. I wondered if he had fed. I knew he was given to prolonged fasts, by way of mortification certainly, and then because his doctor advised it. Thus he killed two birds with one stone. Not a word to a soul, he said. Let it remain between us and—. He broke off, raising a finger, and his eyes, to the ceiling. Heavens, he said, what is that stain? I looked in turn at the ceiling. Damp, I said. Tut tut, he said, how annoying. The words tut tut seemed to me the maddest I had heard. There are times, he said, when one feels like weeping. He got up. I'll go and get my kit, he said. He called that his kit. Alone, my hands clasped until it seemed my knuckles would crack, I asked the Lord for guidance. Without result. That was some consolation. As for Father Ambrose, in view of his alacrity to fetch his kit, it seemed evident to me he suspected nothing. Or did it amuse him to see how far I would go? Or did it tickle him to have me commit a sin? I summarised the situation briefly as follows. If knowing I have beer taken he gives me the sacrament, his sin, if sin there be, is as great as mine. I was therefore risking little. He came back with a kind of portable pyx, opened it, and dispatched me without an instant's hesitation. I rose and thanked him warmly. Pah! he said, it's nothing. Now we can talk.

I had nothing else to say to him. All I wanted was to return home as quickly as possible and stuff myself with stew. My soul appeased, I was ravenous. But being slightly in advance of my schedule I resigned myself to allowing him eight minutes. They seemed endless. He informed me that Mrs Clement, the chemist's wife and herself a highly qualified chemist, had fallen, in her laboratory, from the top of a ladder, and broken the neck—. The neck! I cried. Of her femur, he said, can't you let me finish. He added that it was bound to happen. And I, not to be outdone, told him how worried I was about my hens, particularly my grey hen, which would neither brood nor lay and for the past month and more had done nothing but sit with her arse in the dust, from morning to night. Like Job, haha, he said. I too said haha. What a joy it is to laugh, from time to time, he said. Is it not? I said. It is peculiar to man, he said. So I have noticed, I said. A brief silence ensued. What do you feed her on? he said. Corn chiefly, I said. Cooked or raw? he said. Both, I said. I added that she ate nothing any more. Nothing! he cried. Next to nothing, I said. Animals never laugh, he said. It takes us to find that funny, I said. What? he said. It takes us to find that funny, I said loudly. He mused. Christ never laughed either, he said, so far as we know. He looked at me. Can you wonder? I said. There it is, he said. He smiled sadly. She has not the pip, I hope, he said. I said she had not, certainly not, anything he liked, but not the pip. He meditated. Have you tried bicarbonate? he said. I beg your pardon? I said. Bicarbonate of soda, he said, have you tried it? Why no, I said. Try it! he cried, flushing with pleasure, have her swallow a few dessertspoonfuls, several times a day, for a few months. You'll see, you won't know her. A powder? I said. Bless my heart to be sure, he said. Many thanks, I said, I'll begin today. Such a fine hen, he said, such a good layer. Or rather tomorrow, I said. I had forgotten the chemist was closed. Except in case of emergency. And now that little cordial, he said. I declined.

This interview with Father Ambrose left me with a painful impression. He was still the same dear man, and yet not. I seemed to have surprised, on his face, a lack, how shall I say, a lack of nobility. The host, it is only fair to say, was lying heavy on my stomach. And as I made my way home I felt like one who, having swallowed a pain-killer, is first astonished, then indignant, on obtaining no relief. And I was almost ready to suspect Father Ambrose, alive to my excesses of the fore-noon, of having fobbed me off with unconsecrated bread. Or of mental reservation as he pronounced the magic words. And it was in vile humour that I arrived home, in the pelting rain.

The stew was a great disappointment. Where are the onions? I cried. Gone to nothing, replied Martha. I rushed into the kitchen, to look for the onions I suspected her of having removed from the pot, because she knew how much I liked them. I even rummaged in the bin. Nothing. She watched me mockingly.

I went up to my room again, drew back the curtains on a calamitous sky and lay down. I could not understand what was happening to me. I found it painful at that period not to understand. I tried to pull myself together. In vain. I might have known. My life was running out, I knew not through what breach. I succeeded however in dozing off, which is not so easy, when pain is speculative. And I was marvelling, in that half-sleep, at my half-sleeping, when my son came in, without knocking. Now if there is one thing I abhor, it is someone coming into my room, without knocking. I might just happen to be masturbating, before my cheval-glass. Father with yawning fly and starting eyes, toiling to scatter on the ground his joyless seed, that was no sight for a small boy. Harshly I recalled him to the proprieties. He protested he had knocked twice. If you had knocked a hundred times, I replied, it would not give you the right to come in without being invited. But, he said. But what? I said. You told me to be here at half-past four, he said. There is something, I said, more important in life than punctuality, and that is decorum. Repeat. In that disdainful mouth my phrase put me to shame. He was soaked. What have you been looking at? I said. The liliaceae, papa, he answered. The liliaceae papa! My son had a way of saying papa, when he wanted to hurt me, that was very special. Now listen to me, I said. His face took on an expression of anguished attention. We leave this evening, I said in substance, on a journey. Put on your school suit, the green—. But it's blue, papa, he said. Blue or green, put it on, I said violently. I went on. Put in your little knapsack, the one I gave you for your birthday, your toilet things, one shirt, one pair of socks and seven pairs of drawers. Do you understand? Which shirt, papa? he said. It doesn't matter which shirt, I cried, any shirt! Which shoes am I to wear? he said. You have two pairs of shoes, I said, one for Sundays, and one for weekdays, and you ask me which you are to wear. I sat up. I want none of your lip, I said.

Thus to my son I gave precise instructions. But were they the right ones? Would they stand the test of second thoughts? Would

I not be impelled, in a very short time, to cancel them? I who never changed my mind before my son. The worst was to be feared.

Where are we going, papa? he said. How often had I told him not to ask me questions. And where were we going, in point of fact. Do as you're told, I said. I have an appointment with Mr Py tomorrow, he said. You'll see him another day, I said. But I have an ache, he said. There exist other dentists, I said, Mr Py is not the unique dentist of the northern hemisphere. I added rashly, We are not going into the wilderness. But he's a very good dentist, he said. All dentists are alike, I said. I could have told him to get to hell out of that with his dentist, but no, I reasoned gently with him, I spoke with him as with an equal. I could furthermore have pointed out to him that he was lying when he said he had an ache. He did have an ache, in a bicuspid I believe, but it was over. Py himself had told me so. I have dressed the tooth, he said, your son cannot possibly feel any more pain. I remembered this conversation well. He has naturally very bad teeth, said Py. Naturally, I said, what do you mean, naturally? What are you insinuating? He was born with bad teeth, said Py, and all his life he will have bad teeth. Naturally I shall do what I can. Meaning, I was born with the disposition to do all I can, all my life I shall do all I can, necessarily. Born with bad teeth! As for me, I was down to my incisors, the nippers.

Is it still raining? I said. My son had drawn a small glass from his pocket and was examining the inside of his mouth, prising away his upper lip with his finger. Aaw, he said, without interrupting his inspection. Stop messing about with your mouth! I cried. Go to the window and tell me if it's still raining. He went to the window and told me it was still raining. Is the sky completely overcast? I said. Yes, he said. Not the least rift? I said. No, he said. Draw the curtains, I said. Delicious instants, before one's eyes get used to the dark. Are you still there? I said. He was still there. I asked him what he was waiting for to do as I had told him. If I had been my son I would have left me long ago. He was not worthy of me, not in the same class at all. I could not escape this conclusion. Cold comfort that is, to feel superior to one's son, and hardly sufficient to calm the remorse of having begotten him. May I bring my stamps? he said. My son had two albums, a big one for his collection properly speaking and a small one for the duplicates. I authorised him to bring the latter. When I can give pleasure, without doing violence to my principles, I do so gladly. He withdrew.

Malone Dies

Like *Molloy*, *Malone Dies* is a monologue, but unlike the earlier book this monologue is based on inventive imagination rather than memory. Malone lies in bed, constantly falling asleep, waiting for death to arrive. Unlike Molloy, he is calmer, more stoical, and has largely lost interest in himself in terms of self-pity. His bitterness is frank and curmudgeonly, and his main problem is to overcome his boredom when awake. To pass the time, instead of telling his own story to himself, as did Molloy, he invents new ones, whole families and histories of rural life. The author is now at the height of his powers, and except for a few asides, brief flashes of erudition or wit, he has put aside the cleverness, philosophical conceits and comicry of earlier work to present a fully rounded character who despises the world, his presence in it, and his forthcoming fate too much to be afraid of them. Beckett's first novel to be published in Britain after the war, it received very mixed reviews, although by then *Waiting for Godot* had already been seen on the London stage; but the younger and more open-minded reviewers began to realise that something new and important had arrived in the novel, and *Malone Dies* did much to establish Beckett's reputation among other writers and in the universities.

The extracts given here come from the first pages of the novel, after which some of the invented stories that Malone tells himself to pass the time have been joined up. In the novel, these stories are often separated by Malone's reflections on his physical and moral condition, or on the style in which he is framing his time-passing fictions.

I shall soon be quite dead at last in spite of all. Perhaps next month. Then it will be the month of April or of May. For the year is still young, a thousand little signs tell me so. Perhaps I am wrong, perhaps I shall survive Saint John the Baptist's Day and even the Fourteenth of July, festival of freedom. Indeed I would not put it past me to pant on to the Transfiguration, not to speak of the Assumption. But I do not think so, I do not think I am wrong in saying that these rejoicings will take place in my absence, this year. I have that feeling, I have had it now for some days, and I credit it. But in what does it differ from those that have abused me ever since I was born? No, that is the kind of bait I do not rise to any more, my need for prettiness is gone. I could die to-day, if I wished, merely by making a little effort. But it is just as well to let myself die, quietly, without rushing things. Something must have changed. I will not weigh upon the balance any more, one way or the other. I shall be neutral and inert. No difficulty there. Throes are the only trouble. I must be on my guard against throes. But I am less given to them now, since coming here. Of course I still have my little fits of impatience, from time to time, I must be on my guard against them, for the next fortnight or three weeks. Without exaggeration to be sure, quietly crying and laughing, without working myself up into a state. Yes I shall be natural at last, I shall suffer more, then less, without drawing any conclusions, I shall pay less heed to myself, I shall be neither hot nor cold any more, I shall be tepid, I shall die tepid, without enthusiasm. I shall not watch myself die, that would spoil everything. Have I watched myself live? Have I ever complained? Then why rejoice now? I am content, necessarily, but not to the point of clapping my hands. I was always content, knowing I would be repaid. There he is now, my old debtor. Shall I then fall on his neck? I shall not answer any more questions. I shall even try not to ask myself any more. While waiting I shall tell myself stories, if I can. They will not be the same kind of stories as hitherto, that is all. They will be neither beautiful nor ugly, they will be calm, there will be no ugliness or beauty or fever in them any more, they will be almost lifeless, like the teller. What was that I said? It does not matter. I look forward to their giving me great satisfaction, some satisfaction. I am satisfied, there, I have enough, I am repaid, I need nothing more. Let me say before I go any further that I forgive nobody. I wish them all an atrocious life and then the fires and ice of hell and in the execrable generations to come an honoured name. Enough for this evening.

. . . Does anything remain to be said? A few words about myself perhaps. My body is what is called, unadvisedly perhaps, impotent. There is virtually nothing it can do. Sometimes I miss not being able to crawl around any more. But I am not much given to nostalgia. My arms, once they are in position, can exert a certain force. But I find it hard to guide them. Perhaps the red nucleus has faded. I tremble a little, but only a little. The groaning of the bedstead is part of my life, I would not like it to cease, I mean I would not like it to decrease. It is on my back, that is to say prostrate, no, supine, that I feel best, bony. I lie on my back, but my cheek is on the pillow. I have only to open my eyes to have them begin again, the sky and smoke of mankind. My sight and hearing are very bad, on the vast main no light but reflected gleams. All my senses are trained full on me, me. Dark and silent and stale, I am no prey for them. I am far from the sounds of blood and breath, immured. I shall not speak of my sufferings. Cowering deep down among them I feel nothing. It is there I die, unbeknown to my stupid flesh. That which is seen, that which cries and writhes, my witless remains. Somewhere in this turmoil thought struggles on, it too wide of the mark. It too seeks me, as it always has, where I am not to be found. It too cannot be quiet. On others let it wreak its dying rage, and leave me in peace. Such would seem to be my present state.

The man's name is Saposcat. Like his father's. Christian name? I don't know. He will not need one. His friends call him Sapo. What friends? I don't know. A few words about the boy. This cannot be avoided.

He was a precocious boy. He was not good at his lessons, neither could he see the use of them. He attended his classes with his mind elsewhere, or blank.

He attended his classes with his mind elsewhere. He liked sums, but not the way they were taught. What he liked was the manipulation of concrete numbers. All calculation seemed to him idle in which the nature of the unit was not specified. He made a practice, alone and in company, of mental arithmetic. And the figures then marshalling in his mind thronged it with colours and with forms.

What tedium.

He was the eldest child of poor and sickly parents. He often heard them talk of what they ought to do in order to have better health and more money. He was struck each time by the vagueness of these palavers and not surprised that they never led to anything. His father was a salesman, in a shop. He used to say to his wife, I really must find work for the evenings and the Saturday afternoon. He added, faintly, And the Sunday. His wife would answer, But if you do any more work you'll fall ill. And Mr Saposcat had to allow that he would indeed be ill-advised to forgo his Sunday rest. These people at least are grown up. But his health was not so poor that he could not work in the evenings of the week and on the Saturday afternoon. At what, said his wife, work at what? Perhaps secretarial work of some kind, he said. And who will look after the garden? said his wife. The life of the Saposcats was full of axioms, of which one at least established the criminal absurdity of a garden without roses and with its paths and lawns uncared for. I might perhaps grow vegetables, he said. They cost less to buy, said his wife. Sapo marvelled at these conversations. Think of the price of manure, said his mother. And in the silence which followed Mr Saposcat applied his mind, with the earnestness he brought to everything he did, to the high price of manure which prevented him from supporting his family in greater comfort, while his wife made ready to accuse herself, in her turn, of not doing all she might. But she was easily persuaded that she could not do more without exposing herself to the risk of dying before her time. Think of the doctor's fees we save, said Mr Saposcat. And the chemist's bills, said his wife. Nothing remained but to envisage a smaller house. But we are cramped as it is, said Mrs Saposcat. And it was an understood thing that they would be more and more so with every passing year until the day came when, the departure of the first-born compensating the arrival of the new-born, a kind of equilibrium would be attained. Then little by little the house would empty. And at last they would be all alone, with their memories. It would be time enough then to move. He would be pensioned off, she at her last gasp. They would take a cottage in the country where, having no further need of manure, they could afford to buy it in cartloads. And their children, grateful for the sacrifices made on their behalf, would come to their assistance. It was in this atmosphere of unbridled dream that these conferences usually ended. It was as though the Saposcats drew the strength to live from the prospect of their impotence. But sometimes, before reaching that stage, they paused to consider the case of their first-born. What age is he now? asked Mr Saposcat. His wife provided the information, it being understood that this was of her province. She was always wrong. Mr Saposcat took over the erroneous figure, murmuring it over and over to himself as though it were a question of the rise in price of some indispensable commodity, such as butcher's meat. And at the same time he sought in the appearance of his son some alleviation of what he had just heard. Was it at least a nice sirloin? Sapo looked at his father's face, sad, astonished, loving, disappointed, confident in spite of all. Was it on the cruel flight of the years he brooded, or on the time it was taking his son to command a salary? Sometimes he stated wearily his regret that his son should not be more eager to make himself useful about the place. It is better for him to prepare his examinations, said his wife. Starting from a given theme their minds laboured in unison. They had no conversation properly speaking. They made use of the spoken word in much the same way as the guard of a train makes use of his flags, or of his lantern. Or else they said, This is where we get down. And their son once signalled, they wondered sadly if it was not the mark of superior minds to fail miserably at the written paper and cover themselves with ridicule at the viva voce. They were not always content to gape in silence at the same landscape. At least his health is good, said Mr Saposcat. Not all that, said his wife. But no definite disease, said Mr Saposcat. A nice thing that would be, at his age, said his wife. They did not know why he was committed to a liberal profession. That was yet another thing that went without saying. It was therefore impossible he should be unfitted for it. They thought of him as a doctor for preference. He will look after us when we are old, said Mrs Saposcat. And her husband replied, I see him rather as a surgeon, as though after a certain age people were inoperable.

. . . The summer holidays. In the morning he took private lessons. You'll have us in the poorhouse, said Mrs Saposcat. It's a good investment, said Mr Saposcat. In the afternoon he left the house, with his books under his arm, on the pretext that he worked better in the open air, no, without a word. Once clear of the town he hid his books under a stone and ranged the countryside. It was the season when the labours of the peasants reach their paroxysm and the long bright days are too short for all there is to do. And often they took advantage of the moon to make a last journey between the fields, perhaps far away, and the barn or threshing floor, or to overhaul the machines and get them ready for the impending dawn. The impending dawn.

. . . The Lamberts. The Lamberts found it difficult to live, I mean to make ends meet. There was the man, the woman and two children, a boy and a girl. There at least is something that admits of no controversy. The father was known as Big Lambert, and big he was indeed. He had married his young cousin and was still with her. This was his third or fourth marriage. He had other children here and there, grown men and women imbedded deep in life, hoping for nothing more, from themselves or from others. They helped him, each one according to his means, or the humour of the moment, out of gratitude towards him but for whom they had never seen the light of day, or saying, with indulgence, If it had not been he it would have been someone else. Big Lambert had not a tooth in his head and smoked his cigarettes in a cigarette-holder, while regretting his pipe. He was highly thought of as a bleeder and disjointer of pigs and greatly sought after, I exaggerate, in that capacity. For his fee was lower than the butcher's, and he had even been known to demand no more, in return for his services, than a lump of gammon or a pig's cheek. How plausible all that is. He often spoke of his father with respect and tenderness. His like will not be seen again, he used to say, once I am gone. He must have said this in other words. His great days then fell in December and January, and from February onwards he waited impatiently for the return of that season, the principal event of which is unquestionably the Saviour's birth, in a stable, while wondering if he would be spared till then. Then he would set forth, hugging under his arm, in their case, the great knives so lovingly whetted before the fire the night before, and in his pocket, wrapped in paper, the apron destined to protect his Sunday suit while he worked. And at the thought that he, Big Lambert, was on his way towards that distant homestead where all was in readiness for his coming, and that in spite of his great age he was still needed, and his methods preferred to those of younger men, then his old heart exulted. From these expeditions he reached home late in the night, drunk and exhausted by the long road and the emotions of the day. And for days afterwards he could speak of nothing but the pig he had just dispatched, I would say into the other world if I was not aware that pigs have none but this, to the great affliction of his family. But they did not dare protest, for they feared him. Yes, at an age when most people cringe and cower, as if to apologize for still being present, Lambert was feared and in a position to do as he pleased. And even his young wife had abandoned all hope of bringing him to heel, by means of her cunt, that trump card of young wives. For she knew what he would do to her if she did not open it to him. And he even insisted on her making things easy for him, in ways that often appeared to her exorbitant. And at the least show of rebellion on her part he would run to the wash-house and come back with the battle and beat her until she came round to a better way of thinking. All this by the way. And to return to our pigs, Lambert continued to expatiate, to his near and dear ones, of an evening, while the lamp burned low, on the specimen he had just slaughtered, until the day he was summoned to slaughter another. Then all his conversation was of this new pig, so unlike the other in every respect, so quite unlike, and yet at bottom the same. For all pigs are alike, when you get to know their little ways, struggle, squeal, bleed, squeal, struggle, bleed, squeal and faint away, in more or less the same way exactly, a way that is all their own and could never be imitated by a lamb, for example, or a kid. But once March was out Big Lambert recovered his calm and became his silent self again.

The son, or heir, was a great strapping lad with terrible teeth.

The farm. The farm was in a hollow, flooded in winter and in summer burnt to a cinder. The way to it lay through a fine meadow. But this fine meadow did not belong to the Lamberts, but to other peasants living at a distance. There jonquils and narcissi bloomed in extraordinary profusion, at the appropriate season. And there at nightfall, stealthily, Big Lambert turned loose his goats.

Strange to say this gift that Lambert possessed when it came to sticking pigs seemed of no help to him when it came to rearing them, and it was seldom his own exceeded nine stone. Clapped into a tiny sty on the day of its arrival, in the month of April, it remained there until the day of its death, on Christmas Eve. For Lambert persisted in dreading for his pigs, though every passing year proved him wrong, the thinning effects of exercise. Daylight and fresh air he dreaded for them too. And it was finally a weak pig, blind and lean, that he lay on its back in the box, having tied its legs, and killed, indignantly but without haste, upbraiding it the while for its ingratitude, at the top of his voice. For he could not or would not understand that the pig was not to blame, but he himself, who had coddled it unduly. And he persisted in his error.

Dead world, airless, waterless. That's it, reminisce. Here and there, in the bed of a crater, the shadow of a withered lichen. And nights of three hundred hours. Dearest of lights, wan, pitted, least fatuous of lights. That's it, babble. How long can it have lasted? Five minutes? Ten minutes? Yes, no more, not much more. But my sliver of sky is silvery with it yet. In the old days I used to count, up to three hundred, four hundred, and with other things too, the showers, the bells, the chatter of the sparrows at dawn, or with nothing, for no reason, for the sake of counting, and then I divided, by sixty. That passed the time, I was time, I devoured the world. Not now, any more. A man changes. As he gets on.

In the filthy kitchen, with its earth floor, Sapo had his place, by the window. Big Lambert and his son left their work, came and shook his hand, then went away, leaving him with the mother and the daughter. But they too had their work, they too went away and left him, alone. There was so much work, so little time, so few hands. The woman, pausing an instant between two tasks, or in the midst of one, flung up her arms and, in the same breath, unable to sustain their great weight, let them fall again. Then she began to toss them about in a way difficult to describe, and not easy to understand. The movements resembled those, at once frantic and slack, of an arm shaking a duster, or a rag, to rid it of its dust. And so rapid was the trepidation of the limp, empty hands that there seemed to be four or five at the end of each arm, instead of the usual one. At the same time angry unanswerable questions, such as, What's the use? fell from her lips. Her hair came loose and fell about her face. It was thick, grey and dirty, for she had no time to tend it, and her face was pale and thin and as though gouged with worry and its attendant rancours. The bosom – no, what matters is the head and then the hands it calls to its help before all else, that clasp, wring, then sadly resume their labour, lifting the old inert objects and changing their position, bringing them closer together and moving them further apart. But this pantomine and these ejaculations were not intended for any living person. For every day and several times a day she gave way to them, within doors and without. Then she little cared whether she was observed or not, whether what she was doing was urgent or could wait, no, but she dropped everything and began to cry out and gesticulate, the last of all the living as likely as not and dead to what was going on about her. Then she fell silent and stood stockstill a moment, before resuming whatever it was she had abandoned or setting about some new task. Sapo remained alone, by the window, the bowl of goat's milk on the table before him, forgotten. It was summer. The room was dark in spite of the door and window open on the great outer light. Through these narrow openings, far apart, the light poured, lit up a little space, then died, undiffused. It had no steadfastness, no assurance of lasting as long as day lasted. But it entered at every moment, renewed from without, entered and died at every moment, devoured by the dark. And at the last abatement of the inflow the room grew darker and darker until nothing in it was visible any more. For the dark had triumphed. And Sapo, his face turned towards an earth so resplendent that it hurt his eyes, felt at his back and all about him the unconquerable dark, and it licked the light on his face. Sometimes abruptly he turned to face it, letting it envelop and pervade him, with a kind of relief. Then he heard more clearly the sounds of those at work, the daughter calling to her goats, the father cursing his mule. But silence was in the heart of the dark, the silence of dust and the things that would never stir, if left alone. And the ticking of the invisible alarm-clock was as the voice of that silence which, like the dark, would one day triumph too. And then all would be still and dark and all things at rest for ever at last. Finally he took from his pocket the few poor gifts he had brought, laid them on the table and went. But it sometimes happened, before he decided to go, before he went rather, for there was no decision, that a hen, taking advantage of the open door, would venture into the room. No sooner had she crossed the threshold than she paused, one leg hooked up under her breech, her head on one side, blinking, anxious. Then, reassured, she advanced a little further, jerkily, with concertina neck. It was a grey hen, perhaps the grey hen. Sapo got to know her well and, it seemed to him, to be well known by her. If he rose to go she did not fly into a flutter. But perhaps there were several hens, all grey and so alike in other respects that Sapo's eye, avid of resemblances, could not tell between them. Sometimes she was followed by a second, a third and even a fourth, bearing no likeness to her, and but little to one another, in the matter of plumage and entasis. These showed more confidence than the grey, who had led the way and come to no harm. They shone an instant in the light, grew dimmer and dimmer as they advanced, and finally vanished. Silent at first, fearing to betray their presence, they began gradually to scratch and cluck, for contentment, and to relax their soughing feathers. But often the grey hen came alone, or one of the grey hens if you prefer, for that is a thing that will never be known, though it might well have been, without much trouble. For all that was necessary, in order that it might be known whether there was only one grey hen or more than one, was for someone to be present when all the hens came running towards Mrs Lambert as she cried, Tweet! Tweet!, and banged on an old tin with an old spoon. But after all what use would that have been? For it was quite possible there were several grey hens, and yet only one in the habit of coming to the kitchen. And yet the experiment was worth making. For it was quite possible there was only one grey hen, even at feeding-time. Which would have clinched the matter. And yet that is a thing that will never be known. For among those who must have known, some are dead and the others have forgotten. And the day when it was urgent for Sapo to have this point cleared up, and his mind set at rest, it was too late. Then he was sorry he had not understood, in time to profit by it, the importance that those hours were one day to assume, for him, those long hours in that old kitchen where, neither quite indoors nor quite out of doors, he waited to be on his feet again, and in motion, and while waiting noted many things, among them this big, anxious, ashen bird, poised irresolute on the bright threshold, then clucking and clawing behind the range and fidgeting her atrophied wings, soon to be sent flying with a broom and angry cries and soon to return, cautiously, with little hesitant steps, stopping often to listen, opening and shutting her little bright black eyes. And so he went, all unsuspecting, with the fond impression of having been present at everyday scenes of no import. He stooped to cross the threshold and saw before him the well, with its winch, chain and bucket, and often too a long line of tattered washing, swaying and drying in the sun. He went by the

little path he had come by, along the edge of the meadow in the
shadow of the great trees that bordered the stream, its bed a chaos
of gnarled roots, boulders and baked mud. And so he went, often
unnoticed, in spite of his strange walk, his halts and sudden starts.
Or the Lamberts saw him, from far off or from near by, or some
of them from far off and the others from near by, suddenly emerge
from behind the washing and set off down the path. Then they
did not try to detain him or even call goodbye, unresentful at his
leaving them in a way that seemed so lacking in friendliness, for
they knew he meant no harm. Or if at the time they could not
help feeling a little hurt, this feeling was quite dispelled a little
later, when they found on the kitchen-table the crumpled paper-
bag containing a few little articles of haberdashery. And these
humble presents, but oh how useful, and this oh so delicate way
of giving, disarmed them too at the sight of the bowl of goat's milk
only half emptied, or left untouched, and prevented them from
regarding this as an affront, in the way tradition required. But it
would appear on reflection that Sapo's departure can seldom have
escaped them. For at the least moment within sight of their land,
were it only that of a little bird alighting or taking to wing, they
raised their heads and stared with wide eyes. And even on the
road, of which segments were visible more than a mile away,
nothing could happen without their knowledge, and they were
able not only to identify all those who passed along it and whose
remoteness reduced them to the size of a pin's head, but also to
divine whence they were coming, where they were going, and for
what purpose. Then they cried the news to one another, for they
often worked at a great distance apart, or they exchanged signals,
all erect and turned towards the event, for it was one, before
bowing themselves down to the earth again. And at the first spell
of rest taken in common, about the table or elsewhere, each one
gave his version of what had passed and listened to those of the
others. And if at first they were not in agreement about what they
had seen, they talked it over doggedly until they were, in agreement I mean, or until they resigned themselves to never being so.
It was therefore difficult for Sapo to glide away unseen, even in
the deep shadow of the trees that bordered the stream, even supposing him to have been capable of gliding, for his movements
were rather those of one floundering in a quag. And all raised their
heads and watched him as he went, then looked at one another,
before stooping to the earth again. And on each face bent to the

earth there played perhaps a little smile, a little rictus rather, but without malice, each wondering perhaps if the others felt the same thing and making the resolve to ask them at their next meeting. But the face of Sapo, as he stumbled away, now in the shadow of the venerable trees he could not name, now in the brightness of the waving meadow, so erratic was his course, the face of Sapo was as always grave, or rather expressionless. And when he halted it was not the better to think, or the closer to pore upon his dream, but simply because the voice had ceased that told him to go on. Then with his pale eyes he stared down at the earth, blind to its beauty, and to its utility, and to the little wild many-coloured flowers happy among the crops and weeds. But these stations were short-lived, for he was still young. And of a sudden he is off again, on his wanderings, passing from light to shadow, from shadow to light, unheedingly.

When I stop, as just now, the noises begin again, strangely loud, those whose turn it is. So that I seem to have again the hearing of my boyhood. Then in my bed, in the dark, on stormy nights, I could tell from one another, in the outcry without, the leaves, the boughs, the groaning trunks, even the grasses and the house that sheltered me. Each tree had its own cry, just as no two whispered alike, when the air was still. I heard afar the iron gates clashing and dragging at their posts and the wind rushing between their bars. There was nothing, not even the sand on the paths, that did not utter its cry. The still nights too, still as the grave as the saying is, were nights of storm for me, clamorous with countless pantings. These I amused myself with identifying, as I lay there. Yes, I got great amusement, when young, from their so-called silence. The sound I liked best had nothing noble about it. It was the barking of the dogs, at night, in the clusters of hovels up in the hills, where the stone-cutters lived, like generations of stone-cutters before them. It came down to me where I lay, in the house in the plain, wild and soft, at the limit of earshot, soon weary. The dogs of the valley replied with their gross bay all fangs and jaws and foam. From the hills another joy came down, I mean the brief scattered lights that sprang up on their slopes at nightfall, merging in blurs scarcely brighter than the sky, less bright than the stars, and which the palest moon extinguished. They were things that scarcely were, on the confines of silence and dark, and soon ceased. So I reason now, at my ease. Standing before my high window I gave myself to them, waiting for them to end, for my joy to end, straining towards the joy of ended joy. But our business at the moment is less with these futilities than with my ears from which there spring two impetuous tufts of no doubt yellow hair, yellowed by wax and lack of care, and so long that the lobes are hidden. I note then, without emotion, that of late their hearing seems to have improved. Oh not that I was ever even incompletely deaf. But for a long time now I have been hearing things confusedly. There I go again. What I mean is possibly this, that the noises of the world, so various in themselves and which I used to be so clever at distinguishing from one another, had been dinning at me for so long, always the same old noises, as gradually to have merged into a single noise, so that all I heard was one vast continuous buzzing. The volume of sound perceived remained no doubt the same, I had simply lost the faculty of decomposing it. The noises of nature, of mankind and even my own, were all jumbled together in one and the same unbridled gibberish. Enough. I would willingly attribute part of my shall I say my misfortunes to this disordered sense were I not unfortunately rather inclined to look upon it as a blessing. Misfortunes, blessings, I have no time to pick my words, I am in a hurry to be done. And yet no, I am in no hurry. Decidedly this evening I shall say nothing that is not false, I mean nothing that is not calculated to leave me in doubt as to my real intentions. For it is evening, even night, one of the darkest I can remember, I have a short memory. My little finger glides before my pencil across the page and gives warning, falling over the edge, that the end of the line is near. But in the other direction, I mean of course vertically, I have nothing to guide me. I did not want to write, but I had to resign myself to it in the end. It is in order to know where I have got to, where he has got to. At first I did not write, I just said the thing. Then I forgot what I had said. A minimum of memory is indispensable, if one is to live really. Take his family, for example, I really know practically nothing about his family any more. But that does not worry me, there is a record of it somewhere. It is the only way to keep an eye on him. But as far as I myself am concerned the same necessity does not arise, or does it? And yet I write about myself with the same pencil and in the same exercise-book as about him. It is because it is no longer I, I must have said so long ago, but another whose life is just beginning. It is right that he too should have his little chronicle, his memories, his reason, and be able to recognize the good in the bad, the bad in the worst, and so grow gently old all down the unchanging days and die one day like any other day, only shorter. That is my excuse. But there must be others, no less excellent. Yes, it is quite dark. I can see nothing. I can scarcely even see the window-pane, or the wall forming with ιt so sharp a contrast that it often looks like the edge of an abyss. I hear the noise of my little finger as it glides over the paper and then that so different of the pencil following after. That is what surprises me and makes me say that something must have changed. Whence that child I might have been, why not? And I hear also, there we are at last, I hear a choir, far enough away, for me not to hear it when it goes soft. It is a song I know, I don't know how, and when it fades, and when it dies quite away, it goes on inside me, but too slow, or too fast, for when it comes on the air to me again it is not together with mine, but behind, or ahead. It is a mixed choir, or I am greatly deceived. With children too perhaps. I have the absurd feeling it is conducted by a woman. It has been singing the same song for a long time now. They must be rehearsing. It belongs already to the long past, it has uttered for the last time the triumphal cry on which it ends. Can it be Easter Week? Thus with the year Seasons return. If it can, could not this song I have just heard, and which quite frankly is not yet quite stilled within me, could not this song have simply been to the honour and glory of him who was the first to rise from the dead, to him who saved me, twenty centuries in advance? Did I say the first? The final bawl lends colour to this view.

I fear I must have fallen asleep again. In vain I grope, I cannot find my exercise-book. But I still have the pencil in my hand. I shall have to wait for day to break. God knows what I am going to do till then.

I have just written, I fear I must have fallen, etc. I hope this is not too great a distortion of the truth. I now add these few lines, before departing from myself again. I do not depart from myself now with the same avidity as a week ago for example. For this must be going on now for over a week, it must be over a week since I said, I shall soon be quite dead at last, etc. Wrong again. That is not what I said, I could swear to it, that is what I wrote. This last phrase seems familiar, suddenly I seem to have written it somewhere before, or spoken it, word for word. Yes, I shall soon be, etc., that is what I wrote when I realised I did not know what I had said, at the beginning of my say, and subsequently, and that consequently the plan I had formed, to live, and cause to live, at last, to play at last and die alive, was going the way of all my other plans. I think the dawn was not so slow in coming as I had feared, I really do. But I feared nothing, I fear nothing any more. High summer is truly at hand. Turned towards the window I saw the pane shiver at last, before the ghastly sunrise. It is no ordinary pane, it brings me sunset and it brings me sunrise. The exercise-book had fallen to the ground. I took a long time to find it. It was under the bed. How are such things possible? I took a long time to recover it. I had to harpoon it. It is not pierced through and through, but it is in a bad way. It is a thick exercise-book. I hope it will see me out. From now on I shall write on both sides of the page. Where does it come from? I don't know. I found it, just like that, the day I needed it. Knowing perfectly well I had no exercise-book I rummaged in my possessions in the hope of finding one. I was not disappointed, not surprised. If tomorrow I needed an old love-letter I would adopt the same method. It is ruled in squares. The first pages are covered with ciphers and other symbols and diagrams, with here and there a brief phrase. Calculations, I reckon. They seem to stop suddenly, prematurely at all events. As though discouraged. Perhaps it is astronomy, or astrology. I did not look closely. I drew a line, no, I did not even draw a line, and I wrote, Soon I shall be quite dead at last, and so on, without even going on to the next page, which was blank. Good. Now I need not dilate on this exercise-book when it comes to the inventory, but merely say, Item, an exercise-book, giving perhaps the colour of the cover. But I may well lose it between now and then, for good and all. The pencil on the contrary is an old acquaintance, I must have had it about me when I was brought here. It has five faces. It is very short. It is pointed at both ends. A Venus. I hope it will see me out. I was saying I did not depart from myself now with quite the same alacrity. That must be in the natural order of things, all that pertains to me must be written there, including my inability to grasp what order is meant. For I have never seen any sign of any, inside me or outside me. I have pinned my faith to appearances, believing them to be vain. I shall not go into the details. Choke, go down, come up, choke, suppose, deny, affirm, drown. I depart from myself less gladly. Amen. I waited for the dawn. Doing what? I don't know. What I had to do. I watched for the window. I gave rein to my pains, my impotence. And in the end it seemed to me, for a second, that I was going to have a visit!

The summer holidays were drawing to a close. The decisive moment was at hand when the hopes reposed in Sapo were to be fulfilled, or dashed to the ground. He is trained to a hair, said Mr Saposcat. And Mrs Saposcat, whose piety grew warm in times of crisis, prayed for his success. Kneeling at her bedside, in her night-dress, she ejaculated, silently for her husband would not have approved, Oh God grant he pass, grant he pass, grant he scrape through!

When this first ordeal was surmounted there would be others, every year, several times a year. But it seemed to the Saposcats that these would be less terrible than the first which was to give them, or deny them the right to say, He is doing his medicine, or, He is reading for the bar. For they felt that a more or less normal if unintelligent youth, once admitted to the study of these professions, was almost sure to be certified, sooner or later, apt to exercise them. For they had experience of doctors, and of lawyers, like most people.

One day Mr Saposcat sold himself a fountain-pen, at a discount. A Bird. I shall give it to him on the morning of the examination, he said. He took off the long cardboard lid and showed the pen to his wife. Leave it in its box! he cried, as she made to take it in her hand. It lay almost hidden in the scrolled leaflet containing the instructions for use. Mr Saposcat parted the edges of the paper and held up the box for his wife to look inside. But she, instead of looking at the pen, looked at him. He named the price. Might it not be better, she said, to let him have it the day before, to give him time to get used to the nib? You are right, he said, I had not thought of that. Or even two days before, she said, to give him time to change the nib if it does not suit him. A bird, its yellow beak agape to show it was singing, adorned the lid, which Mr Saposcat now put on again. He wrapped with expert hands the box in tissue-paper and slipped over it a narrow rubber band. He was not pleased. It is a medium nib, he said, and it will certainly suit him.

This conversation was renewed the next day. Mr Saposcat said, Might it not be better if we just lent him the pen and told him he could keep it for his own, if he passed? Then we must do so at once, said Mrs Saposcat, otherwise there is no point in it. To which Mr Saposcat, made, after a silence, a first objection, and then, after a second silence, a second objection. He first objected that his son, if he received the pen forthwith, would have time to break it, or lose it, before the paper. He secondly objected that his son, if he received the pen immediately, and assuming he neither broke nor lost it, would have time to get so used to it and, by comparing it with the pens of his less impoverished friends, so familiar with its defects, that its possession would no longer tempt him. I did not know it was an inferior article, said Mrs Saposcat. Mr Saposcat placed his hand on the table-cloth and sat gazing at it for some time. Then he laid down his napkin and left the room. Adrian, cried Mrs Saposcat, come back and finish your sweet! Alone before the table she listened to the steps on the garden-path, clearer, fainter, clearer, fainter.

The Lamberts. One day Sapo arrived at the farm earlier than usual. But do we know what time he usually arrived? Lengthening, fading shadows. He was surprised to see, at a distance, in the midst of the young stubble, the father's big red and white head. His body was in the hole or pit he had dug for his mule, which had died during the night. Edmund came out of the house, wiping his mouth, and joined him. Lambert then climbed out of the hole and the son went down into it. Drawing closer Sapo saw the mule's black corpse. Then all became clear to him. The mule was lying on its side, as was to be expected. The forelegs were stretched out straight and rigid, the hind drawn up under the belly. The yawning jaws, the wreathed lips, the enormous teeth, the bulging eyes, composed a striking death's-head. Edmund handed up to his father the pick, the shovel and the spade and climbed out of the hole. Together they dragged the mule by the legs to the edge of the hole and heaved it in, on its back. The forelegs, pointing towards heaven, projected above the level of the ground. Old Lambert banged them down with his spade. He handed the spade to his son and went towards the house. Edmund began to fill up the hole. Sapo stood watching him. A great calm stole over him. Great calm is an exaggeration. He felt better. The end of a life is always vivifying. Edmund paused to rest, leaned panting on the spade and smiled. There were great pink gaps in his front teeth. Big Lambert sat by the window, smoking, drinking, watching his son. Sapo sat down before him, laid his hand on the table and his head on his hand, thinking he was alone. Between his head and his hand he slipped the other hand and sat there marble still. Louis began to talk. He seemed in good spirits. The mule, in his opinion, had died of old age. He had bought it, two years before, on its way to the slaughter-house. So he could not complain. After the transaction the owner of the mule predicted that it would drop down dead at the first ploughing. But Lambert was a connoisseur of mules. In the case of mules it is the eye that counts, the rest is unimportant. So he looked the mule full in the eye, at the gates of the slaughter-house, and saw it could still be made to serve. And the mule returned his gaze, in the yard of the slaughter-house. As Lambert unfolded his story the slaughter-house loomed larger and larger. Thus the site of the transaction shifted gradually from the road that led to the slaughter-house to the gates of the slaughter-house and thence to the yard itself. Yet a little while and he would have contended for the mule with the knacker. The look in his eye, he said, was like a prayer to me to take him. It was covered with sores, but in the case of mules one should never let oneself be deterred by senile sores. Someone said, He's done ten miles already, you'll never get him home, he'll drop down dead on the road. I thought I might screw six months out of him, said Lambert, and I screwed two years. All the time he told this story he kept his eyes fixed on his son. There they sat, the table between them, in the gloom, one speaking, the other listening, and far removed, the one from what he said, the other from what he heard, and far from each other. The heap of earth was dwindling, the earth shone strangely in the raking evening light, glowing in patches as though with its own fires, in the fading light. Edmund stopped often to rest, leaning on the spade and looking about him. The slaughter-house, said Lambert, that's where I buy my beasts, will you look at that loafer. He went out and set to work, beside his son. They worked together for a time, heedless of each other. Then the son dropped his shovel, turned aside and moved slowly away, passing from toil to rest in a single unbroken movement that did not seem of his doing. The mule was no longer visible. The face of the earth, on which it had plodded its life away, would see it no more, toiling before the plough, or the dray. And Big Lambert would soon be able to plough and harrow the place where it lay, with another mule, or an old horse, or an old ox, bought at the Knacker's yard, knowing that the share would not turn up the putrid flesh or be blunted by the big bones. For he knew how the dead and buried tend, contrary to what one might expect, to rise to the surface, in which they resemble the drowned. And he had made allowance for this when digging the hole. Edmund and his mother passed each other by in silence. She had been to see a neighbour, to borrow a pound of lentils for their supper. She was thinking of the handsome steelyard that had served to weigh them and wondering if it was true. Before her husband too she rapidly passed, without a glance, and in his attitude there was nothing to suggest that he had seen her either. She lit the lamp where it stood at its usual place on the chimney-piece, beside the alarm-clock flanked in its turn by a crucifix hanging from a nail. The clock, being the lowest of the three, had to remain in the middle, and the lamp and crucifix could not change places because of the nail from which the latter was hung. She stood with her forehead and her hands pressed against the wall, until she might turn up the wick. She turned it up and put on the yellow globe which a large hole defaced. Seeing Sapo she first thought he was her daughter. Then her thoughts flew to the absent one. She set down the lamp on the table and the outer world went out. She sat down, emptied out the lentils on the table and began to sort them. So that soon there were two heaps on the table, one big heap getting smaller and one small heap getting bigger. But suddenly with a furious gesture she swept the two together, annihilating thus in less than a second the work of two or three minutes. Then she went away and came back with a saucepan. It won't kill them, she said, and with the heel of her hand she brought the lentils to the edge of the table and over the edge into the saucepan, as if all that mattered was not to be killed, but so clumsily and with such nervous haste that a great number fell wide of the pan to the ground. Then she took up the lamp and went out to fetch wood perhaps, or a lump of fat bacon. Now that it was dark again in the kitchen the dark outside gradually lightened and Sapo, his eye against the window-pane, was able to discern certain shapes, including that of Big Lambert stamping the ground. To stop in the middle of a tedious and perhaps futile task was something that Sapo could readily understand. For a great number of tasks are of this kind, without a doubt, and the only way to end them is to abandon them. She could have gone on sorting her lentils all night and never achieved her purpose, which was to free them from all admixture. But in the end she would have stopped, saying, I have done all I can do. But she would not have done all she could have done. But the moment comes when one desists, because it is the wisest thing to do, discouraged, but not to the extent of undoing all that has been done. But what if her purpose, in sorting the lentils, were not to rid them of all that was not lentil, but only of the greater part, what then? I don't know. Whereas there are other tasks, other days, of which one may fairly safely say that they are finished, though I do not see which. She came back holding the lamp high and a little to one side, so as not to be dazzled. In the other hand she held a white rabbit, by the hindlegs. For whereas the mule had been black, the rabbit had been white. It was dead already, it had ceased to be. There are rabbits that die before they are killed, from sheer fright. They have time to do so while being taken out of the hutch, often by the ears, and disposed in the most convenient position to receive the blow, whether on the back of the neck or on some other part. And often you strike a corpse, without knowing it. For you have just seen the rabbit alive and well behind the wire meshing, nibbling at its leaves. And you congratulate yourself on having succeeded with the first blow, and not caused unnecessary suffering, whereas in reality you have taken all that trouble for nothing. This occurs most frequently at night, fright being greater in the night. Hens on the other hand are more stubborn livers and some have been observed, with the head already off, to cut a few last capers before collapsing. Pigeons too are less impressionable and sometimes even struggle, before choking to death. Mrs Lambert was breathing hard. Little devil! she cried. But Sapo was already far away, trailing his hand in the high waving meadow grasses. Soon afterwards Lambert, then his son, attracted by the savoury smell, entered the kitchen. Sitting at the table, face to face, their eyes averted from each other's eyes, they waited. But the woman, the mother, went to the door and called. Lizzy! she cried, again and again. Then she went back to her range. She had seen the moon. After a silence Lambert declared, I'll kill Whitey tomorrow. Those of course were not the words he used, but that was the meaning. But neither his wife nor his son could approve him, the former because she would have preferred him to kill Blackey, the latter because he held that to kill the kids at such an early stage of their development, either of them, it was all the same to him, would be premature. But Big Lambert told them to hold their tongues and went to the corner to fetch the case containing the knives, three in number. All he had to do was to wipe off the grease and whet them a little on one another. Mrs Lambert went back to the door, listened, called. In the far distance the flock replied. She's coming, she said. But a long time passed before she came. When the meal was over Edmund went up to bed, so as to masturbate in peace and comfort before his sister joined him, for they shared the same room. Not that he was restrained by modesty, when his sister was there. Nor was she, when her brother was there. Their quarters were cramped, certain refinements were not possible. Edmund then went up to bed, for no particular reason. He would have gladly slept with his sister, the father too, I mean the father would have gladly slept with his daughter, the time was long past and gone when he would have gladly slept with his sister. But something held them back. And she did not seem eager. But she was still young. Incest then was in the air. Mrs Lambert, the only member of the household who had no desire to sleep with anybody, saw it coming with indifference. She went out. Alone with his daughter Lambert sat watching her. She was crouched before the range, in an attitude of dejection. He told her to eat and she began to eat the remains of the rabbit, out of the pot, with a spoon. But it is hard to look steadily for any length of time at a fellow-creature, even when you are resolved to, and suddenly Lambert saw his daughter at another place and otherwise engaged than in bringing the spoon up from the pot into her mouth and down from her mouth into the pot again. And yet he could have sworn that he had not taken his eyes off her. He said, To-morrow we'll kill Whitey, you can hold her if you like. But seeing her still so sad, and her cheeks wet with tears, he went towards her.

What tedium. If I went on to the stone? No, it would be the same thing. The Lamberts, the Lamberts, does it matter about the Lamberts? No, not particularly. But while I am with them the other is lost. How are my plans getting on, my plans, I had plans not so long ago. Perhaps I have another ten years ahead of me. The Lamberts! I shall try and go on all the same, a little longer, my thoughts elsewhere, I can't stay here. I shall hear myself talking, afar off, from my far mind, talking of the Lamberts, talking of myself, my mind wandering, far from here, among its ruins.

The Unnamable

The third book of the *Trilogy* is probably one of the half-dozen key works of twentieth-century literature, where Beckett found his ultimate voice in terms of his development up to that time, and where all the protagonists of the earlier novels are linked to a single voice. This new voice has its own presence, not that of the author, nor is it exactly an intervening stage between the author's voice and those of earlier narrators or persons narrated; it is linked as if the other voices had been overheard, as on a crossed line. From first to last there is a sense of urgency which breaks down into a mental panic of awesome complexity, variety, and obsession: knowing what we now know, that the author believed when writing *The Unnamable* that he had little time to live, and to let free his obsessive voices, it becomes clear that *The Unnamable* was, at the time he wrote it, Beckett's most personal and urgent book. It is not easy to read, but neither is it difficult; the language is magnificent in its imagery, and the urgency of the tone has the unerring ring of truth; it can be of no lower coinage than genius, but it is painful to read about such pain without feeling the pain itself. The three extracts that follow come from the beginning, the late middle, and the end of the book. The Unnamable is not only the voice of the narrator who seems to have many masks and presences but only one voice and no name, but he is also that which the voice dare not name, that which lies behind the silence which the voice is holding at bay. *The Unnamable* is the culmination of Beckett's second period, but it also belongs to the third. It finally solves his long struggle to find a way in which he could concentrate the whole human condition into a single person or presence, and into a single speaking voice.

Where now? Who now? When now? Unquestioning. I, say I. Unbelieving. Questions, hypotheses, call them that. Keep going, going on, call that going, call that on. Can it be that one day, off it goes on, that one day I simply stayed in, in where, instead of going out, in the old way, out to spend day and night as far away as possible, it wasn't far. Perhaps that is how it began. You think you are simply resting, the better to act when the time comes, or for no reason, and you soon find yourself powerless ever to do anything again. No matter how it happened. It, say it, not knowing what. Perhaps I simply assented at last to an old thing. But I did nothing. I seem to speak, it is not I, about me, it is not about me. These few general remarks to begin with. What am I to do, what shall I do, what should I do, in my situation, how proceed? By aporia pure and simple? Or by affirmations and negations invalidated as uttered, or sooner or later? Generally speaking. There must be other shifts. Otherwise it would be quite hopeless. But it is quite hopeless. I should mention before going any further, any further on, that I say aporia without knowing what it means. Can one be ephectic otherwise than unawares? I don't know. With the yesses and noes it is different, they will come back to me as I go along and how, like a bird, to shit on them all without exception. The fact would seem to be, if in my situation one may speak of facts, not only that I shall have to speak of things of which I cannot speak, but also, which is even more interesting, but also that I, which is if possible even more interesting, that I shall have to, I forget, no matter. And at the same time I am obliged to speak. I shall never be silent. Never.

I shall not be alone, in the beginning. I am of course alone. Alone. That is soon said. Things have to be soon said. And how can one be sure, in such darkness? I shall have company. In the beginning. A few puppets. Then I'll scatter them, to the winds, if I can. And things, what is the correct attitude to adopt towards things? And, to begin with, are they necessary? What a question.

But I have few illusions, things are to be expected. The best is not to decide anything, in this connection, in advance. If a thing turns up, for some reason or another, take it into consideration. Where there are people, it is said, there are things. Does this mean that when you admit the former you must also admit the latter? Time will tell. The thing to avoid, I don't know why, is the spirit of system. People with things, people without things, things without people, what does it matter, I flatter myself it will not take me long to scatter them, whenever I choose, to the winds. I don't see how. The best would be not to begin. But I have to begin. That is to say I have to go on. Perhaps in the end I shall smother in a throng. Incessant comings and goings, the crush and bustle of a bargain sale. No, no danger. Of that.

Malone is there. Of his mortal liveliness little trace remains. He passes before me at doubtless regular intervals, unless it is I who pass before him. No, once and for all, I do not move. He passes, motionless. But there will not be much on the subject of Malone, from whom there is nothing further to be hoped. Personally I do not intend to be bored. It was while watching him pass that I wondered if we cast a shadow. Impossible to say. He passes close by me, a few feet away, slowly, always in the same direction. I am almost sure it is he. The brimless hat seems to me conclusive. With his two hands he props up his jaw. He passes without a word. Perhaps he does not see me. One of these days I'll challenge him. I'll say, I don't know, I'll say something, I'll think of something when the time comes. There are no days here, but I use the expression. I see him from the waist up, he stops at the waist, as far as I am concerned. The trunk is erect. But I do not know whether he is on his feet or on his knees. He might also be seated. I see him in profile. Sometimes I wonder if it is not Molloy. Perhaps it is Molloy, wearing Malone's hat. But it is more reasonable to suppose it is Malone, wearing his own hat. Oh look, there is the first thing, Malone's hat. I see no other clothes. Perhaps Molloy is not here at all. Could he be, without my knowledge? The place is no doubt vast. Dim intermittent lights suggest a kind of distance. To tell the truth I believe they are all here, at least from Murphy on, I believe we are all here, but so far I have only seen Malone. Another hypothesis, they were here, but are here no longer. I shall examine it after my fashion. Are there other pits, deeper down? To which one accedes by mine? Stupid obsession with depth. Are there other places set aside for us and this one where I am, with Malone, merely their narthex? I thought I had done with preliminaries. No, no, we have all been here forever, we shall all be here forever, I know it.

No more questions. Is not this rather the place where one finishes vanishing? Will the day come when Malone will pass before me no more? Will the day come when Malone will pass before the spot where I was? Will the day come when another will pass before me, before the spot where I was? I have no opinion, on these matters.

Were I not devoid of feeling his beard would fill me with pity. It hangs down, on either side of his chin, in two twists of unequal length. Was there a time when I too revolved thus? No, I have always been sitting here, at this selfsame spot, my hands on my knees, gazing before me like a great horn-owl in an aviary. The tears stream down my cheeks from my unblinking eyes. What makes me weep so? From time to time. There is nothing saddening here. Perhaps it is liquefied brain. Past happiness in any case has clean gone from my memory, assuming it was ever there. If I accomplish other natural functions it is unawares. Nothing ever troubles me. And yet I am troubled. Nothing has ever changed since I have been here. But I dare not infer from this that nothing ever will change. Let us try and see where these considerations lead. I have been here, ever since I began to be, my appearances elsewhere having been put in by other parties. All has proceeded, all this time, in the utmost calm, the most perfect order, apart from one or two manifestations the meaning of which escapes me. No, it is not that their meaning escapes me, my own escapes me just as much. Here all things, no, I shall not say it, being unable to. I owe my existence to no one, these faint fires are not of those that illuminate or burn. Going nowhere, coming from nowhere. Malone passes. These notions of forbears, of houses where lamps are lit at night, and other such, where do they come to me from? And all these questions I ask myself. It is not in a spirit of curiosity. I cannot be silent. About myself I need know nothing. Here all is clear. No, all is not clear. But the discourse must go on. So one invents obscurities. Rhetoric. These lights for instance, which I do not require to mean anything, what is there so strange about them, so wrong? Is it their irregularity, their instability, their shining strong one minute and weak the next, but never beyond the power of one or two candles? Malone appears and disappears with the punctuality of clockwork, always at the same remove, the same velocity, in the same direction, the same attitude. But the play of the lights is truly unpredictable. It is only fair to say that to eyes less knowing than mine they would probably pass unseen. But even to mine do they not sometimes do so? They are perhaps unwavering and fixed and my fitful perceiving the cause of their inconstancy. I hope I may have occasion to revert to this question. But I shall remark without further delay, in order to be sure of doing so, that I am relying on these lights, as indeed on all other similar sources of credible perplexity, to help me continue and perhaps even conclude. I resume, having no alternative. Where was I? Ah yes, from the unexceptionable order which has prevailed here up to date may I infer that such will always be the case? I may of course. But the mere fact of asking myself such a question gives me to reflect. It is in vain I tell myself that its only purpose is to stimulate the lagging discourse, this excellent explanation does not satisfy me. Can it be I am the prey of a genuine preoc-cupation, of a need to know as one might say? I don't know. I'll try it another way. If one day a change were to take place, resulting from a principle of disorder already present, or on its way, what then? That would seem to depend on the nature of the change. No, here all change would be fatal and land me back, there and then, in all the fun of the fair. I'll try it another way. Has nothing really changed since I have been here? No, frankly, hand on heart, wait a second, no, nothing, to my knowledge. But, as I have said, the place may well be vast, as it may well measure twelve feet in diameter. It comes to the same thing, as far as discerning its limits is concerned. I like to think I occupy the centre, but nothing is less certain. In a sense I would be better off at the circumference, since my eyes are always fixed in the same direction. But I am certainly not at the circumference. For if I were it would follow that Molloy, wheeling about me as he does, would issue from the enceinte at every revolution, which is manifestly impossible. But does he in fact wheel, does he not perhaps simply pass before me in a straight line? No, he wheels, I feel i , and about me, like a planet about its sun. And if he made a noise, as he goes, I would hear him all the time, on my right hand, behind my back, on my left hand, before seeing him again. But he makes none, for I am not deaf, of that I am convinced, that is to say half-convinced. From centre to circumference in any case it is a far cry and I may well be situated somewhere between the two. It is equally possible, I do not deny it, that I too am in perpetual motion, accompanied by Malone, as the earth by its moon. In which case there would be no further grounds for my complaining about the disorder of the lights, this being due simply to my insistence on regarding them as always the same lights and viewed always from the same point. All is possible, or almost. But the best is to think of myself as fixed and at the centre of this place, whatever its shape and extent may be. This is also probably the most pleasing to me. In a word, no change apparently since I have been here, disorder of the lights perhaps an illusion, all change to be feared, incomprehensible uneasiness.

. . . what do they want. what have I done to them, what have I done to God, what have they done to God, what has God done to us, nothing, and we've done nothing to him, you can't do anything to him, he can't do anything to us, we're innocent, he's innocent, it's nobody's fault, what's nobody's fault, this state of affairs, what state of affairs, so it is, so be it, don't fret, so it will be, how so, rattling on, dying of thirst, seeking determinedly, what they want, they want me to be, this, that, to howl, stir, crawl out of here, be born, die, listen, I'm listening, it's not enough, I must understand, I'm doing my best, I can't understand, I stop doing my best, I can't do my best, I can't go on, poor devil, neither can they, let them say what they want, give me something to do, something doable to do, poor devils, they can't, they don't know, they're like me, more and more, no more need of them, no more need of anyone, no one can do anything, it's I am talking, thirsting, starving, let it stand, in the ice and in the furnace, you feel nothing, strange, you don't feel a mouth on you, you don't feel your mouth any more, no need of a mouth, the words are everywhere, inside me, outside me, well well, a minute ago I had no thickness, I hear them, no need to hear them, no need of a head, impossible to stop them, impossible to stop, I'm in words, made of words, others' words, what others, the place too, the air, the walls, the floor, the ceiling, all words, the whole world is here with me, I'm the air, the walls, the walled-in one, everything yields, opens, ebbs, flows, like flakes, I'm all these flakes, meeting, mingling, falling asunder, wherever I go I find me, leave me, go towards me, come from me, nothing ever but me, a particle of me, retrieved, lost, gone astray, I'm all these words, all these strangers, this dust of words, with no ground for their settling, no sky for their dispersing, coming together to say, fleeing one another to say, that I am they, all of them, those that merge, those that part, those that never meet, and nothing else, yes, something else, that I'm something quite different, a quite different thing, a wordless thing in an empty place, a hard shut dry cold black place, where nothing stirs, nothing speaks, and that I listen, and that I seek, like a caged beast born of caged beasts born of caged beasts born of caged beasts born in a cage and dead in a cage, born and then dead, born in a cage and then dead in a cage, in a word like a beast, in one of their words, like such a beast, and that I seek, like such a beast, with my little strength, such a beast, with nothing of its species left but fear and fury, no, the fury is past, nothing but fear, nothing of all its due but fear centupled, fear of its shadow, no, blind from birth, of sound then, if you like, we'll have that, one must have something, it's a pity, but there it is, fear of sound, fear of sounds, the sounds of beasts, the sounds of men, sounds in the daytime and sounds at night, that's enough, fear of sounds, all sounds, more or less, more or less fear, all sounds, there's only one, continuous, day and night, what is it, it's steps coming and going, it's voices speaking for a moment, it's bodies groping their way, it's the air, it's things, it's the air among the things, that's enough, that I seek, like it, no, not like it, like me, in my own way, what am I saying, after my fashion, that I seek, what do I seek now, what it is, it must be that, it can only be that, what it is, what it can be, what what can be, what I seek, no, what I hear, now it comes back to me, all back to me, they say I seek what it is I hear, I hear them, now it comes back to me, what it can possibly be, and where it can possibly come from, since all is silent here, and the walls thick, and how I manage, without feeling an ear on me, or a head, or a body, or a soul, how I manage, to do what, how I manage, it's not clear, dear dear, you say it's not clear, something is wanting to make it clear, I'll seek, what is wanting, to make everything clear, I'm always seeking something, it's tiring in the end, and it's only the beginning, how I manage, under such conditions, to do what I'm doing, what am I doing, I must find out what I'm doing, tell me what you're doing and I'll ask you how it's possible, I hear, you say I hear, and that I seek, it's a lie, I seek nothing, nothing any more, no matter, let's leave it, no harking, and that I seek, listen to them now, jogging my memory, seek what, firstly what it is, secondly where it comes from, thirdly how I manage, that's it, now we've got it, thirdly how I manage, to do it, seeing that this, considering that that, inasmuch as God knows what, that's clear now, how I manage to hear, and how I manage to understand, it's a lie, what would I understand with, that's what I'm asking, how I manage to understand, oh not the half, nor the hundredth, nor the five thousandth, let us go on dividing by fifty, nor the quarter millionth, that's enough, but a little nevertheless, it's essential, it's preferable, it's a pity, but there it is, just a little all the same, the least possible, it's appreciable, it's enough, the rough meaning of one expression in a thousand, in ten thousand, let us go on multiplying by ten, nothing more restful than arithmetic, in a hundred thousand, in a million, it's too much, too little . . .

. . . The silence, speak of the silence before going into it, was I there already, I don't know, at every instant I'm there, listen to me speaking of it, I knew it would come, I emerge from it to speak of it, I stay in it to speak of it, if it's I who speak, and it's not, I act as if it were, sometimes I act as if it were, but at length, was I ever there at length, a long stay, I understand nothing about duration, I can't speak of it, oh I know I speak of it, I say never and ever, I speak of the four seasons and the different parts of the day and night, the night has no parts, that's because you are asleep, the seasons must be very similar, perhaps it's springtime now, that's all words they taught me, without making their meaning clear to me, that's how I learnt to reason, I use them all, all the words they showed me, there were columns of them, oh the strange glow all of a sudden, they were on lists, with images opposite, I must have forgotten them, I must have mixed them up, these nameless images I have, these imageless names, these windows I should perhaps rather call doors, at least by some other name, and this word man which is perhaps not the right one for the thing I see when I hear it, but an instant, an hour, and so on, how can they be represented, a life, how could that be made clear to me, here, in the dark, I call that the dark, perhaps it's azure, blank words, but I use them, they keep coming back, all those they showed me, all those I remember, I need them all, to be able to go on, it's a lie, a score would be plenty, tried and trusty, unforgettable, nicely varied, that would be palette enough. I'd mix them, I'd vary them, that would be gamut enough, all the things I'd do if I could, if I wished, if I could wish, no need to wish, that's how it will end, in heart-rending cries, inarticulate murmurs, to be invented, as I go along, improvised, as I groan along, I'll laugh, that's how it will end, in a chuckle, chuck chuck, ow, ha, pa, I'll practise, nyum, hoo, plop, psss, nothing but emotion, bing bang, that's blows, ugh, pooh, what else, oooh, aaah, that's love, enough, it's tiring, hee hee, that's the Abderite, no, the other, in the end, it's the end, the ending end, it's the silence, a few gurgles on the silence, the real silence, not the one where I macerate up to the mouth, up to the ear, that covers me, uncovers me, breathes with me, like a cat with a mouse, that of the drowned, I've drowned, more than once, it wasn't I, suffocated, set fire to me, thumped on my head with wood and iron, it wasn't I, there was no head, no wood, no iron, I didn't do anything to me, I didn't do anything to anyone, no one did anything to me, there is no one, I've looked, no one but me, no, not me either, I've looked everywhere, there must be someone, the voice must belong to someone, I've no objection, what it wants I want, I am it, I've said so, it says so, from time to time it says so, then it says not, I've no objection, I want it to go silent, it wants to go silent, it can't, it does for a second, then it starts again, that's not the real silence, it says that's not the real silence, what can be said of the real silence, I don't know, that I don't know what it is, that there is no such thing, that perhaps there is such a thing, yes, that perhaps there is, somewhere, I'll never know. But when it falters and when it stops, but it falters every instant, it stops every instant, yes, but when it stops for a good few moments, a good few moments, what are a good few moments, what then, murmurs, then it must be murmurs, and listening, someone listening, no need of an ear, no need of a mouth, the voice listens, as when it speaks, listens to its silence, that makes a murmur, that makes a voice, a small voice, the same voice only small, it sticks in the throat, there's the throat again, there's the mouth again, it fills the ear, there's the ear again, then I vomit, someone vomits, someone starts vomiting again, that must be how it happens, I have no explanations to offer, none to demand, the comma will come where I'll drown for good, then the silence, I believe it this evening, still this evening, how it drags on, I've no objection, perhaps it's springtime, violets, no, that's autumn, there's a time for everything, for the things that pass, the things that end, they could never get me to understand that, the things that stir, depart, return, a light changing, they could never get me to see that, and death into the bargain, a voice dying, that's a good one, silence at last, not a murmur, no air, no one listening, not for the likes of me, amen, on we go. Enormous prison, like a hundred thousand cathedrals, never anything else any more, from this time forth, and in it, somewhere, perhaps, riveted, tiny, the prisoner, how can he be found, how false this space is, what falseness instantly, to want to draw that round you, to want to put a being there, a cell would be plenty, if I gave up, if only I could give up, before beginning, before beginning again, what breathlessness, that's right, ejaculations, that helps you on, that puts off the fatal hour, no, the reverse, I don't know, start again, in this immensity, this obscurity, go through the motions of starting again, you who can't stir, you who never started, you the who, go through the motions, what motions, you can't stir, you launch your voice, it dies away in the vault, it calls that a vault, perhaps it's the abyss, those are words, it speaks of a prison, I've no objection, vast enough for a whole people, for me alone, or waiting for me, I'll go there now, I'll try and go there now, I can't stir, I'm there already, I must be there already, perhaps I'm not alone, perhaps a whole people is here, and the voice its voice, coming to me fitfully, we would have lived, been free a moment, now we talk about it, each one to himself, each one out loud for himself, and we listen, a whole people, talking and listening, all together, that would ex, no, I'm alone, perhaps the first, or perhaps the last, talking alone, listening alone, alone alone, the others are gone, they have been stilled, their voices stilled, their listening stilled, one by one, at each new-coming, another will come, I won't be the last, I'll be with the others, I'll be as gone, in the silence, it won't be I, it's not I, I'm not there yet, I'll go there now, I'll try and go there now, no use trying, I wait for my turn, my turn to go there, my turn to talk there, my turn to listen there, my turn to wait there for my turn to go, to be as gone, it's unending, it will be unending, gone where, where do you go from there, you must go somewhere else, wait somewhere else, for your turn to go again, and so on, a whole people, or I alone, and come back, and begin again, no, go on, go on again, it's a circuit, a long circuit, I know it well, I must know it well, it's a lie, I can't stir, I haven't stirred, I launch the voice, I hear a voice, there is nowhere but here, there are not two places, there are not two prisons, it's my parlour, it's a parlour, where I wait for nothing, I don't know where it is, I don't know what it's like, that's no business of mine, I don't know if it's big, or if it's small, or if it's closed, if it's open that's right, reiterate, that helps you on, open on what, there is nothing else, only it, open on the void, open on the nothing, I've no objection, those are words, open on the silence, looking out on the silence, straight out, why not, all this time on the brink of silence, I knew it, on a rock, lashed to a rock, in the midst of silence, its great swell rears towards me, I'm streaming with it, it's an image, those are words, it's a body, it's not I, I knew it wouldn't be I, I'm not outside, I'm inside, I'm in something, I'm shut up, the silence is outside, outside, inside, there is nothing but here, and the silence outside, nothing but this voice and the silence all round, no need of walls, yes, we must have walls, I need walls, good and thick, I need a prison, I was right, for me alone, I'll go there now, I'll put me in it, I'm there already, I'll start looking for me now, I'm there somewhere, it won't be I, no matter, I'll say it's I, perhaps it will be I, perhaps that's all they're waiting for, there they are again, to give me quittance, waiting for me to say I'm someone, to say I'm somewhere, to put me out, into the silence, I see nothing, it's because there is nothing, or it's because I have no eyes, or both, that makes three possibilities, to choose from, but do I really see nothing, it's not the moment to tell a lie, but how can you not tell a lie, what an idea, a voice like this, who can check it, it tries everything, it's blind, it seeks me blindly, in the dark, it seeks a mouth, to enter into, who can query it, there is no other, you'd need a head, you'd need things, I don't know, I look too often as if I knew, it's the voice does that, it goes all knowing, to make me think I know, to make me think it's mine, it has no interest in eyes, it says I have none, or that they are no use to me, then it speaks of tears, then it speaks of gleams, it is truly at a loss, gleams, yes, far, or near, distances, you know, measurements, enough said, gleams, as at dawn, then dying, as at evening, or flaring up, they do that too, blaze up more dazzling than snow, for a second, that's short, then fizzle out, that's true enough, if you like, one forgets, I forget, I say I see nothing, or I say it's all in my head, as if I felt a head on me, that's all hypotheses, lies, these gleams too, they were to save me, they were to devour me, that came to nothing, I see nothing, either because of this or else on account of that, and these images at which they watered me, like a camel, before the desert, I don't know, more lies, just for the fun of it, fun, what fun we've had, what fun of it, all lies, that's soon said, you must say soon, it's the regulations. The place, I'll make it all the same, I'll make it in my head, I'll draw it out of my memory, I'll gather it all about me, I'll make myself a head, I'll make myself a memory, I have only to listen, the voice will tell me everything, tell it to me again, everything I need, in dribs and drabs, breathless, it's like a confession, a last confession, you think it's finished, then it starts off again, there were so many sins, the memory is so bad, the words don't come, the words fail, the breath fails, no, it's something else, it's an indictment, a dying voice accusing, accusing me, you must accuse someone, a culprit is indispensable, it speaks of my sins, it speaks of my head, it says it's mine, it says that I repent, that I want to be punished, better than I am, that I want to go, give myself up, a victim is essential, I have only to listen, it will show me my hiding-place, what it's like, where the door is, if there's a door, and whereabouts I am in it, and what lies between us, how the land lies, what kind of country, whether it's sea, or whether it's mountain, and the way to take, so that I may go, make my escape, give myself up, come to the place where the axe falls, without further ceremony, on all who come from here, I'm not the first, I won't be the first, it will best me in the end, it has bested better than me, it will tell me what to do, in order to rise, move, act like a body endowed with despair, that's how I reason, that's how I hear myself reasoning, all lies, it's not me they're calling, not me they're talking about, it's not yet my turn, it's someone else's turn, that's why I can't stir, that's why I don't feel a body on me, I'm not suffering enough yet, it's not yet my turn, not suffering enough to be able to stir, to have a body, complete with head, to be able to understand, to have eyes to light the way, I merely hear, without understanding, without being able to profit by it, by what I hear, to do what, to rise and go and be done with hearing, I don't hear everything, that must be it, the important things escape me, it's not my turn, the topographical and anatomical information in particular is lost on me, no, I hear everything, what difference does it make, the moment it's not my turn, my turn to understand, my turn to live, my turn of the life-screw, it calls that living, the space of the way from here to the door, it's all there, in what I hear, somewhere, if all has been said, all this long time, all must have been said, but it's not my turn to know what, to know what I am, where I am, and what I should do to stop being it, to stop being there, that's coherent, so as to be another, no, the same, I don't know, depart into life, travel the road, find the door, find the axe, perhaps it's a cord, for the neck, for the throat, for the cords, or fingers, I'll have eyes, I'll see fingers, it will be the silence, perhaps it's a drop, find the door, open the door, drop, into the silence, it won't be I, I'll stay here, or there, more likely there, it will never be I, that's all I know, it's all been done already, said and said again, the departure, the body that rises, the way, in colour, the arrival, the door that opens, closes again, it was never I, I've never stirred, I've listened, I must have spoken, why deny it, why not admit it, after all, I deny nothing, I admit nothing, I say what I hear, I hear what I say, I don't know, one or the other, or both, that makes three possibilities, pick your fancy, all these stories about travellers, these stories about paralytics, all are mine, I must be extremely old, or it's memory playing tricks, if only I knew if I've lived, if I live, if I'll live, that would simplify everything, impossible to find out, that's where you're buggered, I haven't stirred, that's all I know, no, I know something else, it's not I, I always forget that, I resume, you must resume, never stirred from here, never stopped telling stories, to myself, hardly hearing them, hearing something else, listening for something else, wondering now and then where I got them from, was I in the land of the living, were they in mine, and where, where do I store them, in my head, I don't feel a head on me, and what do I tell them with, with my mouth, same remark, and what do I hear them with, and so on, the old rigmarole, it can't be I, or it's because I pay no heed, it's such an old habit, I do it without heeding, or as if I were somewhere else, there I am far again, there I am the absentee again, it's his turn again now, he who neither speaks nor listens, who has neither body nor soul, it's something else he has, he must have something, he must be somewhere, he is made of silence, there's a pretty analysis, he's in the silence, he's the one to be sought, the one to be, the one to be spoken of, the one to speak, but he can't speak, then I could stop, I'd be he, I'd be the silence, I'd be back in the silence, we'd be reunited, his story the story to be told, but he has no story, he hasn't been in story, it's not certain, he's in his own story, unimaginable, unspeakable, that doesn't matter, the attempt must be made, in the old stories incomprehensibly mine, to find his, it must be there somewhere, it must have been mine, before being his, I'll recognise it, in the end I'll recognise it, the story of the silence that he never left, that I should never have left, that I may never find again, that I may find again, then it will be he, it will be I, it will be the place, the silence, the end, the beginning, the beginning again, how can I say it, that's all words, they're all I have, and not many of them, the words fail, the voice fails, so be it, I know that well,

it will be the silence, full of murmurs, distant cries, the usual
silence, spent listening, spent waiting, waiting for the voice, the
cries abate, like all cries, that is to say they stop, the murmurs
cease, they give up, the voice begins again, it begins trying again,
quick now before there is none left, no voice left, nothing left but
the core of murmurs, distant cries, quick now and try again, with
the words that remain, try what, I don't know, I've forgotten, it
doesn't matter, I never knew, to have them carry me into my
story, the words that remain, my old story, which I've forgotten,
far from here, through the noise, through the door, into the
silence, that must be it, it's too late, perhaps it's too late, perhaps
they have, how would I know, in the silence you don't know,
perhaps it's the door, perhaps I'm at the door, that would surprise
me, perhaps it's I, perhaps somewhere or other it was I, I can
depart, all this time I've journeyed without knowing it, it's I now
at the door, what door, what's a door doing here, it's the last
words, the true last, or it's the murmurs, the murmurs are coming,
I know that well, no, not even that, you talk of murmurs, distant
cries, as long as you can talk, you talk of them before and you talk
of them after, more lies, it will be the silence, the one that doesn't
last, spent listening, spent waiting, for it to be broken, for the
voice to break it, perhaps there's no other, I don't know, it's not
worth having, that's all I know, it's not I, that's all I know, it's
not mine, it's the only one I ever had, that's a lie, I must have had
the other, the one that lasts, but it didn't last, I don't understand,
that is to say it did, it still lasts, I'm still in it, I left myself behind
in it, I'm waiting for me there, no, there you don't wait, you don't
listen, I don't know, perhaps it's a dream, all a dream, that would
surprise me, I'll wake, in the silence, and never sleep again, it will
be I, or dream, dream again, dream of a silence, a dream silence,
full of murmurs, I don't know, that's all words, never wake, all
words, there's nothing else, you must go on, that's all I know,
they're going to stop, I know that well, I can feel it, they're going
to abandon me, it will be the silence, for a moment, a good few
moments, or it will be mine, the lasting one, that didn't last, that
still lasts, it will be I, you must go on, I can't go on, you must go
on, I'll go on, you must say words, as long as there are any, until
they find me, until they say me, strange pain, strange sin, you
must go on, perhaps it's done already, perhaps they have said me
already, perhaps they have carried me to the threshold of my story,
before the door that opens on my story, that would surprise me,

if it opens, it will be I, it will be the silence, where I am, I don't know, I'll never know, in the silence you don't know, you must go on, I can't go on, I'll go on.

Waiting for Godot

Waiting for Godot was written between Malone Dies and The Unnamable and was Beckett's second play written in French. The first, entitled Eleutheria, has never been released. A complete break from the theatre of the 1940s, it is a return to the poetic theatre of myth, with many echoes of the old Greek drama and frequent similarities to the surrealists in the ambiguities and contradictions in which it abounds. Does the second act occur one day after the first, or are there several days, weeks, or even years in between? The memories of the two tramps are dim and they disagree. The stage instructions are, 'Next day. Same time. Same place.' The boots that Estragon has left front stage at the end of the first act are still there, although he claims that they no longer fit him, but there are indications that the first act is in the autumn and the second in the spring, and in the period intervening between the two acts Pozzo, the bullying master who was self-confidently taking his servant Lucky to market to sell him, has gone blind and is now helpless and dependent on Lucky, who, having been capable in Act I of delivering an abstruse medieval sermon, has now inexplicably been struck dumb.

The situations of Godot are puzzling and part of the fascination of the play, but it is in the shape of the speeches, the poetical style that Beckett had developed to convey the anguish of humanity, that the greatness of the play lies. A great tenderness and an insistent humour pervade it, so that the two tramps, the reflective Vladimir and the more instinctive Estragon, instantly attract our sympathy and enable us to see ourselves in a new light. Little happens during the two acts. There is time to be filled, and the tramps fill it as best they can, by alternating gestures of warmth and hostility, by threatening to leave each other, by making up games, and by curiously exploring their own capacity for cruelty. In a way they are the most real people in the Beckett canon, not prototypes, nor abstractions, nor personifications of an idea. The following extract is from the end of the play. Just as the boredom of the day was becoming intolerable for the tramps, they hear Pozzo and Lucky returning and are amazed to discover their changed condition. Pozzo is weak and hardly able to stand, clutching the rope attached to Lucky's neck. Vladimir and Estragon are delighted and want them to stay as long as possible. Assistance in passing the time has arrived, and the rest of the day will have its entertainment. Pozzo falls and is unable to rise. They speculate whether to rob him, but lack the courage. They show willingness to help, partly in the hope of reward and partly because of the rarity of the occasion. As Vladimir says,

'Let us do something while we have the chance! It is not every day that we are needed. Not indeed that we personally are needed. Others would meet the case equally well, if not better. To all mankind they were addressed, those cries for help still ringing in our ears! But at this place, at this moment of time, all mankind is us, whether we like it or not. Let us make the most of it, before it is too late! Let us represent worthily for once the foul brood to which a cruel fate consigned us!'

The pages that follow have tremendous dramatic force, leading up to Pozzo's outburst which contains the very core of Beckettian anguish and despair at the incomprehensibility and cruelty of life, the shortness and the waste of it, and man's compulsion, in spite of it, to go on. Pozzo is quoted by Vladimir in the beautifully controlled soliloquy that follows, when having given in to despair, he abruptly pulls himself back, in one of the most poignant and beautiful moments in the whole theatrical repertory.

POZZO: Who are you?

VLADIMIR: Do you not recognise us?

POZZO: I am blind.

Silence.

ESTRAGON: Perhaps he can see into the future.

VLADIMIR: Since when?

POZZO: I used to have wonderful sight – but are you friends?

ESTRAGON: (*laughing noisily*). He wants to know if we are friends!

VLADIMIR: No, he means friends of his.

ESTRAGON: Well?

VLADIMIR: We've proved we are, by helping him.

ESTRAGON: Exactly. Would we have helped him if we weren't his friends?

VLADIMIR: Possibly.

ESTRAGON: True.

VLADIMIR: Don't let's quibble about that now.

POZZO: You are not highwaymen?

ESTRAGON: Highwaymen! Do we look like highwaymen?

VLADIMIR: Damn it, can't you see the man is blind!

ESTRAGON: Damn it, so he is. (*Pause.*) So he says.

POZZO: Don't leave me!

VLADIMIR: No question of it.

ESTRAGON: For the moment.

POZZO: What time is it?

VLADIMIR: (*inspecting the sky*). Seven o'clock . . . eight o'clock . . .

ESTRAGON: That depends what time of year it is.

POZZO: Is it evening?

Silence. Vladimir and Estragon scrutinise the sunset.

ESTRAGON: It's rising.

VLADIMIR: Impossible.

ESTRAGON: Perhaps it's the dawn.

VLADIMIR: Don't be a fool. It's the west over there.

ESTRAGON: How do you know?

POZZO: (*anguished*). Is it evening?

VLADIMIR: Anyway it hasn't moved.

ESTRAGON: I tell you it's rising.

POZZO: Why don't you answer me?

ESTRAGON: Give us a chance.

VLADIMIR: (*reassuring*). It's evening, sir, it's evening, night is drawing nigh. My friend here would have me doubt it and I must confess he shook me for a moment. But it is not for nothing I have lived through this long day and I can assure you it is very near the end of its repertory. (*Pause.*) How do you feel now?

ESTRAGON: How much longer must we cart him round? (*They half release him, catch him again as he falls.*) We are not caryatids!

VLADIMIR: You were saying your sight used to be good, if I heard you right.

POZZO: Wonderful! Wonderful, wonderful sight!
Silence.

ESTRAGON: (*irritably*). Expand! Expand!

VLADIMIR: Let him alone. Can't you see he's thinking of the days when he was happy? (*Pause.*) *Memoria praeteritorum bonorum* – that must be unpleasant.

ESTRAGON: We wouldn't know.

VLADIMIR: And it came on you all of a sudden?

POZZO: Quite wonderful!

VLADIMIR: I'm asking you if it came on you all of a sudden.

POZZO: I woke up one fine day as blind as Fortune. (*Pause.*) Sometimes I wonder if I'm not still asleep.

VLADIMIR: And when was that?

POZZO: I don't know.

VLADIMIR: But no later than yesterday—

POZZO: (*violently*). Don't question me! The blind have no notion of time. The things of time are hidden from them too.

VLADIMIR: Well just fancy that! I could have sworn it was just the opposite.

ESTRAGON: I'm going.

POZZO: Where are we?

VLADIMIR: I couldn't tell you.

POZZO: It isn't by any chance the place known as the Board?

VLADIMIR: Never heard of it.

POZZO: What is it like?

VLADIMIR: (*looking round*). It's indescribable. It's like nothing. There's nothing. There's a tree.

POZZO: Then it's not the Board.

ESTRAGON: (*sagging*). Some diversion!

POZZO: Where is my menial?

VLADIMIR: He's about somewhere.

POZZO: Why doesn't he answer when I call?

VLADIMIR: I don't know. He seems to be sleeping. Perhaps he's dead.

POZZO: What happened exactly?

ESTRAGON: Exactly!

VLADIMIR: The two of you slipped. (*Pause.*) And fell.

POZZO: Go and see is he hurt.

VLADIMIR: We can't leave you.

POZZO: You needn't both go.

VLADIMIR: (*to Estragon*). You go.

ESTRAGON: After what he did to me? Never!

POZZO: Yes yes, let your friend go, he stinks so. (*Silence.*) What is he waiting for?

VLADIMIR: What are you waiting for?

ESTRAGON: I'm waiting for Godot.

Silence.

VLADIMIR: What exactly should he do?

POZZO: Well to begin with he should pull on the rope, as hard as he likes so long as he doesn't strangle him. He usually responds to that. If not he should give him a taste of his boot, in the face and the privates as far as possible.

VLADIMIR: (*to Estragon*). You see, you've nothing to be afraid of. It's even an opportunity to revenge yourself.

ESTRAGON: And if he defends himself?

POZZO: No no, he never defends himself.

VLADIMIR: I'll come flying to the rescue.

ESTRAGON: Don't take your eyes off me.

He goes towards Lucky.

VLADIMIR: Make sure he's alive before you start. No point in exerting yourself if he's dead.

ESTRAGON: (*bending over Lucky*). He's breathing.
VLADIMIR: Then let him have it.
With sudden fury Estragon starts kicking Lucky, hurling abuse at him as he does so. But he hurts his foot and moves away, limping and groaning. Lucky stirs.
ESTRAGON: Oh the brute!
He sits down on the mound and tries to take off his boot. But he soon desists and disposes himself for sleep, his arms on his knees and his head on his arms.
POZZO: What's gone wrong now?
VLADIMIR: My friend has hurt himself.
POZZO: And Lucky?
VLADIMIR: So it is he?
POZZO: What?
VLADIMIR: It is Lucky?
POZZO: I don't understand.
VLADIMIR: And you are Pozzo?
POZZO: Certainly I am Pozzo.
VLADIMIR: The same as yesterday?
POZZO: Yesterday?
VLADIMIR: We met yesterday. (*Silence.*) Do you not remember?
POZZO: I don't remember having met anyone yesterday. But tomorrow I won't remember having met anyone today. So don't count on me to enlighten you.
VLADIMIR: But—
POZZO: Enough. Up pig!
VLADIMIR: You were bringing him to the fair to sell him. You spoke to us. He danced. He thought. You had your sight.
POZZO: As you please. Let me go! (*Vladimir moves away.*) Up!
Lucky gets up, gathers up his burdens.
VLADIMIR: Where do you go from here?
POZZO: On. (*Lucky, laden down, takes his place before Pozzo.*) Whip! (*Lucky puts everything down, looks for whip, finds it, puts it into Pozzo's hand, takes up everything again.*) Rope!
Lucky puts everything down, puts end of the rope into Pozzo's hand, takes up everything again.
VLADIMIR: What is there in the bag?
POZZO: Sand. (*He jerks the rope.*) On!

VLADIMIR: Don't go yet!

POZZO: I'm going.

VLADIMIR: What do you do when you fall far from help?

POZZO: We wait till we can get up. Then we go on. On!

VLADIMIR: Before you go tell him to sing!

POZZO: Who?

VLADIMIR: Lucky.

POZZO: To sing?

VLADIMIR: Yes. Or to think. Or to recite.

POZZO: But he's dumb.

VLADIMIR: Dumb!

POZZO: Dumb. He can't even groan.

VLADIMIR: Dumb! Since when?

POZZO: (*suddenly furious*). Have you not done tormenting me with your accursed time! It's abominable! When! When! One day, is that not enough for you, one day like any other day, one day he went dumb, one day I went blind, one day we'll go deaf, one day we were born, one day we shall die, the same day, the same second, is that not enough for you? (*Calmer.*) They give birth astride of a grave, the light gleams an instant, then it's night once more.

(*He jerks the rope.*) On!

Exeunt Pozzo and Lucky. Vladimir follows them to the edge of the stage, looks after them. The noise of falling, reinforced by mimic of Vladimir, announces that they are down again. Silence. Vladimir goes towards Estragon, contemplates him a moment, then shakes him awake.

ESTRAGON: (*wild gestures, incoherent words. Finally*). Why will you never let me sleep?

VLADIMIR: I felt lonely.

ESTRAGON: I was dreaming I was happy.

VLADIMIR: That passed the time.

ESTRAGON: I was dreaming that—

VLADIMIR: (*violently*). Don't tell me! (*Silence.*) I wonder is he really blind.

ESTRAGON: Blind? Who?

VLADIMIR: Pozzo.

ESTRAGON: Blind?

VLADIMIR: He told us he was blind.

ESTRAGON: Well what about it?

VLADIMIR: It seemed to me he saw us.

ESTRAGON: You dreamt it. (*Pause.*) Let's go. We can't. Ah! (*Pause.*) Are you sure it wasn't him?

VLADIMIR: Who?

ESTRAGON: Godot.

VLADIMIR: But who?

ESTRAGON: Pozzo.

VLADIMIR: Not at all! (*Less sure.*) Not at all! (*Still less sure.*) Not at all!

ESTRAGON: I suppose I might as well get up. (*He gets up painfully.*) Ow! Didi!

VLADIMIR: I don't know what to think any more.

ESTRAGON: My feet! (*He sits down, tries to take off his boots.*) Help me!

VLADIMIR: Was I sleeping, while the others suffered? Am I sleeping now? Tomorrow, when I wake, or think I do, what shall I say of today? That with Estragon my friend, at this place, until the fall of night, I waited for Godot? That Pozzo passed, with his carrier, and that he spoke to us? Probably. But in all that what truth will there be? (*Estragon, having struggled with his boots in vain, is dozing off again. Vladimir stares at him.*) He'll know nothing. He'll tell me about the blows he received and I'll give him a carrot. (*Pause.*) Astride of a grave and a difficult birth. Down in the hole, lingeringly, the grave-digger puts on the forceps. We have time to grow old. The air is full of our cries. (*He listens.*) But habit is a great deadener. (*He looks again at Estragon.*) At me too someone is looking, of me too someone is saying, He is sleeping, he knows nothing, let him sleep on. (*Pause.*) I can't go on! (*Pause.*) What have I said?

Texts for Nothing

The thirteen *Texts for Nothing* were written concurrently with the *Trilogy* and are especially close to *The Unnamable* in tone. Each text contains a voice that asks questions, complaining or trying to define its own condition. Number IV is largely quoted in the introduction. Number XIII, given here in full, the last of the series, has a telling phrase borrowed from it by the author for the collection of short prose which appeared in 1967, *No's Knife*: 'And whose shame ... at having to hear, having to say ... so many lies ... whose the screaming silence of no's knife in yes's wound, it wonders.' *No's Knife* contained all the short prose that the author was willing to have published at that time.

The *Texts for Nothing* are in a sense footnotes to the main text, short outbursts wired to the nerve-endings, which can be considered as variant cadenzas to the novels or as extra soliloquies to the plays.

Weaker still the weak old voice that tried in vain to make me, dying away as much as to say it's going from here to try elsewhere, or dying down, there's no telling, as much as to say it's going to cease, give up trying. No voice ever but it in my life, it says, if speaking of me one can speak of life, and it can, it still can, or if not of life, there it dies, if this, if that, if speaking of me, there it dies, but who can the greater can the less, once you've spoken of me you can speak of anything, up to the point where, up to the time when, there it dies, it can't go on, it's been its death, speaking of me, here or elsewhere, it says, it murmurs. Whose voice, no one's, there is no one, there's a voice without a mouth, and somewhere a kind of hearing, something compelled to hear, and somewhere a hand, it calls that a hand, it wants to make a hand, or if not a hand something somewhere that can leave a trace, of what is made, of what is said, you can't do with less, no, that's romancing, more romancing, there is nothing but a voice murmuring a trace. A trace, it wants to leave a trace, yes, like air leaves among the leaves, among the grass, among the sand, it's with that it would make a life, but soon it will be the end, it won't be long now, there won't be any life, there won't have been any life, there will be silence, the air quite still that trembled once an instant, the tiny flurry of dust quite settled. Air, dust, there is no air here, nor anything to make dust, and to speak of instants, to speak of once, is to speak of nothing, but there it is, those are the expressions it employs. It has always spoken, it will always speak, of things that don't exist, or only exist elsewhere, if you like, if you must, if that may be called existing. Unfortunately it is not a question of elsewhere, but of here, ah there are the words out at last, out again, that was the only chance, get out of here and go elsewhere, go where time passes and atoms assemble an instant, where the voice belongs perhaps, where it sometimes says it must have belonged, to be able to speak of such figments. Yes, out of here, but how when here is empty, not a speck of dust, not a breath, the voice's breath alone, it breathes in vain, nothing is made. If I were here, if it could have made me, how I would pity it, for having spoken so long in vain, no, that won't do, it wouldn't have spoken in vain if I were here, and I wouldn't pity it if it had made me, I'd curse it, or bless it, it would be in my mouth, cursing, blessing, whom, what, it wouldn't be able to say, in my mouth it wouldn't have much to say, that had so much to say in vain. But this pity, all the same, it wonders, this pity that is in the air, though no air here for pity, but it's the expression, it wonders should it stop and wonder what pity is doing here and if it's not hope gleaming, another expression, evilly among the imaginary ashes, the faint hope of a faint being after all, human in kind, tears in its eyes before they've had time to open, no, no more stopping and wondering, about that or anything else, nothing will stop it any more, in its fall, or in its rise, perhaps it will end on a castrato scream. True there was never much talk of the heart, literal or figurative, but that's no reason for hoping, what, that one day there will be one, to send up above to break in the galanty show, pity. But what more is it waiting for now, when there's no doubt left, no choice left, to stick a sock in its death-rattle, yet another locution. To have rounded off its cock-and-bullshit in a coda worthy of the rest? Last everlasting questions, infant languors in the end sheets, last images, end of dream, of being past, passing and to be, end of lie. Is it possible, is that the possible thing at last, the extinction of this black nothing and its impossible shades, the end of the farce of making and the silencing of silence, it wonders, that voice which is silence, or it's me, there's no telling, it's all the same dream, the same silence, it and me, it and him, him and me, and all our train, and all theirs, and all theirs, but whose, whose dream, whose silence, old questions, last questions, ours who are dream and silence, but it's ended, we're ended who never were, soon there will be nothing where there was never anything, last images. And whose the shame, at every mute micro-millisyllable, and unshakable infinity of remorse delving ever dee-per in its bite, at having to hear, having to say, fainter than the faintest murmur, so many lies, so many times the same lie lyingly denied, whose the screaming silence of no's knife in yes's wound, it wonders. And wonders what has become of the wish to know, it is gone, the heart is gone, the head is gone, no one feels anything, asks anything, seeks anything, says anything, hears anything, there is only silence. It's not true, yes, it's true, it's true and it's not true, there is silence and there is not silence, there is no one and there is someone, nothing prevents anything. And were the voice to cease quite at last, the old ceasing voice, it would not be true, as it is not true that it speaks, it can't speak, it can't cease. And were there one day to be here, where there are no days, which is no place, born of the impossible voice the unmakable being, and a gleam of light, still all would be silent and empty and dark, as now, as soon now, when all will be ended, all said, it says, it murmurs.

'Text for Nothing XIII'

The Duthuit Dialogues

The English-language magazine *Transition* appeared in Paris during the 1930s and was a principal vehicle for important new writing from those American and British émigrés who lived in or around Paris, mostly ignored by commercial publishers and uninterested in the mainstream literature of the time. Most of *Finnegans Wake* appeared in *Transition* as 'Work in Progress', and other contributors included most of the surrealists and expressionists in translation, and also Gertrude Stein, Hart Crane, Hemingway, Dylan Thomas, and Beckett; the latter in particular did many translations for the magazine. *Transition* closed down during the war, was started after it again by Georges Duthuit, an art critic and friend of Beckett's, by an agreement with the previous editor, Eugène Jolas, because at the time only pre-war magazines could get a paper quota.

Beckett and Duthuit met frequently in cafés, discussed art, and played chess. The play *Endgame* is constructed in the shape of a chess game, as are the three dialogues, based on their conversations, that Beckett later put onto paper. Each dialogue is tied to their discussion of one of the painters Tal Coat, Masson, and Bram van Velde. The painting in question is really only a jumping-off point for Beckett to outline Duthuit's basic critical view of the nature of art as a foil for his own more generalised ideas about creativity in general and the relationship of art to life. The cut-and-thrust of the dialogues has the crispness of a fast chess game, using all Beckett's economy of language. In the first dialogue, discussing Tal Coat, Duthuit praises the painter for being 'committed neither to truth nor beauty, twin tyrannies of nature', but is countered by Beckett for not being revolutionary enough. Beckett complains that the old masters of Italian painting 'never stirred from the field of the possible, however much they may have enlarged it'. Well-painted painting is not enough: art must do more than 'disturb the plane of the feasible'. He agrees there could be logically no other plane for the creative artist, but continues:

Beckett – Yet I speak of an art turning from it in disgust, weary of puny exploits, weary of pretending to be able, of being able, of doing a little better the same old thing, of going a little further along a dreary road.

Duthuit – And preferring what?

B. – The expression that there is nothing to express, nothing with which to express, nothing from which to express, no power to express, no desire to express, together with the obligation to express.

Duthuit points out that 'that is a violently extreme and personal point of view' and of little relevance to the argument in question. Beckett makes no reply, ending the dialogue. He allows himself to be bested by the Frenchman in each of the three discussions, but makes his points forcefully none the less.

In the second dialogue, starting from the need to search for a difficulty, detecting an unwelcome facility in Masson's painting, Beckett eludes Duthuit's admiration for Masson's conquests of the 'servitude of space' and his successful use of expression to create joyful forms where 'the object remains sovereign'. Logically out-argued at every turn, Beckett moves sideways and talks of his 'dream of an art unresentful of its insuperable indigence and too proud for the farce of giving and receiving', only to be calmly routed by Duthuit:

Duthuit – Masson himself, having remarked that western perspective is no more than a series of traps for the capture of objects, declares that their possession does not interest him. He congratulates Bonnard for having, in his last works, 'gone beyond possessive space in every shape and form, far from surveys and bounds, to the point where all possession is dissolved'. I agree that there is a long cry from Bonnard to that impoverished painting, 'authentically fruitless, incapable of any image whatsoever', to which you aspire, and towards which too, who knows, unconsciously perhaps, Masson tends. But must we really deplore the painting that admits 'the things and creatures of spring, resplendent with desire and affirmation, ephemeral no doubt, but immortally reiterant', not in order to benefit by them, not in order to enjoy them, but in order that what is tolerable and radiant in the world may continue? Are we really to deplore the painting that is a rallying, among the things of time that pass and hurry us away, towards a time that endures and gives increase?

The dialogue ends amusingly with a stage direction: 'Beckett – (Exit weeping)'. The third dialogue, given here in full, contains in Beckett's long speech – it can hardly be called an argument – a personal statement akin to the 'nothing to express' bombshell of the first dialogue. Nowhere else is Beckett so explicit about his perverse and individual approach to art, although in his essay on Proust and some of the early critical writing due to be published in 1983 (under the title *Disjecta*) he makes other, equally contro-versial comments on aesthetics, to show how far removed he is from those who see the arts principally as a method of making life more tolerable, or as a chain of development whereby every historical stage leads to artistic advance, or who see art simply as individual expression, licensed or tolerated by society. To Beckett, failure is what the human condition is all about, and art can be no different. If art has a purpose it should be to enable us to see tragedy with greater depth and to increase the agony (this must be taken half seriously and half tongue-in-cheek). Probably every artist ultimately sees himself in terms of failure, with the greater his acclaim, the greater the gap between the goal and achievement. What Beckett is really saying is that the artist is doomed to attempt the impossible and, because it is impossible, doomed not to achieve it. Nevertheless without the attempt, the goal and its impossibility would not even be sighted, and of course failure of the type and on the scale that Beckett is talking about can be and is magnificent. Beckett's very personal ability to create vacuums of meaning to exclude beautiful form (which hides the pain at the core of the message) creates such tension both in his readers and in the forms themselves that awareness of that beauty must surface, just as all the things removed from the vacuum will spawn there again.

The dialogues are short, delightful, perfectly shaped, and very revealing: in them Beckett gives himself away, wickedly loses every argument, creates some fascinating *non sequiturs*, and leaves the reader with much to puzzle out for himself.

B. – Frenchman, fire first.

D. – Speaking of Tal Coat and Masson you invoked an art of a different order, not only from theirs, but from any achieved up to date. Am I right in thinking that you had van Velde in mind when making this sweeping distinction?

B. – Yes. I think he is the first to accept a certain situation and to consent to a certain act.

D. – Would it be too much to ask you to state again, as simply as possible, the situation and act that you conceive to be his?

B. – The situation is that of him who is helpless, cannot act, in the event cannot paint, since he is obliged to paint. The act is of him who, helpless, unable to act, acts, in the event paints, since he is obliged to paint.

D. – Why is he obliged to paint?

B. – I don't know.

D. – Why is he helpless to paint?

B. – Because there is nothing to paint and nothing to paint with.

D. – And the result, you say, is art of a new order?

B. – Among those whom we call great artists, I can think of none whose concern was not predominantly with his expressive possibilities, those of his vehicle, those of humanity. The assumption underlying all painting is that the domain of the maker is the domain of the feasible. The much to express, the little to express, the ability to express much, the ability to express little, merge in the common anxiety to express as much as possible, or as truly as possible, or as finely as possible, to the best of one's ability. What—

D. – One moment. Are you suggesting that the painting of van Velde is inexpressive?

B. – (A fortnight later) Yes.

D. – You realise the absurdity of what you advance?

B. – I hope I do.

D. – What you say amounts to this: the form of expression known as painting, since for obscure reasons we are obliged to speak of painting, has had to wait for van Velde to be rid of the misapprehension under which it has laboured so long and so bravely, namely, that its function was to express, by means of paint.

B. – Others have felt that art is not necessarily expression. But the numerous attempts made to make painting independent of its occasion have only succeeded in enlarging its repertory. I suggest that van Velde is the first whose painting is bereft, rid if you prefer, of occasion in every shape and form, ideal as well as material, and the first whose hands have not been tied by the certitude that expression is an impossible act.

D. – But might it not be suggested, even by one tolerant of this fantastic theory, that the occasion of his painting is his predicament, and that it is expressive of the impossibility to express?

B. – No more ingenious method could be devised for restoring him, safe and sound, to the bosom of Saint Luke. But let us, for once, be foolish enough not to turn tail. All have turned wisely tail, before the ultimate penury, back to the mere misery where destitute virtuous mothers may steal bread for their starving brats. There is more than a difference of degree between being short, short of the world, short of self, and being without these esteemed commodities. The one is a predicament, the other not.

D. – But you have already spoken of the predicament of van Velde.

B. – I should not have done so.

D. – You prefer the purer view that here at last is a painter who does not paint, does not pretend to paint. Come, come, my dear fellow, make some kind of connected statement and then go away.

B. – Would it not be enough if I simply went away?

D. – No. You have begun. Finish. Begin again and go on until you have finished. Then go away. Try and bear in mind that the subject under discussion is not yourself, nor the Sufist Al-Haqq, but a particular Dutchman by name van Velde, hitherto erroneously referred to as an *artiste peintre*.

B. – How would it be if I first said what I am pleased to fancy he is, fancy he does, and then that it is more than likely that he is and does quite otherwise? Would not that be an excellent issue out of all our afflictions? He happy, you happy, I happy, all three bubbling over with happiness.

D. – Do as you please. But get it over.

B. – There are many ways in which the thing I am trying in vain to say may be tried in vain to be said. I have experimented, as you know, both in public and in private, under duress, through faintness of heart, through weakness of mind, with two or three hundred. The pathetic antithesis possession-poverty was perhaps not the most tedious. But we begin to weary of it, do we not? The realisation that art has always been bourgeois, though it may dull our pain before the achievements of the socially progressive, is finally of scant interest. The analysis of the relation between the artist and his occasion, a relation always regarded as indispensable, does not seem to have been very productive either, the reason being perhaps that it lost its way in disquisitions on the nature of occasion. It is obvious that for the artist obsessed with his expressive vocation, anything and everything is doomed to become occasion, including, as is apparently to some extent the case with Masson, the pursuit of occasion, and the every man his own wife experiments of the spiritual Kandinsky. No painting is more replete than Mondrian's. But if the occasion appears as an unstable term of relation, the artist, who is the other term, is hardly less so, thanks to his warren of modes and attitudes. The objections to this dualist view of the creative process are unconvincing. Two things are established, however precariously: the aliment, from fruits on plates to low mathematics and self-commiseration, and its manner of dispatch. All that should concern us is the acute and increasing anxiety of the relation itself, as though shadowed more and more darkly by a sense of invalidity, of inadequacy, of existence at the expense of all that it excludes, all that it blinds to. The history of painting, here we go again, is the history of its attempts to escape from this sense of failure, by means of more authentic, more ample, less exclusive relations between representer and representee, in a kind of tropism towards a light as to the nature of which the best opinions continue to vary, and with a kind of Pythagorean terror, as though the irrationality of pi were an offence against the deity, not to mention his creature. My case, since I am in the dock, is that van Velde is the first to desist from this aestheticised automatism, the first to submit wholly to the incoercible absence of relation, in the absence of terms or, if you like, in the presence of unavailable terms, the first to admit that to be an artist is to fail, as no other dare fail, that failure is his world and the shrink from it desertion, art and craft, good housekeeping, living. No, no, allow me to expire. I know that all that is required now, in order to bring even this horrible matter to an acceptable conclusion, is to make of this submission, this admission, this fidelity to failure, a new occasion, a new term of relation, and of the act which, unable to act, obliged to act, he makes, an expressive act, even if only of itself, of its impossibility, of its obligation. I know that my inability to do so places myself, and perhaps an innocent, in what I think is still called an unenviable situation, familiar to psychiatrists. For what is this coloured plane, that was not there before. I don't know what it is, having never seen anything like it before. It seems to have nothing to do with art, in any case, if my memories are correct. (Prepares to go.)

D. – Are you not forgetting something?

B. – Surely that is enough?

D. – I understood your number was to have two parts. The first was to consist in your saying what you – er – thought. This I am prepared to believe you have done. The second—

B. – (Remembering, warmly) Yes, yes, I am mistaken, I am mistaken.

The Poems

This section contains a small selection of Samuel Beckett's poetry. As with the Dialogues, the poems are very revealing of the author's attitudes and outlook, often expressing a Beckettian concept that we know from his other work in a new or briefer way.

The first poem, 'Whoroscope', was written overnight in 1930, as a last-minute entry for a prize, for a poem on the subject of time, given by Nancy Cunard; it won. A dramatic monologue, a little in the manner of Browning, it owes something to T. S. Eliot's *Waste Land*, especially in the notes, which in the event are more useful to the reader than those in Eliot's poem. The speaker is Descartes, and the poem is clever, if eccentric. 'The Vulture', inspired by Goethe, gives an image of the sky enclosed in a skull that in one form or another was to be used by Beckett again. 'Malacoda' is about death in the family. Malacoda himself, one of Dante's monsters in the *Divine Comedy*, is the undertaker who comes to measure the corpse while the widow is taken out to the garden. The line 'must it be it must be' presumably refers to the famous Beethoven incident when as a joke the composer wrote a tune to these words, refusing a favour to his secretary Schindler; the tune later surfaced in his final quartet as a dialogue with death.

Of the other poems 'Cascando', a love poem, is as emotional an outburst as Beckett has ever allowed himself. 'Vive morte', in French, has been included because it is such a perfect short evocation of the cruelties of spring. Perhaps it will be translated one day. The next three are justly famous and were all originally translated from French.

'Lady Love' and 'Scarcely Disfigured' are translations from Eluard, given as examples of how perfectly Beckett can catch the feeling of another poet.

Whoroscope

What's that?
An egg?
By the brothers Boot it stinks fresh.
Give it to Gillot.

Galileo how are you
and his consecutive thirds!
The vile old Copernican lead-swinging son of a sutler!
We're moving he said we're off – Porca Madonna!
the way a boatswain would be, or a sack-of-potatoey charging
                                        Pretender.
That's not moving, that's *moving*.   10

What's that?
A little green fry or a mushroomy one?
Two lashed ovaries with prostisciutto?
How long did she womb it, the feathery one?
Three days and four nights?
Give it to Gillot.

Faulhaber, Beeckman and Peter the Red,
come now in the cloudy avalanche or Gassendi's sun-red
                                        crystally cloud
and I'll pebble you all your hen-and-a-half ones
or I'll pebble a lens under the quilt in the midst of day.   20

To think he was my own brother, Peter the Bruiser,
and not a syllogism out of him
no more than if Pa were still in it.
Hey! pass over those coppers,
sweet milled sweat of my burning liver!
Them were the days I sat in the hot-cupboard throwing Jesuits
                                        out of the skylight.

Who's that? Hals?
Let him wait.

My squinty doaty!
I hid and you sook.   .   30

And Francine my precious fruit of a house-and-parlour foetus!
What an exfoliation!
Her little grey flayed epidermis and scarlet tonsils!
My one child
scourged by a fever to stagnant murky blood –
blood!
Oh Harvey belovèd
how shall the red and white, the many in the few,
(dear bloodswirling Harvey)
eddy through that cracked beater?   40
And the fourth Henry came to the crypt of the arrow.

What's that?
How long?
Sit on it.

A wind of evil flung my despair of ease
against the sharp spires of the one
lady:
not once or twice but . . . .
(Kip of Christ hatch it!)
in one sun's drowning   50
(Jesuitasters please copy).
So on with the silk hose over the knitted, and the morbid
                                                      leather –
what am I saying! the gentle canvas –
and away to Ancona on the bright Adriatic,
and farewell for a space to the yellow key of the Rosicrucians.
They don't know what the master of them that do did,
that the nose is touched by the kiss of all foul and sweet air,
and the drums, and the throne of the faecal inlet,
and the eyes by its zig-zags.
So we drink Him and eat Him   60
and the watery Beaune and the stale cubes of Hovis
because He can jig
as near or as far from His Jigging Self
and as sad or lively as the chalice or the tray asks.
How's that, Antonio?

In the name of Bacon will you chicken me up that egg.
Shall I swallow cave-phantoms?

Anna Maria!
She reads Moses and says her love is crucified.
Leider! Leider! she bloomed and withered,   70
a pale abusive parakeet in a mainstreet window.

No I believe every word of it I assure you.
Fallor, ergo sum!
The coy old frôleur!
He tolle'd and legge'd
and he buttoned on his redemptorist waistcoat.
No matter, let it pass.
I'm a bold boy I know
so I'm not my son
(even if I were a concierge)   80
nor Joachim my father's
but the chip of a perfect block that's neither old nor new,
the lonely petal of a great high bright rose.

Are you ripe at last,
my slim pale double-breasted turd?
How rich she smells,
this abortion of a fledgling!
I will eat it with a fish fork.
White and yolk and feathers.
Then I will rise and move moving   90
towards Rahab of the snows,
the murdering matinal pope-confessed amazon,
Christina the ripper.
Oh Weulles spare the blood of a Frank
who has climbed the bitter steps,
(René du Perron . . . . !)
and grant me my second
starless inscrutable hour.

                                                       (1930)

NOTES
René Descartes, Seigneur du Perron, liked his omelette made of eggs hatched
from eight to ten days; shorter or longer under the hen and the result, he says, is
disgusting.
He kept his own birthday to himself so that no astrologer could cast his nativity.
The shuttle of a ripening egg combs the warp of his days.

line 3   In 1640 the brothers Boot refuted Aristotle in Dublin.

4   Descartes passed on the easier problems in analytical geometry to his valet Gillot.

5–10   Refer to his contempt for Galileo Jr, (whom he confused with the more musical Galileo Sr), and to his expedient sophistry concerning the movement of the earth.

17   He solved problems submitted by these mathematicians.

21–26   The attempt at swindling on the part of his elder brother Pierre de la Bretaillière – The money he received as a soldier.

27   Franz Hals.

29–30   As a child he played with a little cross-eyed girl.

31–35   His daughter died of scarlet fever at the age of six.

37–40   Honoured Harvey for his discovery of the circulation of the blood, but would not admit that he had explained the motion of the heart.

41   The heart of Henri iv was received at the Jesuit college of La Flèche while Descartes was still a student there.

45–53   His visions and pilgrimage to Loretto.

56–65   His Eucharistic sophistry, in reply to the Jansenist Antoine Arnauld, who challenged him to reconcile his doctrine of matter with the doctrine of transubstantiation.

68   Schurmann, the Dutch blue-stocking, a pious pupil of Voët, the adversary of Descartes.

73–76   Saint Augustine has a revelation in the shrubbery and reads Saint Paul.

77–83   He proves God by exhaustion.

91–93   Christina, queen of Sweden. At Stockholm, in November, she required Descartes, who had remained in bed till midday all his life, to be with her at five o'clock in the morning.

94   Weulles, a Peripatetic Dutch physician at the Swedish court, and an enemy of Descartes.

The Vulture

dragging his hunger through the sky
of my skull shell of sky and earth

stooping to the prone who must
soon take up their life and walk

mocked by a tissue that may not serve
till hunger earth and sky be offal

Malacoda

thrice he came
the undertaker's man
impassible behind his scutal bowler
to measure
is he not paid to measure
this incorruptible in the vestibule
this malebranca knee-deep in the lilies
Malacoda knee-deep in the lilies
Malacoda for all the expert awe
that felts his perineum mutes his signal
sighing up through the heavy air
must it be it must be it must be
find the weeds engage them in the garden
hear she may see she need not

to coffin
with assistant ungulata
find the weeds engage their attention
hear she must see she need not

to cover
to be sure cover cover all over
your targe allow me hold your sulphur
divine dogday glass set fair
stay Scarmilion stay stay
lay this Huysum on the box
mind the imago it is he
hear she must see she must
all aboard all souls
half-mast aye aye

nay

Cascando

1

why not merely the despaired of
occasion of
wordshed

is it not better abort than be barren

the hours after you are gone are so leaden
they will always start dragging too soon
the grapples clawing blindly the bed of want
bringing up the bones the old loves
sockets filled once with eyes like yours
all always is it better too soon than never
the black want splashing their faces
saying again nine days never floated the loved
nor nine months
nor nine lives

2

saying again
if you do not teach me I shall not learn
saying again there is a last
even of last times
last times of begging
last times of loving
of knowing not knowing pretending
a last even of last times of saying
if you do not love me I shall not be loved
if I do not love you I shall not love

the churn of stale words in the heart again
love love love thud of the old plunger
pestling the unalterable
whey of words

terrified again
of not loving
of loving and not you

of being loved and not by you
of knowing not knowing pretending
pretending

I and all the others that will love you
if they love you

3

unless they love you

(1936)

vive morte ma seule saison
lis blancs chrysanthèmes
nids vifs abandonnés
boue des feuilles d'avril
beaux jours gris de givre

my way is in the sand flowing
between the shingle and the dune
the summer rain rains on my life
on me my life harrying fleeing
to its beginning to its end

my peace is there in the receding mist
when I may cease from treading these long shifting thresholds
and live the space of a door
that opens and shuts

what would I do without this world faceless incurious
where to be lasts but an instant where every instant
spills in the void the ignorance of having been
without this wave where in the end
body and shadow together are engulfed
what would I do without this silence where the murmurs die

the pantings the frenzies towards succour towards love
without this sky that soars
above its ballast dust

what would I do what I did yesterday and the day before
peering out of my deadlight looking for another
wandering like me eddying far from all the living
in a convulsive space
among the voices voiceless
that throng my hiddenness

I would like my love to die
and the rain to be raining on the graveyard
and on me walking the streets
mourning her who thought she loved me

(Translations from Guillaume Appolinaire)

Lady Love

She is standing on my lids
And her hair is in my hair
She has the colour of my eye
She has the body of my hand
In my shade she is engulfed
As a stone against the sky

She will never close her eyes
And she does not let me sleep
And her dreams in the bright day
Make the suns evaporate
And me laugh cry and laugh
Speak when I have nothing to say

(Dying of not Dying, 1924)

Scarcely disfigured

Farewell sadness
Greeting sadness
Thou art inscribed in the lines of the ceiling
Thou art inscribed in the eyes that I love
Thou art not altogether want
For the poorest lips denounce thee
Smiling
Greeting sadness
Love of the bodies that are lovable
Mightiness of love that lovable
Starts up as a bodiless beast
Head of hope defeated
Sadness countenance of beauty

(The Immediate Life, 1932)

Endgame

Endgame was Beckett's second published play. The French production of Roger Blin came for a short season to the Royal Court in 1957 and both it and Georges Devine's later English production were badly received by almost all the London critics. Only Harold Hobson in the *Sunday Times* recognised the deep poetic feeling and the humour in this great tragic play. It was only after the famous Paris production of 1964 with Patrick Magee and Jack Macgowran in the roles of Hamm and Clov, a production that with minor changes transferred to the Aldwych in London, that *Endgame* was recognised as the masterpiece it is. Less ambiguous than *Godot*, more claustrophobic and more direct, it has a fascination of its own. The situation is that of a hammer (Hamm) and three nails (Clov is French Clou, Nell is Nail, and Nagg is German Nagel). Hamm is dying in a world that appears to be coming to an end, taking a grim satisfaction in the prospect of all life being extinguished. He is confined to his chair, and throughout the length of the play discards with reluctant resignation the further prospects of food, of painkiller, of retaining his servant Clov on whom he is totally dependent, of using the pole that enables him to move his wheelchair, or holding the toy dog on which he lavishes his affection. His parents Nagg and Nell, having lost their legs many years previously in a bicycle accident, live in dustbins from which they occasionally emerge to be cursed by their son for engendering him. His mother dies, and Hamm, knowing that Clov is leaving him, prepares for his last battle, first to outlive his father and then to face the inevitable without the help of the few objects that have given him comfort in his last days, and to face it with dignity.

Hamm soliloquises grimly in terms of the last moves in chess, a king evading checkmate as long as possible with grim asides on Christian theology: *'Get out of here and love one another! Lick your neighbour as yourself!'* He echoes Pozzo's gravedigger aphorism when he says: *'The end is in the beginning and yet you go on.'*

Clov prepares to leave, hating Hamm for past wrongs and yet pitying him.

HAMM: It's the end, Clov, we've come to the end. I don't need you any more.
Pause.
CLOV: Lucky for you.
He goes towards door.
HAMM: Leave me the gaff.
Clov gives him the gaff, goes towards door, halts, looks at alarm-clock, takes it down, looks round for a better place to put it, goes to bins, puts it on lid of Nagg's bin. Pause.
CLOV: I'll leave you.
He goes towards door.
HAMM: Before you go . . . (*Clov halts near door*) . . . say something.
CLOV: There is nothing to say.
HAMM: A few words . . . to ponder . . . in my heart.
CLOV: Your heart!
HAMM: Yes. (*Pause. Forcibly.*) Yes! (*Pause.*) With the rest, in the end, the shadows, the murmurs, all the trouble, to end up with. (*Pause.*) Clov . . . He never spoke to me. Then, in the end, before he went, without my having asked him, he spoke to me. He said . . .
CLOV: (*despairingly*). Ah . . . !
HAMM: Something . . . from your heart.
CLOV: My heart!
HAMM: A few words . . . from your heart.
Pause.
CLOV: (*fixed gaze, tonelessly, towards auditorium*). They said to me, That's love, yes yes, not a doubt, now you see how—
HAMM: Articulate!
CLOV: (*as before*). How easy it is. They said to me, That's friendship, yes yes, no question, you've found it. They said to me, Here's the place, stop, raise your head and

look at all that beauty. That order! They said to me,
Come now, you're not a brute beast, think upon these
things and you'll see how all becomes clear. And simple!
They said to me, What skilled attention they get, all
these dying of their wounds.

HAMM: Enough!

CLOV: (*as before*). I say to myself – sometimes, Clov, you must
learn to suffer better than that if you want them to
weary of punishing you – one day. I say to myself –
sometimes, Clov, you must be there better than that if
you want them to let you go – one day. But I feel too
old, and too far, to form new habits. Good, it'll never
end, I'll never go. (*Pause.*) Then one day, suddenly, it
ends, it changes, I don't understand, it dies, or it's me,
I don't understand that either. I ask the words that
remain – sleeping, waking, morning, evening. They have
nothing to say. (*Pause.*) I open the door of the cell and
go. I am so bowed I see only my feet, if I open my eyes,
and between my legs a little trail of black dust. I say to
myself that the earth is extinguished, though I never saw
it lit. (*Pause.*) It's easy going. (*Pause.*) When I fall I'll
weep for happiness.
Pause. He goes towards door.

HAMM: Clov! (*Clov halts, without turning.*) Nothing. (*Clov moves
on.*) Clov!
Clov halts, without turning.

CLOV: This is what we call making an exit.

HAMM: I'm obliged to you, Clov. For your services.

CLOV: (*turning, sharply*). Ah pardon, it's I am obliged to you.

HAMM: It's we are obliged to each other. (*Pause, Clov goes
towards door.*) One thing more. (*Clov halts.*) A last
favour. (*Exit Clov.*) Cover me with the sheet. (*Long
pause.*) No? Good. (*Pause.*) Me to play. (*Pause. Wearily.*)
Old endgame lost of old, play and lose and have done
with losing. (*Pause. More animated.*) Let me see.
(*Pause.*) Ah yes! (*He tries to move the chair, using the gaff
as before. Enter Clov, dressed for the road. Panama hat,
tweed coat, raincoat over his arm, umbrella, bag. He halts
by the door, and stands there, impassive and motionless, his
eyes fixed on Hamm, till the end. Hamm gives up.*) Good.

(*Pause.*) Discard. (*He throws away the gaff, makes to throw away the dog, thinks better of it.*) Take it easy. (*Pause.*) And now? (*Pause.*) Raise hat. (*He raises his toque.*) Peace to our . . . arses. (*Pause.*) And put on again. (*He puts on his toque.*) Deuce. (*Pause. He takes off his glasses.*) Wipe. (*He takes out his handkerchief and, without unfolding it, wipes his glasses.*) And put on again. (*He puts on his glasses, puts back the handkerchief in his pocket.*) We're coming. A few more squirms like that and I'll call. (*Pause.*) A little poetry. (*Pause.*) You prayed— (*Pause. He corrects himself.*) You CRIED for night; it comes— (*Pause. He corrects himself.*) It FALLS: now cry in darkness. (*He repeats, chanting.*) You cried for night; it falls; now cry in darkness. (*Pause.*) Nicely put, that. (*Pause.*) And now? (*Pause.*) Moments for nothing, now as always, time was never and time is over, reckoning closed and story ended. (*Pause. Narrative tone.*) If he could have his child with him . . . (*Pause.*) It was the moment I was waiting for. (*Pause.*) You don't want to abandon him? You want him to bloom while you are withering? Be there to solace your last million last moments? (*Pause.*) He doesn't realise, all he knows is hunger, and cold, and death to crown it all. But you! You ought to know what the earth is like, nowadays. Oh, I put him before his responsibilities! (*Pause. Normal tone.*) Well, there we are, there I am, that's enough. (*He raises the whistle to his lips, hesitates, drops it. Pause.*) Yes, truly! (*He whistles. Pause. Louder. Pause.*) Good. (*Pause.*) Father! (*Pause. Louder.*) Father! (*Pause.*) Good. (*Pause.*) We're coming. (*Pause.*) And to end up with? (*Pause.*) Discard. (*He throws away the dog. He tears the whistle from his neck.*) With my compliments. (*He throws whistle towards auditorium. Pause. He sniffs. Soft.*) Clov! (*Long pause.*) No? Good. (*He takes out the handkerchief.*) Since that's the way we're playing it . . . (*he unfolds handkerchief*) . . . let's play it that way . . . (*he unfolds*) . . . and speak no more about it . . . (*he finishes unfolding*) . . . speak no more. (*He holds the handkerchief spread out before him.*) Old stancher! (*Pause.*) You . . . remain.

Pause. He covers his face with handkerchief, lowers his arms to armrests, remains motionless.
Brief tableau.

CURTAIN

The Voice
Reduces

How It Is

Written a decade after *The Unnamable*, *How It Is* came when Beckett's reputation was well established. He was by then one of the most discussed living novelists and playwrights, whose work inspired strong passions for and against. *The Unnamable*, which has no physical setting except inside the mind, was written when Beckett had not yet had the experience of watching his plays on stage or working with theatrical people. Seeing his work in rehearsal as well as inside his head was an encouragement to give a physically described locale once again to a novel. This is an immense area of mud, through which beings are crawling, dragging their possessions, tied in sacks, behind them. Constant effort, a cross between swimming and crawling, is necessary not to be dragged down. The narrator of *How It Is*, himself unnamed, meets others while crawling through the mud; one called Pim is most often mentioned. A long extract from the novel has been given in the introduction (page 32). The narrator, increasingly panic-struck as he feels himself sinking, questions and receives answers from another voice that may be in himself. The following, the closing pages of *How It Is*, is very similar to the end of *The Unnamable*, except that it ends with quotation marks indicating that that's how it *was*, and that after Pim that is how it *is*, so that another voice, not the same one that sank screaming in the mud, is now speaking: the agony has all been a quotation, a story.

my life a voice without quaqua on all sides words scraps then nothing then again more words more scraps the same ill-spoken ill-heard then nothing vast stretch of time then in me in the vault bone-white if there were a light bits and scraps ten seconds fifteen seconds ill-heard ill-murmured ill-heart ill-recorded my whole life a gibberish garbled sixfold

the panting stops I hear it my life I have it murmur it it's preferable more logical for Kram to note and if we are innumerable then Krams innumerable if you like or one alone my Kram mine alone he's enough here where justice reigns one life all life not two lives our justice one Kram not one of us there's reason in me yet his son begets his son leaves the light Kram goes back up into the light to end his days

or no Kram that too when the panting stops an ear above some-where above and unto it the murmur ascending and if we are innumerable then murmurs innumerable all alike our justice one life everywhere ill-told ill-heart quaqua on all sides then within when the panting stops ten seconds fifteen seconds in the little chamber all bone-white if there were a light oakum of old words ill-heard ill-murmured that murmur those murmurs

fallen in the mud from our mouths innumerable and ascending to where there is an ear a mind to understand a means of noting a care for us the wish to note the curiosity to understand an ear to hear even ill these scraps of other scraps of an antique rigmarole

immemorial imperishable like us the ear we're talking of an ear above in the light and in that case for us days of great gaiety in that untiring listening to this unchanging drone the faint sign of a change some day nay even of an end in all honour and justice or for which as for us each time the first and in that case no problem

or of the fragile kind made for the blackbirds when to the day the long night yields at last and to the night a little later the interminable day but us this life how it was how it is how most certainly it will be not made for that a second time next per shaving and in that case no surprise to be expected either

all that among other things so many others ill-spoken ill-heard ill-remembered to the sole end that there may be white on white trace of so many and so many words ill-given ill-received ill-rendered to the mud and whose ear in these conditions the gift of understanding the care for us the means of noting what does it matter

whose his in charge of the sacks the sacks and food these words again the sack as we have seen

the sack as we have seen there being occasions when the sack as we have seen is more than a mere larder for us yes moments when if needs be it may appear more than a mere larder to us

those words of old in their place of old end of part three and last present formulation at the end before the silence the panting without pause the animal in want of air the mouth murmuring them to the mud and the continuation of old when the panting stops ten words fifteen words a murmur to the mud

and later much later these aeons my God when it stops again ten more fifteen more in me a murmur scarce a breath then from mouth to mud brief kiss brush of lips faint kiss

namely string them together last reasonings namely these sacks these sacks one must understand try and understand these sacks innumerable with us here for our journeys innumerable on this narrow track one foot two foot all here in position already like us all here in position at the inconceivable start of this caravan no impossible

impossible that at every journey we should have had to scale a mountain of sacks and should still have and should for ever have each one of us at every journey in order to reach his victim to scale a mountain of sacks our progress as we have seen while admittedly laborious yet the terrain the terrain try and understand no accidents no asperities our justice

last reasonings last figures number 777777 leaves number 777776 on his way unwitting towards number 777778 finds the sack without which he would not go far appropriates it to himself and continues on his way the same to be taken by number 777776 in his turn and after him by number 777775 and so back to the unimaginable number 1 each one no sooner on his way then he finds the sack indispensable to his journey and not to be relinquished till a little before arrival as we have seen

whence if all the sacks in position like us at the beginning that hypothesis such an acervation of sacks on the track nay concentrated in a little room since each finds his as we have seen his sack we are talking of our sacks no sooner his tormentor forsaken as he must if he is ever to reach his victim as we have seen if his victim is ever to be reached

such an acervation of sacks at the very outset that all progress impossible and no sooner imparted to the caravan the unthinkable first impulsion than arrested for ever and frozen in injustice

then from left to right or west to east the atrocious spectacle on into the black night of boundless futurity of the abandoned tormentor never to be victim then a little space then his brief journey done prostrate at the foot of a mountain of provisions the victim never to be tormentor then a great space then another abandoned so on infinitely

for clear as day that similarly obstructed without exception each and every section of track or segment between consecutive couples consecutive abandons according as one considers it the track we're talking of the track its sections or segments before the departures or during the journeys the panting stops and clear as day that similarly obstructed without exception each and every section or segment and for the same reasons our justice

thus need for the billionth time part three and last present formulation at the end before the silence the panting without pause
if we are to be possible our couplings journeys and abandons need
of one not one of us an intelligence somewhere a love who all along
the track at the right places according as we need them deposits
our sacks

ten yards fifteen yards to the east of the couples the abandoned
according as deposited before the departures or during the journeys
those are the right places

and to whom given our number not unreasonable to attribute
exceptional powers or else at his beck assistants innumerable and
to whom in pursuance of the principle of parsimony not excessive
at times ten seconds fifteen seconds to assign the ear which Kram
eliminated our murmur demands otherwise desert flower

and that minimum of intelligence without which it were an ear like
ours and that strange care for us not to be found among us and
the wish and ability to note which we have not

cumulation of offices most understandable if it will be kindly
considered that to hear and note one of our murmurs is to hear
and note them all

and sudden light on the sacks at what moment renewed at some
moment in the life of the couples since it is while the victim
journeys as we have seen and indeed see that the abandoned
tormentor murmurs or else ring the knell while following the
hearse it's possible too there's a poor light

and to whom at times not extravagant to impute that voice quaqua
the voice of us all of which now when the panting stops ten seconds
fifteen seconds definitely the last scraps to have come down to us
and in what a state

there he is then at last that not one of us there we are then at last
who listens to himself and who when he lends his ear to our
murmur does no more than lend it to a story of his own devising
ill-inspired ill-told and so ancient so forgotten at each telling that
ours may seem faithful that we murmur to the mud to him

and this life in the dark and mud its joys and sorrows journeys intimacies and abandons as with a single voice perpetually broken now one half of us and now the other we exhale it pretty much the same as the one he had devised

and of which untiringly every twenty or forty years according to certain of our figures he recalls to our abandoned the essential features

and this anonymous voice self-styled quaqua the voice of us all that was without on all sides then in us when the panting stops bits and scraps barely audible certainly distorted there it is at last the voice of him who before listening to us murmur what we are tells us what we are as best he can

of him to whom we are further indebted for our unfailing rations which enable us to advance without pause or rest

of him who God knows who could blame him must sometimes wonder if to these perpetual revictuallings narrations and auditions he might not put an end without ceasing to maintain us in some kind of being without end and some kind of justice without flaw who could blame him

and if finally he might not with profit revise us by means for example of a pronouncement to the effect that this diversity is not our portion nor these refreshing transitions from solitary travellers to tormentors of our immediate fellows and from abandoned tormentors to their victims

nor all this black air that breathes through our ranks and enshrines as in a thebaïd our couples and our solitudes as well of the journey as of the abandon

but that in reality we are one and all from the unthinkable first to the no less unthinkable last glued together in a vast imbrication of flesh without breach or fissure

for as we have seen part two how it was with Pim the coming into contact of mouth and ear leads to a slight overlapping of flesh in the region of the shoulders and that linked thus bodily together each one of us is at the same time Bom and Pim tormentor and tormented pedant and dunce wooer and wooed speechless and reafflicted with speech in the dark the mud nothing to emend there

there he is then again last figures the inevitable number 777777 at the instant when he buries the opener in the arse of number 777778 and is rewarded by a feeble cry cut short as we have seen by the thump on skull who on being stimulated at the same instant and in the same way by number 777776 makes his own private moan which same fate

something wrong there

and who at the instant when clawed in the armpit by number 777776 he sings applies the same treatment to number 777778 with no less success

so on and similarly all along the chain in both directions for all our other joys and sorrows all we extort and endure from one another from the one to the other inconceivable end of this immeasurable wallow

formulation to be adjusted assuredly in the light of our limits and possibilities but which will always present this advantage that by eliminating all journeys all abandons it eliminates at the same stroke all occasion of sacks and voices quaqua then in us when the panting stops

and the procession which seemed as if it must be eternal our justice the advantage of stopping it without prejudice to a single one among us for try and stop it without first closing our ranks and of two things one

it is stopped at the season of our couples and in that case one half of us tormentors in perpetuity victims in perpetuity the other

it is stopped at the season of our journeys and in that case solitude guaranteed for all assuredly but not in justice since the traveller to whom life owes a victim will never have another and never another tormentor the abandoned to whom life owes one and other iniquities leave them dark pant wilder one is enough last scraps very last when the panting stops try and catch them last murmurs very last

namely first to have done with this not one of us

his dream of putting an end to our journeys abandons need of sustenance and murmurs

to the extenuating purveyances of every description that devolve on him in consequence

without being reduced on that account to whelming us one and all even to the unimaginable last at one stroke in this black mud and nothing on its surface ever more to sully it

in justice and the safeguard of our essential activites

this new formulation namely this new life to have done with that

sudden question if in spite of this conglomeration of all our bodies we are not still the object of a slow translation from west to east one is tempted

if it will kindly be considered that while it is in our interest as tormentors to remain where we are as victims our urge is to move on

and that of these two aspirations warring in each heart it would be normal for the latter to triumph if only narrowly

for as we have seen in the days that word again of journeys and abandons a most remarkable thing when you come to think of it only the victims journeyed

the tormentors as though struck numb with stupor instead of giving chase right leg right arm push pull ten yards fifteen yards lying where abandoned penalty perhaps of their recent exertions but effect also of our justice though in what this diminished by a general free for all one does not see

involving for one and all the same obligation precisely that of fleeing without fear while pursuing without hope

and if it is still possible at this late hour to conceive of other worlds

as just as ours but less exquisitely organized

one perhaps there is one perhaps somewhere merciful enough to shelter such frolics where no one ever abandons anyone and no one ever waits for anyone and never two bodies touch

and if it may seem strange that without food to sustain us we can drag ourselves thus by the mere grace of our united net sufferings from west to east towards an inexistent peace we are invited kindly to consider

that for the likes of us and no matter how we are recounted there is more nourishment in a cry nay a sigh torn from one whose only good is silence or in speech extorted from one at last delivered from its use than sardines can ever offer

to have done then at last with all that last scraps very last when he panting stops and this voice to have done with this voice namely this life

this not one of us harping harping mad too with weariness to have done with him

has he not staring him in the face I quote on a solution more simple by far and by far more radical

a formulation that would eliminate him completely and so admit him to that peace at least while rendering me in the same breath sole responsible for this unqualifiable murmur of which consequently here the last scraps at last very last

in the familiar form of questions I am said to ask myself and answers I am said to give myself however unlikely that may appear last scraps very last when the panting stops last murmurs very last however unlikely that may appear

if all that all that yes if all that is not how shall I say no answer if all that is not false yes

all these calculations yes explanations yes the whole story from beginning to end yes completely false yes

that wasn't how it was no not at all no how then no answer how was it then no answer HOW WAS IT screams good

there was something yes but nothing of all that no all balls from start to finish yes this voice quaqua yes all balls yes only one voice here yes mine yes when the panting stops yes

when the panting stops yes so that was true yes the panting yes the murmur yes in the dark yes in the mud yes to the mud yes

hard to believe too yes that I have a voice yes in me yes when the panting stops yes not at other times no and that I murmur yes I yes in the dark yes in the mud yes for nothing yes I yes but it must be believed yes

and the mud yes the dark yes the mud and the dark are true yes nothing to regret there no

but all this business of voices yes quaqua yes of other worlds yes of someone in another world yes whose kind of dream I am yes said to be yes that he dreams all the time yes tells all the time yes his only dream yes his only story yes

all this business of sacks deposited yes at the end of a cord no doubt yes of an ear listening to me yes a care for me yes an ability to note yes all that all balls yes Krim and Kram yes all balls yes

and all this business of above yes light yes skies yes a little blue yes a little white yes the earth turning yes bright and less bright yes little scenes yes all balls yes the women yes the dog yes the prayers yes the homes yes all balls yes and this business of a procession no answer this business of a procession yes never any procession no nor any journey no never any Pim no nor any Bom no never anyone no only me no answer only me yes so that was true yes it was true about me yes and what's my name no answer WHAT'S MY NAME screams good

only me in any case yes alone yes in the mud yes the dark yes that holds yes the mud and the dark hold yes nothing to regret there no with my sack no I beg your pardon no no sack either no not even a sack with me no

only me yes alone yes with my voice yes my murmur yes when the panting stops yes all that holds yes panting yes worse and worse no answer WORSE AND WORSE yes flat on my belly yes in the mud yes the dark yes nothing to emend there no the arms spread yes like a cross no answer LIKE A CROSS no answer YES OR NO yes

never crawled no in an amble no right leg right arm push pull ten yards fifteen yards no never stirred no never made to suffer no never suffered no answer NEVER SUFFERED no never abandoned no never was abandoned no so that's life here no answer THAT'S MY LIFE HERE screams good

alone in the mud yes the dark yes sure yes panting yes someone hears me no no one hears me no murmuring sometimes yes when the panting stops yes not at other times no in the mud yes to the mud yes my voice yes mine yes not another's no mine alone yes sure yes when the panting stops yes on and off yes a few words yes a few scraps yes that no one hears no but less and less no answer LESS AND LESS yes

so things may change no answer end no answer I may choke no answer sink no answer sully the mud no more no answer the dark no answer trouble the peace no more no answer the silence no answer die no answer DIE screams I MAY DIE screams I SHALL DIE screams good

good good end at last of part three and last that's how it was end of quotation after Pim how it is

Happy Days

Happy Days was written in English and had its first performance in London at the Royal Court Theatre with Brenda Bruce, rather a traditional actress who must have found the author's presence in the theatre during rehearsals extremely daunting, because she never returned to the role. The play has been amply described in the introduction and does not need further explanation. Its force is most evident to women and certainly it has had great impact on most of its interpreters; in France, Madeleine Renaud can almost be said to have devoted most of her later career to it. Certainly men and women view the everyday tragedy of ageing and loss of powers and capabilities in rather different ways. It has been said that women have greater outer resignation to life and men greater inner, but this is by no means true as a general statement. Outer appearances are obviously extremely important to women and Winnie's insistence on maintaining her everyday rituals and outward cheerfulness is very close to everyday life. The beginning of the first act follows, together with stage directions, to the point when Winnie's husband Willie comes from behind the mound and gives her an opportunity to greet him caustically but with affection. Note the very precise stage directions.

Act One

Expanse of scorched grass rising centre to low mound. Gentle slopes down to front and either side of stage. Back an abrupter fall to stage level. Maximum of simplicity and symmetry.

Blazing light.

Very pompier trompe-l'oeil backcloth to represent unbroken plain and sky receding to meet in far distance.

Embedded up to above her waist in exact centre of mound, WINNIE. *About fifty, well-preserved, blonde for preference, plump, arms and shoulders bare, low bodice, big bosom, pearl necklace. She is discovered sleeping, her arms on the ground before her, her head on her arms. Beside her on ground to her left a capacious black bag, shopping variety, and to her right a collapsible collapsed parasol, beak of handle emerging from sheath.*

To her right and rear, lying asleep on ground, hidden by mound, WILLIE.

Long pause. A bell rings piercingly, say ten seconds, stops. She does not move. Pause. Bell more piercingly, say five seconds. She wakes. Bell stops. She raises her head, gazes front. Long pause. She straightens up, lays her hands flat on ground, throws back her head and gazes at zenith. Long pause.

WINNIE: (*gazing at zenith*). Another heavenly day. (*Pause. Head back level, eyes front, pause. She clasps hands to breast, closes eyes. Lips move in inaudible prayer, say ten seconds. Lips still. Hands remain clasped. Low.*) For Jesus Christ sake Amen. (*Eyes open, hands unclasp, return to mound. Pause. She clasps hands to breast again, closes eyes, lips move again in inaudible addendum, say five seconds. Low.*) World without end Amen. (*Eyes open, hands unclasp, return to mound. Pause.*) Begin, Winnie. (*Pause.*) Begin your day, Winnie. (*Pause. She turns to*

*bag, rummages in it without moving it from its place,
brings out toothbrush, rummages again, brings out flat tube
of toothpaste, turns back front, unscrews cap of tube, lays
cap on ground, squeezes with difficulty small blob of paste
on brush, holds tube in one hand and brushes teeth with
other. She turns modestly aside and back to her right to spit
out behind mound. In this position her eyes rest on* WILLIE.
*She spits out. She cranes a little farther back and down.
Loud.)* Hoo-oo! *(Pause. Louder.)* Hoo-oo! *(Pause.
Tender smile as she turns back front, lays down brush.)*
Poor Willie – *(examines tube, smile off)* – running out –
(looks for cap) – ah well – *(finds cap)* – can't be helped –
(screws on cap) – just one of those old things – *(lays
down tube)* – another of those old things – *(turns
towards bag)* – just can't be cured – *(rummages in bag)* –
cannot be cured – *(brings out small mirror, turns back
front)* – ah yes – *(inspects teeth in mirror)* – poor dear
Willie – *(testing upper front teeth with thumb, indistinctly)*
– good Lord! – *(pulling back upper lip to inspect gums,
do.)* – good God! – *(pulling back corner of mouth, mouth
open, do.)* – ah well – *(other corner, do.)* – no worse –
(abandons inspection, normal speech) – no better, no
worse – *(lays down mirror)* – no change – *(wipes fingers
on grass)* – no pain – *(looks for toothbrush)* – hardly any
– *(takes up toothbrush)* – great thing that – *(examines
handle of brush)* – nothing like it – *(examines handle,
reads)* – pure . . . what? – *(pause)* – what? – *(lays down
brush)* – ah yes – *(turns towards bag)* – poor Willie –
(rummages in bag) – no zest – *(rummages)* – for anything
– *(brings out spectacles in case)* – no interest – *(turns back
front)* – in life – *(takes spectacles from case)* – poor dear
Willie – *(lays down case)* – sleep for ever – *(opens
spectacles)* – marvellous gift – *(puts on spectacles)* –
nothing to touch it – *(looks for toothbrush)* – in my
opinion – *(takes up toothbrush)* – always said so –
(examines handle of brush) – wish I had it – *(examines
handle, reads)* – genuine . . . pure . . . what? – *(lays
down brush)* – blind next – *(takes off spectacles)* – ah
well – *(lays down spectacles)* – seen enough – *(feels in
bodice for handkerchief)* – I suppose – *(takes out folded
handkerchief)* – by now – *(shakes out handkerchief)* –

what are those wonderful lines – (*wipes one eye*) – woe woe is me – (*wipes the other*) – to see what I see – (*looks for spectacles*) – ah yes – (*takes up spectacles*) – wouldn't miss it – (*starts polishing spectacles, breathing on lenses*) – or would I? – (*polishes*) – holy light – (*polishes*) – bob up out of dark – (*polishes*) – blaze of hellish light. (*Stops polishing, raises face to sky, pause, head back level, resumes polishing, stops polishing, cranes back to her right and down.*) Hoo-oo! (*Pause. Tender smile as she turns back front and resumes polishing. Smile off.*) Marvellous gift – (*stops polishing, lays down spectacles*) – wish I had it – (*folds handkerchief*) – ah well – (*puts handkerchief back in bodice*) – can't complain – (*looks for spectacles*) – no no – (*takes up spectacles*) – mustn't complain – (*holds up spectacles, looks through lens*) – so much to be thankful for – (*looks through other lens*) – no pain – (*puts on spectacles*) – hardly any – (*looks for toothbrush*) – wonderful thing that – (*takes up toothbrush*) – nothing like it – (*examines handle of brush*) – slight headache sometimes – (*examines handle, reads*) – guaranteed . . . genuine . . . pure . . . what? – (*looks closer*) – genuine pure . . . – (*takes handkerchief from bodice*) – ah yes – (*shakes out handkerchief*) – occasional mild migraine – (*starts wiping handle of brush*) – it comes – (*wipes*) – then goes – (*wiping mechanically*) – ah yes – (*wiping*) – many mercies – (*wiping*) – great mercies – (*stops wiping, fixed lost gaze, brokenly*) – prayers perhaps not for naught – (*pause, do.*) – first thing – (*pause, do.*) – last thing – (*head down, resumes wiping, stops wiping, head up, calmed, wipes eyes, folds handkerchief, puts it back in bodice, examines handle of brush, reads*) – fully guaranteed . . . genuine pure . . . – (*looks closer*) – genuine pure . . . – (*Takes off spectacles, lays them and brush down, gazes before her.*) Old things. (*Pause.*) Old eyes. (*Long pause.*) On, Winnie. (*She casts about her, sees parasol, considers it at length, takes it up and develops from sheath a handle of surprising length. Holding butt of parasol in right hand she cranes back and down to her right to hang over* WILLIE.) Hoo-oo! (*Pause.*) Willie! (*Pause.*) Wonderful gift. (*She strikes down at him with beak of parasol.*) Wish I had it. (*She strikes again. The*

parasol slips from her grasp and falls behind mound. It is
immediately restored to her by WILLIE'S *invisible hand.*)
Thank you, dear. (*She transfers parasol to left hand,*
turns back front and examines right palm.) Damp.
(*Returns parasol to right hand, examines left palm.*) Ah
well, no worse. (*Head up, cheerfully.*) No better, no
worse, no change. (*Pause. Do.*) No pain. (*Cranes back*
to look down at WILLIE, *holding parasol by butt as*
before.) Don't go off on me again now dear will you
please, I may need you. (*Pause.*) No hurry, no hurry,
just don't curl up on me again. (*Turns back front, lays*
down parasol, examines palms together, wipes them on
grass.) Perhaps a shade off colour just the same. (*Turns*
to bag, rummages in it, brings out revolver, holds it up,
kisses it rapidly, puts it back, rummages, brings out almost
empty bottle of red medicine, turns back front, looks for
spectacles, puts them on, reads label.) Loss of spirits . . .
lack of keenness . . . want of appetite . . . infants . . .
children . . . adults . . . six level . . . tablespoonfuls
daily – (*head up, smile*) – the old style! – (*smile off, head*
down, reads) – daily . . . before and after . . . meals
. . . instantaneous . . . (*looks closer*) . . . improvement.
(*Takes off spectacles, lays them down, holds up bottle at*
arm's length to see level, unscrews cap, swigs it off head
well back, tosses cap and bottle away in WILLIE'S
direction. Sound of breaking glass.) Ah that's better!
(*Turns to bag, rummages in it, brings out lipstick, turns*
back front, examines lipstick.) Running out. (*Looks for*
spectacles.) Ah well. (*Puts on spectacles, looks for mirror.*)
Mustn't complain. (*Takes up mirror, starts doing lips.*)
What is that wonderful line? (*Lips.*) Oh fleeting joys –
(*lips*) – oh something lasting woe. (*Lips. She is*
interrupted by disturbance from WILLIE. *He is sitting up.*
She lowers lipstick and mirror and cranes back and down
to look at him. Pause. Top back of WILLIE'S *bald head,*
trickling blood, rises to view above slope, comes to rest.
WINNIE *pushes up her spectacles. Pause. His hand appears*
with handkerchief, spreads it on skull, disappears. Pause.
The hand appears with boater, club ribbon, settles it on
head, rakish angle, disappears. Pause. WINNIE *cranes a*

little further back and down.) Slip on your drawers, dear, before you get singed. (*Pause.*) No? (*Pause.*) Oh I see, you still have some of that stuff left. (*Pause.*) Work it well in, dear. (*Pause.*) Now the other. (*Pause. She turns back front, gazes before her. Happy expression.*) Oh this is going to be another happy day! (*Pause. Happy expression off. She pulls down spectacles and resumes lips.* WILLIE *opens newspaper, hands invisible. Tops of yellow sheets appear on either side of his head.* WINNIE *finishes lips, inspects them in mirror held a little further away.*) Ensign crimson. (WILLIE *turns page.* WINNIE *lays down lipstick and mirror, turns towards bag.*) Pale flag.

WILLIE *turns page.* WINNIE *rummages in bag, brings out small ornate brimless hat with crumpled feather, turns back front, straightens hat, smooths feather, raises it towards head, arrests gesture as* WILLIE *reads.*

WILLIE: His Grace and Most Reverend Father in God Dr Carolus Hunter dead in tub.
Pause.

WINNIE: (*gazing front, hat in hand, tone of fervent reminiscence*). Charlie Hunter! (*Pause.*) I close my eyes – (*she takes off spectacles and does so, hat in one hand, spectacles in other,* WILLIE *turns page*) – and am sitting on his knees again, in the back garden at Borough Green, under the horse-beech. (*Pause. She opens eyes, puts on spectacles, fiddles with hat.*) Oh the happy memories!
Pause. She raises hat towards head, arrests gesture as WILLIE *reads.*

WILLIE: Opening for smart youth.
Pause. She raises hat towards head, arrests gesture, takes off spectacles, gazes front, hat in one hand, spectacles in other.

WINNIE: My first ball! (*Long pause.*) My second ball! (*Long pause. Closes eyes.*) My first kiss! (*Pause.* WILLIE *turns page.* WINNIE *opens eyes.*) A Mr Johnson, or Johnston, or perhaps I should say John*stone*. Very bushy moustache, very tawny. (*Reverently.*) Almost ginger! (*Pause.*) Within a toolshed, though whose I cannot conceive. We had no toolshed and he most certainly had no toolshed. (*Closes eyes.*) I see the piles of pots. (*Pause.*) The tangles of bast. (*Pause.*) The shadows deepening among the rafters.

Pause. She opens eyes, puts on spectacles, raises hat towards head, arrests gesture as WILLIE *reads.*

WILLIE: Wanted bright boy.

Pause. WINNIE *puts on hat hurriedly, looks for mirror.* WILLIE *turns page.* WINNIE *takes up mirror, inspects hat, lays down mirror, turns towards bag. Paper disappears.* WINNIE *rummages in bag, brings out magnifying-glass, turns back front, looks for toothbrush. Paper reappears, folded, and begins to fan* WILLIE'S *face, hand invisible.* WINNIE *takes up toothbrush and examines handle through glass.*

WINNIE: Fully guaranteed . . . (WILLIE *stops fanning*) . . . genuine pure . . . (*Pause.* WILLIE *resumes fanning.* WINNIE *looks closer, reads.*) Fully guaranteed . . . (WILLIE *stops fanning*) . . . genuine pure . . . (*Pause.* WILLIE *resumes fanning.* WINNIE *lays down glass and brush, takes handkerchief from bodice, takes off and polishes spectacles, puts on spectacles, looks for glass, takes up and polishes glass, lays down glass, looks for brush, takes up brush and wipes handle, lays down brush, puts handkerchief back in bodice, looks for glass, takes up glass, looks for brush, takes up brush and examines handle through glass.*) Fully guaranteed . . . (WILLIE *stops fanning*) . . . genuine pure . . . (*pause,* WILLIE *resumes fanning*) . . . hog's . . . (WILLIE *stops fanning, pause*) . . . setae. (*Pause.* WINNIE *lays down glass and brush, paper disappears,* WINNIE *takes off spectacles, lays them down, gazes front.*) Hog's setae. (*Pause.*) That is what I find so wonderful, that not a day goes by – (*smile*) – to speak in the old style – (*smile off*) – hardly a day, without some addition to one's knowledge however trifling, the addition I mean, provided one takes the pains. (WILLIE'S *hand reappears with a postcard which he examines close to eyes.*) And if for some strange reason no further pains are possible, why then just close the eyes – (*she does so*) – and wait for the day to come – (*opens eyes*) – the happy day to come when flesh melts at so many degrees and the night of the moon has so many hundred hours. (*Pause.*) That is what I find so comforting when I lose heart and envy the brute beast. (*Turning towards* WILLIE.) I hope you are taking in – (*She sees postcard, bends lower.*) What is that you have there, Willie, may I see? (*She reaches down with hand and* WILLIE *hands her card. The hairy forearm appears above slope, raised in gesture of giving, the hand open to take back, and remains in this position till card is returned.* WINNIE *turns back front and examines card.*) Heavens what are they up to! (*She looks for spectacles, puts them on and examines card.*) No but this is just genuine pure filth! (*Examines card.*) Make any nice-minded person want to vomit! (*Impatience of* WILLIE'S *fingers. She looks for glass, takes it up and examines card through glass. Long pause.*) What does that creature in the background think he's doing? (*Looks closer.*) Oh no really! (*Impatience of fingers. Last long look. She lays down glass, takes edge of card between right forefinger and thumb, averts head, takes nose between left forefinger and thumb.*) Pah! (*Drops card.*) Take it away! (WILLIE'S *arm disappears. His hand reappears immediately, holding card.* WINNIE *takes off spectacles, lays them down, gazes before her. During what follows* WILLIE *continues to relish card, varying angles and distance from his eyes.*) Hog's setae. (*Puzzled expression.*) What exactly is a hog? (*Pause. Do.*) A sow of course I know, but a hog . . . (*Puzzled expression off.*) Oh well what does it matter, that is what I always say, it will come back, that is what I find so wonderful, all comes back. (*Pause.*) All? (*Pause.*) No, not all. (*Smile.*) No no. (*Smile off.*) Not quite. (*Pause.*) A part. (*Pause.*) Floats up, one fine day, out of the blue. (*Pause.*) That is what I find so wonderful. (*Pause. She turns towards bag. Hand and card disappear. She makes to rummage in bag, arrests gesture.*) No. (*She turns back front. Smile.*) No no. (*Smile off.*) Gently Winnie. (*She gazes front.* WILLIE'S *hand reappears, takes off hat, disappears with hat.*) What then? (*Hand reappears, takes handkerchief from skull, disappears with handkerchief. Sharply, as to one not paying attention.*) Winnie! (WILLIE *bows head out of sight.*) What is the alternative? (*Pause.*) What is the al— (WILLIE *blows*

*nose loud and long, head and hands invisible. She turns to
look at him. Pause. Head reappears. Pause. Hand
reappears with handkerchief, spreads it on skull,
disappears. Pause. Hand reappears with boater, settles it
on head, rakish angle, disappears. Pause.*) Would I had
let you sleep on. (*She turns back front. Intermittent
plucking at grass, head up and down, to animate
following.*) Ah yes, if only I could bear to be alone, I
mean prattle away with not a soul to hear. (*Pause.*) Not
that I flatter myself you hear much, no Willie, God
forbid. (*Pause.*) Days perhaps when you hear nothing.
(*Pause.*) But days too when you answer. (*Pause.*) So
that I may say at all times, even when you do not
answer and perhaps hear nothing, something of this is
being heard, I am not merely talking to myself, that is
in the wilderness, a thing I could never bear to do –
for any length of time. (*Pause.*) That is what enables
me to go on, go on talking that is. (*Pause.*) Whereas if
you were to die – (*smile*) – to speak in the old style –
(*smile off*) – or go away and leave me, then what would
I do, what *could* I do, all day long, I mean between the
bell for waking and the bell for sleep? (*Pause.*) Simply
gaze before me with compressed lips. (*Long pause while
she does so. No more plucking.*) Not another word as
long as I drew breath, nothing to break the silence of
this place. (*Pause.*) Save possibly, now and then, every
now and then, a sigh into my looking-glass. (*Pause.*)
Or a brief . . . gale of laughter, should I happen to see
the old joke again. (*Pause. Smile appears, broadens and
seems about to culminate in laugh when suddenly replaced
by expression of anxiety.*) My hair! (*Pause.*) Did I brush
and comb my hair? (*Pause.*) I may have done. (*Pause.*)
Normally I do. (*Pause.*) There is so little one *can* do.
(*Pause.*) One does it all. (*Pause.*) All one can. (*Pause.*)
'Tis only human. (*Pause.*) Human nature. (*She begins
to inspect mound, looks up.*) Human weakness. (*She
resumes inspection of mound, looks up.*) Natural
weakness. (*She resumes inspection of mound.*) I see no
comb. (*Inspects.*) Nor any hairbrush. (*Looks up.
Puzzled expression. She turns to bag, rummages in it.*)
The comb is here. (*Back front. Puzzled expression. Back

to bag. *Rummages*.) The brush is here. (*Back front.
Puzzled expression*.) Perhaps I put them back, after use.
(*Pause. Do*.) But normally I do not put things back,
after use, no, I leave them lying about and put them
back all together, at the end of the day. (*Smile*.) To
speak in the old style. (*Pause*.) The sweet old style.
(*Smile off*.) And yet . . . I seem . . . to remember . . .
(*Suddenly careless*.) Oh well, what does it matter, that is
what I always say, I shall simply brush and comb them
later on, purely and simply, I have the whole – (*Pause.
Puzzled*.) Them? (*Pause*.) Or it? (*Pause*.) Brush and
comb it? (*Pause*.) Sounds improper somehow. (*Pause.
Turning a little towards* WILLIE.) What would you say,
Willie? (*Pause. Turning a little further*.) What would
you say, Willie, speaking of your hair, them or it?
(*Pause*.) The hair on your head, I mean. (*Pause.
Turning a little further*.) The hair on your head, Willie,
what would you say speaking of the hair on your head,
them or it?
Long pause.

WILLIE: It.
WINNIE: (*turning back front, joyful*). Oh you arc going to talk to
me today, this is going to be a happy day! (*Pause. Joy
off*.) Another happy day.

Come and Go

Nobody except the author, who has been silent on the subject, knows the full meaning of the title of *Come and Go*; there is certainly more to it than a description of three women, sitting on a log, each of whom knows some terrible secret about one of the others until by permutations of leaving the stage, one by one, enabling the terrible information to be exchanged between the other two, we end up with the same stage picture of the three women on the log in reverse order, each knowing the worst about the other two but not about herself. The author has found a combination of crossed hands whereby one of the three, Flo, can hold the two gloved left hands of the other two before her last line, 'I can feel the rings': a reference to the vanished dreams of marital happiness that will never happen, because the stage direction state that there are no rings; the audience knows all are doomed.

CHARACTERS

Flo
Vi
Ru
(Ages undeterminable)

> *Sitting centre side by side stage right to left Flo, Vi and Ru.*
> *Very erect, facing front, hands clasped in laps.*
> *Silence.*

VI: When did we three last meet?

RU: Let us not speak.
> *Silence.*
> *Exit Vi right.*
> *Silence.*

FLO: Ru.

RU: Yes.

FLO: What do you think of Vi?

RU: I see little change. (*Flo moves to centre seat, whispers in Ru's ear. Appalled.*) Oh! (*They look at each other. Flo puts her finger to her lips.*) Does she not realise?

FLO: God grant not.
> *Enter Vi. Flo and Ru turn back front, resume pose. Vi sits right.*
> *Silence.*

FLO: Just sit together as we used to, in the playground at Miss Wade's.

RU: On the log.
> *Silence.*
> *Exit Flo left.*
> *Silence.*

RU: Vi.

VI: Yes.

RU: How do you find Flo?

VI: She seems much the same. (*Ru moves to centre seat, whispers in Vi's ear. Appalled.*) Oh! (*They look at each other. Ru puts her finger to her lips.*) Has she not been told?

RU: God forbid.
Enter Flo. Ru and Vi turn back front, resume pose. Flo sits left.
Silence.

RU: Holding hands . . . that way.

FLO: Dreaming of . . . love.
Silence.
Exit Ru right.
Silence.

VI: Flo.

FLO: Yes.

VI: How do you think Ru is looking?

FLO: One sees little in this light. (*Vi moves to centre seat, whispers in Flo's ear. Appalled.*) Oh! (*They look at each other. Vi puts her finger to her lips.*) Does she not know?

VI: Please God not.
Enter Ru. Vi and Flo turn back front, resume pose. Ru sits right.
Silence.

VI: May we not speak of the old days? (*Silence.*) Of what came after? (*Silence.*) Shall we hold hands in the old way?
After a moment they join hands as follows: Vi's right hand with Ru's right hand, Vi's left hand with Flo's left hand, Flo's right hand with Ru's left hand, Vi's arms being above Ru's left arm and Flo's right arm. The three pairs of clasped hands rest on the three laps.
Silence.

FLO: I can feel the rings.
Silence.

CURTAIN

NOTES

Successive positions

I	FLO	VI	RU
2	{ FLO		RU
	{	FLO	RU
3	VI	FLO	RU
4	{ VI		RU
	{ VI	RU	
5	VI	RU	FLO
6	{ VI		FLO
	{	VI	FLO
7	RU	VI	FLO

Hands

RU	VI	FLO

Lighting
Soft, from above only and concentrated on playing area. Rest of stage as dark as possible.

Costume
Full-length coats, buttoned high, dull violet (Ru), dull red (Vi), dull yellow (Flo). Drab nondescript hats with enough brim to shade faces. Apart from colour differentiation three figures as alike as possible. Light shoes with rubber soles. Hands made up to be as visible as possible. No rings apparent.

Seat
Narrow benchlike seat, without back, just long enough to accommodate three figures almost touching. As little visible as possible. It should not be clear what they are sitting on.

Exits
The figures are not seen to go off stage. They should disappear a few steps from lit area. If dark not sufficient to allow this, recourse should be had to screens or drapes as little visible as possible. Exits and entrances slow, without sound of feet.

Ohs
Three very different sounds.

Voices
As low as compatible with audibility. Colourless except for three 'ohs' and two lines following.

(*No performance of this play may be given without a licence from John Calder (Publishers) Ltd, 18 Brewer Street, London W1R 4AS.*)

Imagination Dead Imagine

This is perhaps the first important work of Beckett's minimalist phase, the first in a series of residua which the author edited down from longer texts, or extracted from work in progress that he felt unable to continue. *Imagination* was the last item in the earlier Beckett reader; at the time it seemed that the author was running out of subject-matter, but inventing a new language to describe imagination itself. But his new departure has proved a rich vein, fusing word and image into a new form of prose poetry. This short but pungent text describes two bodies that 'lie still in the stress of that storm, or of a worse storm, or in the black dark for good, or the great whiteness unchanging'. Such images have led to a re-evaluation of Beckett, not only as a writer, but as a conceptual painter who paints in words.

No trace anywhere of life, you say, pah, no difficulty there, imagination not dead yet, yes, dead, good, imagination dead imagine. Islands, waters, azure, verdure, one glimpse and vanished, endlessly, omit. Till all white in the whiteness the rotunda. No way in, go in, measure. Diameter three feet, three feet from ground to summit of the vault. Two diameters at right angles AB CD divide the white ground into two semicircles ACB BDA. Lying on the ground two white bodies, each in its semicircle. White too the vault and the round wall eighteen inches high from which it springs. Go back out, a plain rotunda, all white in the whiteness, go back in, rap, solid throughout, a ring as in the imagination the ring of bone. The light that makes all so white no visible source, all shines with the same white shine, ground, wall, vault, bodies, no shadow. Strong heat, surfaces hot but not burning to the touch, bodies sweating. Go back out, move back, the little fabric vanishes, ascend, it vanishes, all white in the whiteness, descend, go back in. Emptiness, silence, heat, whiteness, wait, the light goes down, all grows dark together, ground, wall, vault, bodies, say twenty seconds, all the greys, the light goes out, all vanishes. At the same time the temperature goes down, to reach its minimum, say freezing-point, at the same instant that the black is reached, which may seem strange. Wait, more or less long, light and heat come back, all grows white and hot together, ground, wall, vault, bodies, say twenty seconds, all the greys, till the initial level is reached whence the fall began. More or less long, for there may intervene, experience shows, between end of fall and beginning of rise, pauses of varying length, from the fraction of the second to what would have seemed, in other times, other places, an eternity. Same remark for the other pause, between end of rise and beginning of fall. The extremes, as long as they last, are perfectly stable, which in the case of the temperature may seem strange, in the beginning. It is possible too, experience shows, for rise and fall to stop short at any point and mark a pause, more or less long, before resuming, or reversing, the rise now fall, the fall rise, these in their turn to be completed, or to stop short and mark a pause, more or less long, before resuming, or again reversing, and so on, till finally one or the other extreme is reached. Such variations of rise and fall, combining in countless rhythms, commonly attend the passage from white and heat to black and cold, and vice versa. The extremes alone are stable as is stressed by the vibration to be observed when a pause occurs at some intermediate stage, no matter what its level and duration. Then all vibrates, ground, wall, vault, bodies, ashen or leaden or between the two, as may be. But on the whole, experience shows, such uncertain passage is not common. And most often, when the light begins to fail, and along with it the heat, the movement continues unbroken until, in the space of some twenty seconds, pitch black is reached and at the same instant say freezing-point. Same remark for the reverse movement, towards heat and whiteness. Next most frequent is the fall or rise with pauses of varying length in these feverish greys, without at any moment reversal of the movement. But whatever its uncertainties the return sooner or later to a temporary calm seems assured, for the moment, in the black dark or the great whiteness, with attendant temperature, world still proof against enduring tumult. Rediscovered miraculously after what absence in perfect voids it is no longer quite the same, from this point of view, but there is no other. Externally all is as before and the sighting of the little fabric quite as much a matter of chance, its whiteness merging in the surrounding whiteness. But go in and now briefer lulls and never twice the same storm. Light and heat remain linked as though supplied by the same source of which still no trace. Still on the ground, bent in three, the head against the wall at B, the arse against the wall at A, the knees against the wall between B and C, the feet against the wall between C and A, that is to say inscribed in the semicircle ACB, merging in the white ground were it not for the long hair of strangely imperfect whiteness, the white body of a woman finally. Similarly inscribed in the other semicircle, against the wall his head at A, his arse at B, his knees between A and D, his feet between D and B, the partner. On their right sides therefore both and back to back head to arse. Hold a mirror to their lips, it mists. With their left hands they hold their left legs a little below the knee, with their right hands their left arms a little above the elbow. In this agitated light, its great white calm now so rare and brief, inspection is not easy. Sweat and mirror notwithstanding they might well pass for inanimate but for the left eyes which at incalculable intervals suddenly open wide and gaze in unblinking exposure long beyond what is humanly possible. Piercing pale blue the effect is striking, in the beginning. Never the two gazes together except once, when the beginning of one overlapped the end of the other, for about ten seconds. Neither fat nor thin, big nor small, the bodies seem whole and in fairly good condition, to judge by the surfaces exposed to view. The faces too, assuming the two sides of a piece, seem to want nothing essential. Between their absolute stillness and the convulsive light the contrast is striking, in the beginning, for one who still remembers having been struck by the contrary. It is clear however, from a thousand little signs too long to imagine, that they are not sleeping. Only murmur ah, no more, in this silence, and at the same instant for the eye of prey the infinitesimal shudder instantaneously suppressed. Leave them there, sweating and icy, there is better elsewhere. No, life ends and no, there is nothing elsewhere, and no question now of ever finding again that white speck lost in whiteness, to see if they still lie still in the stress of that storm, or of a worse storm, or in the black dark for good, or the great whiteness unchanging, and if not what they are doing.

Lessness

In its brevity, its pictorial impact, the way the layers of meaning unfold within each other, and perhaps most of all in the way the author ends his short texts with lyrical paragraphs containing images of almost unearthly beauty, *Lessness* occupies a unique position in the late writing. It is a novel in miniature and was separately published as such. It has a special relevance to our atomic age: the author may have had a nuclear explosion in mind as one possible cause of the calamity that overtook the little band of survivors who 'will curse God again as in the blessed days faced with the open sky'.

Ruins true refuge long last towards which so many false time out of mind. All sides endlessness earth sky as one no sound no stir. Grey face two pale blue little body heart beating only upright. Blacked out fallen open four walls over backwards true refuge issueless.

Scattered ruins same grey as the sand ash grey true refuge. Four square all light sheer white blank planes all gone from mind. Never was but grey air timeless no sound figment the passing light. No sound no stir ash grey sky mirrored earth mirrored sky. Never but this changelessness dream the passing hour.

He will curse God again as in the blessed days face to the open sky the passing deluge. Little body grey face features crack and little holes two pale blue. Blank planes sheer white eye calm long last all gone from mind.

Figment light never was but grey air timeless no sound. Blank planes touch close sheer white all gone from mind. Little body ash grey locked rigid heart beating face to endlessness. On him will rain again as in the blessed days of blue the passing cloud. Four square true refuge long last four walls over backwards no sound.

Grey sky no cloud no sound no stir earth ash grey sand. Little body same grey as the earth sky ruins only upright. Ash grey all sides earth sky as one all sides endlessness.

He will stir in the sand there will be stir in the sky the air the sand. Never but in dream the happy dream only one time to serve. Little body little block heart beating ash grey only upright. Earth sky as one all sides endlessness little body only upright. In the sand no hold one step more in the endlessness he will make it. No sound not a breath same grey all sides earth sky body ruins.

Slow black with ruin true refuge four walls over backwards no sound. Legs a single block arms fast to sides little body face to endlessness. Never but in vanished dream the passing hour long short. Only upright little body grey smooth no relief a few holes. One step in the ruins in the sand on his back in the endlessness he will make it. Never but dream the days and nights made of dreams of other nights better days. He will live again the space of a step it will be day and night again over him the endlessness.

In four split asunder over backwards true refuge issueless scattered ruins. Little body little block genitals overrun arse a single block grey crack overrun. True refuge long last issueless scattered down four walls over backwards no sound. All sides endlessness earth sky as one no stir not a breath. Blank planes sheer white calm eye light of reason all gone from mind. Scattered ruins ash grey all sides true refuge long last issueless.

Ash grey little body only upright heart beating face to endlessness. Old love new love as in the blessed days unhappiness will reign again. Earth sand same grey as the air sky ruins body fine ash grey sand. Light refuge sheer white blank planes all gone from mind. Flatness endless little body only upright same grey all sides earth sky body ruins. Face to white calm touch close eye calm long last all gone from mind. One step more one alone all alone in the sand no hold he will make it.

Blacked out fallen open true refuge issueless towards which so many false time out of mind. Never but silence such that in imagination this wild laughter these cries. Head through calm eye all light white calm all gone from mind. Figment dawn dispeller of figments and the other called dusk.

He will go on his back face to the sky open again over him the ruins the sand the endlessness. Grey air timeless earth sky as one same grey as the ruins flatness endless. It will be day and night again over him the endlessness the air heart will beat again. True refuge long last scattered ruins same grey as the sand.

Face to calm eye touch close all calm all white all gone from mind. Never but imagined the blue in a wild imagining the blue celeste of poesy. Little void mighty light four square all white blank planes all gone from mind. Never was but grey air timeless no stir not a breath. Heart beating little body only upright grey face features overrun two pale blue. Light white touch close head through calm eye light of reason all gone from mind.

Little body same grey as the earth sky ruins only upright. No sound not a breath same grey all sides earth sky body ruins. Blacked out fallen open four walls over backwards true refuge issueless.

No sound no stir ash grey sky mirrored earth mirrored sky. Grey air timeless earth sky as one same grey as the ruins flatness endless. In the sand no hold one step more in the endlessness he will make it. It will be day and night again over him the endlessness the air heart will beat again.

Figment light never was but grey air timeless no sound. All sides endlessness earth sky as one no stir not a breath. On him will rain again as in the blessed days of blue the passing cloud. Grey sky no cloud no sound no stir earth ash grey sand.

Little void mighty light four square all white blank planes all gone from mind. Flatness endless little body only upright same grey all sides earth sky body ruins. Scattered ruins same grey as the sand ash grey true refuge. Four square true refuge long last four walls over backwards no sound. Never but this changelessness dream the passing hour. Never was but grey air timeless no sound figment the passing light.

In four split asunder over backwards true refuge issueless scattered ruins. He will live again the space of a step it will be day and night again over him the endlessness. Face to white calm touch close eye calm long last all gone from mind. Grey face two pale blue little body heart beating only upright. He will go on his back face to the sky open again over him the ruins the sand the endlessness. Earth sand same grey as the air sky ruins body fine ash grey sand. Blank planes touch close sheer white all gone from mind.

Heart beating little body only upright grey face features overrun two pale blue. Only upright little body grey smooth no relief a few holes. Never but dream the days and nights made of dreams of other nights better days. He will stir in the sand there will be stir in the sky the air the sand. One step in the ruins in the sand on his back in the endlessness he will make it. Never but silence such that in imagination this wild laughter these cries.

True refuge long last scattered ruins same grey as the sand. Never was but grey air timeless no stir not a breath. Blank planes sheer white calm eye light of reason all gone from mind. Never but in vanished dream the passing hour long short. Four square all light sheer white blanks planes all gone from mind.

Blacked out fallen open true refuge issueless towards which so many false time out of mind. Head through calm eye all light white calm all gone from mind. Old love new love as in the blessed days unhappiness will reign again. Ash grey all sides earth sky as one all sides endlessness. Scattered ruins ash grey all sides true refuge long last issueless. Never but in dream the happy dream only one time to serve. Little body grey face features crack and little holes two pale blue.

Ruins true refuge long last towards which so many false time out of mind. Never but imagined the blue in a wild imagining the blue celeste of poesy. Light white touch close head through calm eye light of reason all gone from mind.

Slow black with ruin true refuge four walls over backwards no sound. Earth sky as one all sides endlessness little body only upright. One step more one alone all alone in the sand no hold he will make it. Ash grey little body only upright heart beating face to endlessness. Light refuge sheer white blank planes all gone from mind. All sides endlessness earth sky as one no sound no stir.

Legs a single block arms fast to sides little body face to endlessness. True refuge long last issueless scattered down four walls over backwards no sound. Blank planes sheer white eye calm long last all gone from mind. He will curse God again as in the blessed days face to the open sky the passing deluge. Face to calm eye touch close all calm all white all gone from mind.

Little body little block heart beating ash grey only upright. Little body ash grey locked rigid heart beating face to endlessness. Little body little block genitals overrun arse a single block grey crack overrun. Figment dawn dispeller of figments and the other called dusk.

Still

This short description of a presence sitting at a window as the sun sets is a beautiful evocation of stillness. It has the exact description of body movements that one associates with those French writers like Alain Robbe-Grillet who taught us how to read significance into even the flattest descriptions. *Ill Seen Ill Said* may be a later and more menacing variation of the window-watching described here.

Bright at last close of a dark day the sun shines out at last and goes down. Sitting quite still at valley window normally turn head now and see it the sun low in the southwest sinking. Even get up certain moods and go stand by western window quite still watching it sink and then the afterglow. Always quite still some reason some time past this hour at open window facing south in small upright wicker chair with armrests. Eyes stare out unseeing till first movement some time past close though unseeing still while still light. Quite still again then all quite quiet apparently till eyes open again while still light though less. Normally turn head now ninety degrees to watch sun which if already gone then fading afterglow. Even get up certain moods and go stand by western window till quite dark and even some evenings some reason long after. Eyes then open again while still light and close again in what if not quite a single movement almost. Quite still again then at open window facing south over the valley in this wicker chair though actually close inspection not still at all but trembling all over. Close inspection namely detail by detail all over to add up finally to this whole not still at all but trembling all over. But casually in this failing light impression dead still even the hands clearly trembling and the breast faint rise and fall. Legs side by side broken right angles at the knees as in that old statue some old god twanged at sunrise and again at sunset. Trunk likewise dead plumb right up to top of skull seen from behind including nape clear of chairback. Arms likewise broken right angles at the elbows forearms along armrests just right length forearms and rests for hands clenched lightly to rest on ends. So quite still again then all quite quiet apparently eyes closed which to anticipate when they open again if they do in time then dark or some degree of starlight or moonlight or both. Normally watch night fall however long from this narrow chair or standing by western window quite still either case. Quite still namely staring at some one thing alone such as tree or bush a detail alone if near if far the whole if far enough till it goes.

Or by eastern window certain moods staring at some point on the hillside such as that beech in whose shade once quite still till it goes. Chair some reason always same place same position facing south as though clamped down whereas in reality no lighter no more movable imaginable. Or anywhere any ope staring out at nothing just failing light quite still till quite dark though of course no such thing just less light still when less did not seem possible. Quite still then all this time eyes open when discovered then closed then opened and closed again no other movement any kind though of course not still at all when suddenly or so it looks this movement impossible to follow let alone describe. The right hand slowly opening leaves the armrest taking with it the whole forearm complete with elbow and slowly rises opening further as it goes and turning a little deasil till midway to the head it hesitates and hangs half open trembling in mid air. Hangs there as if half inclined to return that is sink back slowly closing as it goes and turning the other way till as and where it began clenched lightly on end of rest. Here because of what comes now not midway to the head but almost there before it hesitates and hangs there trembling as if half inclined etc. Half no but on the verge when in its turn the head moves from its place forward and down among the ready fingers where no sooner received and held it weighs on down till elbow meeting armrest brings this last movement to an end and all still once more. Here back a little way to that suspense before head to rescue as if hand's need the greater and on down in what if not quite a single movement almost till elbow against rest. All quite still again then head in hand namely thumb on outer edge of right socket index ditto left and middle on left cheekbone plus as the hours pass lesser contacts each more or less now more now less with the faint stirrings of the various parts as night wears on. As if even in the dark eyes closed not enough and perhaps even more than ever necessary against that no such thing the further shelter of the hand. Leave it so all quite still or try listening to the sounds all quite still head in hand listening for a sound.

Company and *Ill Seen Ill Said*

Company and *Ill Seen Ill Said* are both products of Beckett's seventies. Although characterised by an equanimity that in Beckett we associate with an observer looking and describing from outside, the calm might be deceptive. In *Company*, the company is a voice talking to the subject who recognises still another voice, that of his past creations. There is also the voice of the book's narration and the silent voice of the person who listens to the company, is spoken to in the second person, and told his own memories. At the end it is revealed that the company and all the other voices are fables, so that ultimately the only voice is that which objectively relates the first line describing the 'voice that comes to one in the dark' and which hears, as does the subject, the truth revealed:

Till finally you hear how words are coming to an end. With every inane word a little nearer to the last. And how the fable too. The fable of one with you in the dark. The fable of one fabling of one with you in the dark. And how better in the end labour lost and silence. And you as you always were.

Alone.

Ill Seen Ill Said is another matter altogether. As the closing extract in this volume, it might be said to be already opening up a new late phase. As with much of the work of recent years it is ghost-haunted, picturing a woman who is 'ill seen' and sometimes 'ill half seen' and sometimes not seen at all. Her cabin seems to grow and encroach on the surrounding land, and the book implies that this is not a good thing. There is a zone of pasture which is perhaps where she is most easily seen or caught, because her presence is always spectral, and she is not as safe in the pasture as she is in the zone of stones, which may in fact be a graveyard or a witches' circle because there is reference to 'The twelve'. The implication of a coven is very strong. Aside from the twelve there is another: 'yes yes she has one', who may be her dead husband in the graveyard that she goes to visit but who the text implies 'has her' (one of the twelve, the devil or the shade of her husband?).

James Joyce made it plain that he wished to keep academics

busy studying his work for the next three hundred years, and undoubtedly Beckett's puzzles will do the same, but the very ambiguity, the series of alternative scenarios, and tantalising hints that he provides for his readers give a positive fillip to the enjoyment of studying these texts to coax out meaning. There is no more reason why a Beckett text should yield up all its treasures at once than a modern musical work or painting. Enjoyment lies partly in the initial shock of meeting whatever speaks loudest in the style and imagery, and this increases with time as we enter into the work itself, finding new meanings and trying to read the mind of the artist. With its cadences, descriptions, passages reminiscent of the ghosts in *Footfalls*, the text of *Ill Seen* shines with a brilliance from which it is difficult not to sense a whiff of evil.

The extract from *Company* given here is from the middle of the short novel. The voice is speaking to the subject, reminding him of the past and present, where he was and where he is, and it includes an unforgettable childhood memory. The passage from *Ill Seen Ill Said* comes from the opening pages, the description of the woman, the cabin and her sorties out, which culminate at the end of the book in what we must assume is her relish of the end of life . . . but yet another meaning could be inferred if something else is waiting beyond that void she breathes. The author's voice constantly intervenes, stopping him from revealing too much.

If this *Samuel Beckett Reader* ends provocatively, it is because Samuel Beckett has always been provocative, and his four most recent works have many meanings. Two of them depict older women dead or dying, two of them are about men dreaming up companionship for consolation or company. What the reader or the viewer gets is the wash of the mystique, eerie figures to haunt the memory, and phrases that one constantly wishes to read again.

Beckett means different things to different readers, a prophet of the world turned into a wasteland, and of human life reduced either to screaming consciousness or to such a stillness that only the very observant eye can see that the mind still thinks with a voice that is reaching ever further to ask the eternal questions of human existence – where from, why, where to, how? Each one of us must ultimately find his or her own answers. Samuel Beckett at least has shown us how we can frame the questions.

From Company

The light there was then. On your back in the dark the light there was then. Sunless cloudless brightness. You slip away at break of day and climb to your hiding place on the hillside. A nook in the gorse. East beyond the sea the faint shape of high mountain. Seventy miles away according to your Longman. For the third or fourth time in your life. The first time you told them and were derided. All you had seen was cloud. So now you hoard it in your heart with the rest. Back home at nightfall supperless to bed. You lie in the dark and are back in that light. Straining out from your nest in the gorse with your eyes across the water till they ache. You close them while you count a hundred. Then open and strain again. Again and again. Till in the end it is there. Palest blue against the pale sky. You lie in the dark and are back in that light. Fall asleep in that sunless cloudless light. Sleep till morning light.

Deviser of the voice and of its hearer and of himself. Deviser of himself for company. Leave it at that. He speaks of himself as of another. He says speaking of himself, He speaks of himself as of another. Himself he devises too for company. Leave it at that. Confusion too is company up to a point. Better hope deferred than none. Up to a point. Till the heart starts to sicken. Company too up to a point. Better a sick heart than none. Till it starts to break. So speaking of himself he concludes for the time being, For the time being leave it at that.

In the same dark as his creature or in another not yet imagined. Nor in what position. Whether standing or sitting or lying or in some other position in the dark. These are among the matters yet to be imagined. Matters of which as yet no inkling. The test is company. Which of the two darks is the better company. Which of all imaginable positions has the most to offer in the way of company. And similarly for the other matters yet to be imagined. Such as if such decisions irreversible. Let him for example after due imagination decide in favour of the supine position or prone and this in practice prove less companionable than anticipated. May he then or may he not replace it by another? Such as huddled with his legs drawn up within the semi-circle of his arms and his head on his knees. Or in motion. Crawling on all fours. Another in another dark or in the same crawling on all fours devising it all

for company. Or some other form of motion. The possible encounters. A dead rat. What an addition to company that would
be! A rat long dead.

Might not the hearer be improved? Made more companionable if
not downright human. Mentally perhaps there is room for en-
livenment. An attempt at reflexion at least. At recall. At speech
even. Conation of some kind however feeble. A trace of emotion.
Signs of distress. A sense of failure. Without loss of character.
Delicate ground. But physically? Must he lie inert to the end?
Only the eyelids stirring on and off since technically they must.
To let in and shut out the dark. Might he not cross his feet? On
and off. Now left on right and now a little later the reverse. No.
Quite out of keeping. He lie with crossed feet? One glance dispels.
Some movement of the hands? A hand. A clenching and unclench-
ing. Difficult to justify. Or raised to brush away a fly. But there
are no flies. Then why not let there be? The temptation is great.
Let there be a fly. For him to brush away. A live fly mistaking
him for dead. Made aware of its error and renewing it incontinent.
What an addition to company that would be! A live fly mistaking
him for dead. But no. He would not brush away a fly.

You take pity on a hedgehog out in the cold and put it in an old
hatbox with some worms. This box with the hog inside you then
place in a disused hutch wedging the door open for the poor
creature to come and go at will. To go in search of food and having
eaten to regain the warmth and security of its box in the hutch.
There then is the hedgehog in its box in the hutch with enough
worms to tide it over. A last look to make sure all is as it should
be before taking yourself off to look for something else to pass the
time heavy already on your hands at that tender age. The glow at
your good deed is slower than usual to cool and fade. You glowed
readily in those days but seldom for long. Hardly had the glow
been kindled by some good deed on your part or by some little
triumph over your rivals or by a word of praise from your parents
or mentors when it would begin to cool and fade leaving you in a
very short time as chill and dim as before. Even in those days.
But not this day. It was on an autumn afternoon you found the
hedgehog and took pity on it in the way described and you were
still the better for it when your bedtime came. Kneeling at your
bedside you included it the hedgehog in your detailed prayer to

269

God to bless all you loved. And tossing in your warm bed waiting for sleep to come you were still faintly glowing at the thought of what a fortunate hedgehog it was to have crossed your path as it did. A narrow clay path edged with sere box edging. As you stood there wondering how best to pass the time till bedtime it parted the edging on the one side and was making straight for the edging on the other when you entered its life. Now the next morning not only was the glow spent but a great uneasiness had taken its place. A suspicion that all was perhaps not as it should be. That rather than do as you did you had perhaps better let good alone and the hedgehog pursue its way. Days if not weeks passed before you could bring yourself to return to the hutch. You have never forgotten what you found then. You are on your back in the dark and have never forgotten what you found then. The mush. The stench.

Impending for some time the following. Need for company not continuous. Moments when his own unrelieved a relief. Intrusion of voice at such. Similarly image of hearer. Similarly his own. Regret then at having brought them about and problem how dispel them. Finally what meant by his own unrelieved? What possible relief? Leave it at that for the moment.

Let the hearer be named H. Aspirate. Haitch. You Haitch are on your back in the dark. And let him know his name. No longer any question of his overhearing. Of his not being meant. Though logically none in any case. Of words murmured in his ear to wonder if to him! So he is. So that faint uneasiness lost. That faint hope. To one with so few occasions to feel. So inapt to feel. Asking nothing better in so far as he can ask anything than to feel nothing. Is it desirable? No. Would he gain thereby in companionability? No. Then let him not be named H. Let him be again as he was. The hearer. Unnamable. You.

Imagine closer the place where he lies. Within reason. To its form and dimensions a clue is given by the voice afar. Receding afar or there with abrupt saltation or resuming there after pause. From above and from all sides and levels with equal remoteness at its most remote. At no time from below. So far. Suggesting one lying on the floor of a hemispherical chamber of generous diameter with ear dead centre. How generous? Given faintness of voice at its least faint some sixty feet should suffice or thirty from ear to any given point of encompassing surface. So much for form and dimensions. And composition? What and where clue to that if any anywhere. Reserve for the moment. Basalt is tempting. Black basalt. But reserve for the moment. So he imagines to himself as voice and hearer pall. But further imagination shows him to have imagined ill. For with what right affirm of a faint sound that it is a less faint made fainter by farness and not a true faint near at hand? Or of a faint fading to fainter that it recedes and not in situ decreases. If with none then no light from the voice on the place where our old hearer lies. In immeasurable dark. Contourless. Leave it at that for the moment. Adding only, What kind of imagination is this so reason-ridden? A kind of its own.

Another devising it all for company. In the same dark as his creature or in another. Quick imagine. The same.

Might not the voice be improved? Made more companionable. Say changing now for some time past though no tense in the dark in that dim mind. All at once over and in train and to come. But for the other say for some time past some improvement. Same flat tone as initially imagined and same repetitiousness. No improving those. But less mobility. Less variety of faintness. As if seeking optimum position. From which to discharge with greatest effect. The ideal amplitude for effortless audition. Neither offending the ear with loudness nor through converse excess constraining it to strain. How far more companionable such an organ than it initially in haste imagined. How far more likely to achieve its object. To have the hearer have a past and acknowledge it. You were born on an Easter Friday after long labour. Yes I remember. The sun had not long sunk behind the larches. Yes I remember. As best to erode the drop must strike unwavering. Upon the place beneath.

From Ill Seen Ill Said

From where she lies she sees Venus rise. On. From where she lies when the skies are clear she sees Venus rise followed by the sun. Then she rails at the source of all life. On. At evening when the skies are clear she savours its star's revenge. At the other window. Rigid upright on her old chair she watches for the radiant one. Her old deal spindlebacked kitchen chair. It emerges from out the last rays and sinking ever brighter is engulfed in its turn. On. She sits on erect and rigid in the deepening gloom. Such helplessness to move she cannot help. Heading on foot for a particular point often she freezes on the way. Unable till long after to move on not knowing whither or for what purpose. Down on her knees especially she finds it hard not to remain so forever. Hand resting on hand on some convenient support. Such as the foot of her bed. And on them her head. There then she sits as though turned to stone face to the night. Save for the white of her hair and faintly bluish white of face and hands all is black. For an eye no need of light to see. All this in the present as had she the misfortune to be still of this world.

The cabin. Its situation. Careful. On. At the inexistent centre of a formless place. Rather more circular than otherwise finally. Flat to be sure. To cross it in a straight line takes her from five to ten minutes. Depending on her speed and radius taken. Here she who loves to – here she who now can only stray never strays. Stones increasingly abound. Ever scanter even the rankest weed. Meagre pastures hem it round on which it slowly gains. With none to gainsay. To have gainsaid. As if doomed to spread. How come a cabin in such a place? How came? Careful. Before replying that in the far past at the time of its building there was clover growing to its very walls. Implying furthermore that it the culprit. And from it as from an evil core that the what is the wrong word the evil spread. And none to urge – none to have urged its demolition. As if doomed to endure. Question answered. Chalkstones of striking effect in the light of the moon. Let it be in opposition when the skies are clear. Quick then still under the spell of Venus quick to the other window to see the other marvel rise. How whiter and whiter as it climbs it whitens more and more the stones. Rigid with face and hands against the pane she stands and marvels long.

The two zones form a roughly circular whole. As though outlined by a trembling hand. Diameter. Careful. Say one furlong. On an average. Beyond the unknown. Mercifully. The feeling at times of being below sea level. Especially at night when the skies are clear. Invisible nearby sea. Inaudible. The entire surface under grass. Once clear of the zone of stones. Save where it has receded from the chalky soil. Innumerable white scabs all shapes and sizes. Of striking effect in the light of the moon. In the way of animals ovines only. After long hesitation. They are white and make do with little. Whence suddenly come no knowing nor whither as suddenly gone. Unshepherded they stray as they list. Flowers? Careful. Alone the odd crocus still at lambing time. And man? Shut of at last? Alas no. For will she not be surprised one day to find him gone? Surprised no she is beyond surprise. How many? A figure come what may. Twelve. Wherewith to furnish the horizon's narrow round. She raises her eyes and sees one. Turns away and sees another. So on. Always afar. Still or receding. She never once saw one come toward her. Or she forgets. She forgets. Are they always the same? Do they see her? Enough.

A moor would have better met the case. Were there a case better to meet. There had to be lambs. Rightly or wrongly. A moor would have allowed of them. Lambs for their whiteness. And for other reasons as yet obscure. Another reason. And so that there may be none. At lambing time. That from one moment to the next she may raise her eyes to find them gone. A moor would have allowed of them. In any case too late. And what lambs. No trace of frolic. White splotches in the grass. Aloof from the unheeding ewes. Still. Then a moment straying. Then still again. To think there is still life in this age. Gently gently.

She is drawn to a certain spot. At times. There stands a stone. It it is draws her. Rounded rectangular block three times as high as wide. Four. Her stature now. Her lowly stature. When it draws she must to it. She cannot see it from her door. Blindfold she could find her way. With herself she has no more converse. Never had much. Now none. As had she the misfortune to be still of this world. But when the stone draws then to her feet the prayer, Take her. Especially at night when the skies are clear. With moon or without. They take her and halt her before it. There she too as if of stone. But black. Sometimes in the light of the moon. Mostly of the stars alone. Does she envy it?

To the imaginary stranger the dwelling appears deserted. Under constant watch it betrays no sign of life. The eye glued to one or the other window has nothing but black drapes for its pains. Motionless against the door he listens long. No sound. Knocks. No answer. Watches all night in vain for the least glimmer. Returns at last to his own and avows, No one. She shows herself only to her own. But she has no own. Yes yes she has one. And who has her.

There was a time when she did not appear in the zone of stones. A long time. Was not therefore to be seen going out or coming in. When she appeared only in the pastures. Was not therefore to be seen leaving them. Save as though by enchantment. But little by little she began to appear. In the zone of stones. First darkly. Then more and more plain. Till in detail she could be seen crossing the threshold both ways and closing the door behind her. Then a time when within her walls she did not appear. A long time. But little by little she began to appear. Within her walls. Darkly. Time truth to tell still current. Though she within them no more. This long time.

Yes within her walls so far at the window only. At one or the other window. Rapt before the sky. And only half seen so far a pallet and a ghostly chair. Ill half seen. And how in her faint comings and goings she suddenly stops dead. And how hard set to rise up from off her knees. But there too little by little she begins to appear more plain. Within her walls. As well as other objects. Such as under her pillow – such as deep in some recess this still shadowy album. Perhaps in time be by her when she takes it on her knees. See the old fingers fumble through the pages. And what scenes they can possibly be that draw the head down lower still and hold it in thrall. In the meantime who knows no more than withered flowers. No more!

Bibliography

Available Works by Samuel Beckett

This bibliography includes all works available at the time of publication in book form in the UK written by Samuel Beckett. Pre-war articles, translations, and occasional writing that are not available have not been included. Nevertheless since he won the Nobel Prize in 1969, Mr Beckett has in many instances acceded to the wishes of his various publishers, so that the list of earlier work now available is much increased. He has also been very active with new writing in the last few years.

The dates given are the dates of original publication, in brackets if different from the current trade edition. The order is chronological.

The number of books written about Samuel Beckett staggers the imagination, and so does the great quantity of critical material in different journals. A selection is listed here of the more important books, in some cases with a commentary.

Novels, Short Stories and Other Prose

More Pricks Than Kicks. Short Stories. (Chatto and Windus 1934, special edition for scholars, *hors commerce*, Calder and Boyars 1966.) Trade edition Calder and Boyars 1970, Picador 1977.

Murphy. A novel. (Routledge 1938, John Calder (Publishers) Ltd 1963.) John Calder (Publishers) Ltd 1977, Picador 1973.

Watt. A novel. (Olympia Press 1953, John Calder (Publishers) Ltd 1963.) John Calder (Publishers) Ltd 1976.

Mercier and Camier. A novel. Calder and Boyars 1974. *Mercier and Camier* was written in French after the war but suppressed by the author until 1970 when it appeared in the original. The author then translated it for British publication.

First Love. Calder and Boyars 1973. This novella was also written in the 1940s in French and suppressed by the author until 1970 when it appeared in France and subsequently in the author's translation. It was later collected into *Four Novellas*.

Four Novellas: 'First Love'; 'The Expelled'; 'The Calmative'; 'The End'. The last three of these novellas were collected for the first time in English in *No's Knife*, Calder and Boyars 1967, later reprinted together with 'First Love' as *Four Novellas*, John Calder (Publishers) Ltd 1977, Penguin Books 1981.

Molloy. A novel. (French publication 1951.) John Calder (Publishers) Ltd 1959 in one volume with *Malone Dies* and *The Unnamable*. Published individually 1966. Picador 1979.

Malone Dies. A novel. (French publication 1951.) John Calder (Publishers) Ltd 1958. As part of *Trilogy* 1959. In Picador in one volume with *Molloy* and *The Unnamable* 1979.

The Unnamable. A novel. (French publication 1953.) John Calder (Publishers) Ltd 1959 in one volume with *Molloy* and *Malone Dies*. Published separately Calder and Boyars 1975. In one volume with *Molloy* and *Malone Dies*, Picador 1979.

From an Abandoned Work. Prose fragment. (Faber and Faber 1958.) Also in *No's Knife*, Calder and Boyars 1967; *Six Residua*, John Calder (Publishers) Ltd 1978.

How It Is. A novel. John Calder (Publishers) Ltd 1964. Reprinted John Calder (Publishers) Ltd 1977.

Imagination Dead Imagine. Short text, residue of a novel. Calder and Boyars 1966. Also in *No's Knife*, Calder and Boyars 1967. Collected in *Six Residua*, John Calder (Publishers) Ltd 1978.

No's Knife. Collected short prose in four sections: three stories, 'The Calmative', 'The End' and 'The Expelled'; thirteen *Texts for Nothing*; 'From An Abandoned Work'; and three residua, 'Enough', 'Imagination Dead Imagine' and 'Ping'. Calder and Boyars 1967. Later broken up into separate volumes as follows: *Four Novellas* (the three stories and 'First Love'), John Calder (Publishers) Ltd 1977; *Texts for Nothing*, Calder and Boyars 1974; *Six Residua* ('From An Abandoned Work' and three residua to which 'Lessness' and 'The Lost Ones' were later added), John Calder (Publishers) Ltd 1978.

Lessness. (French publication 1969.) Calder and Boyars 1970. Collected in *Six Residua*, John Calder (Publishers) Ltd 1978.

The Lost Ones. (French publication 1971.) Calder and Boyars 1972. Later collected in *Six Residua*, John Calder (Publishers) Ltd 1978.

Still. Calder and Boyars 1973. Written in English. Collected in *For To End Yet Again*, John Calder (Publishers) Ltd 1976.

For To End Yet Again. (French publication 1976.) Contains: 'For To End Yet Again'; 'Still'; 'He is Barehead'; 'Horn Came Always'; 'Afar a Bird'; 'I Gave up Before Birth'; 'Closed Place'; 'Old Earth'.

All Strange Away. (Gotham Book Mart 1976.) John Calder (Publishers) Ltd 1979.

Six Residua. Collected texts: 'From an Abandoned Work'; 'Enough'; 'Imagination Dead Imagine'; 'Ping'; 'Lessness'; 'The Lost Ones'. John Calder (Publishers) Ltd 1978.

Company. John Calder (Publishers) Ltd 1980. Picador 1982.

Ill Seen Ill Said. (French publication 1981.) John Calder (Publishers) Ltd 1982.

Worstword Ho. Short novel. John Calder (Publishers) Ltd 1983.

Dramatic Works

Human Wishes. A fragment. (Written 1937.) In *Disjecta*. John Calder (Publishers) Ltd 1983.

Waiting for Godot. (French publication 1952.) A play in two acts. Faber and Faber 1956.

Endgame. Play in one act. (French publication 1957.) Faber and Faber 1958. Published in one volume with *Act Without Words I*.

Act Without Words I. Mime. Faber and Faber 1958. Published in one volume with *Endgame*. Later collected in *Collected Shorter Plays*, Faber and Faber 1983.

All That Fall. Radio play. BBC commission. Faber and Faber 1957.

Krapp's Last Tape. Play in one act. Faber and Faber 1960. Published in one volume with *Embers*. Later collected in *Collected Shorter Plays*, Faber and Faber 1983.

Embers. Radio play. Faber and Faber 1960. Published in one volume with *Krapp's Last Tape*. Later collected in *Collected Shorter Plays*, Faber and Faber 1983.

Act Without Words II. Mime. (French publication 1963.) Faber and Faber 1967. Later collected in *Collected Shorter Plays*, Faber and Faber 1983.

The Old Tune. Adaptation from *La Manivelle* by Robert Pinget. Calder and Boyars 1963. Published in *Plays Volume One* by Robert Pinget. Later collected in *Collected Shorter Plays*, Faber and Faber 1983.

Happy Days. Play in two acts. Faber and Faber 1962.

Words and Music. Radio play. Faber and Faber 1964. Published together with *Play* and *Cascando*. Later collected in *Collected Shorter Plays*, Faber and Faber 1983.

Cascando. Radio play. (French publication 1963.) Faber and Faber

1964. Published together with *Play* and *Words and Music*. Later collected in *Collected Shorter Plays*, Faber and Faber 1983.

Play. Play in one act. Faber and Faber 1964. Published together with *Words and Music* and *Cascando*. Later collected in *Collected Shorter Plays*, Faber and Faber 1983.

Film. Short film scenario. (Written 1963.) Faber and Faber 1967. Later collected in *Collected Shorter Plays*, Faber and Faber 1983.

Come and Go. Dramaticule. Calder and Boyars 1967. Later collected in *Collected Shorter Plays*, Faber and Faber 1983.

Eh Joe. Television play. Faber and Faber 1967. Later collected in *Collected Shorter Plays*, Faber and Faber 1983.

Breath. Thirty-second play. Written for *Oh Calcutta*. Collected in *Collected Shorter Plays*, Faber and Faber 1983.

Not I. Faber and Faber 1973. Collected in *Collected Shorter Plays*, Faber and Faber 1983.

That Time. Faber and Faber 1974. Collected in *Collected Shorter Plays*, Faber and Faber 1983.

Footfalls. Faber and Faber 1975. Collected in *Collected Shorter Plays*, Faber and Faber 1983.

Ghost Trio. Television play. Faber and Faber 1976. Collected in *Collected Shorter Plays*, Faber and Faber 1983.

. . . but the clouds . . . Television play. Faber and Faber 1976. Collected in *Collected Shorter Plays*, Faber and Faber 1983.

Rockaby. *Collected Shorter Plays*, Faber and Faber 1983.

Ohio Impromptu. *Collected Shorter Plays*, Faber and Faber 1983.

A Piece of Monologue. Monologue for stage. *Collected Shorter Plays*, Faber and Faber 1983.

Square (Quadrat). Television play first written for German television. *Collected Shorter Plays*, Faber and Faber 1983.

Catastrophe. Play. Written in French for special Havel evening at Avignon 1982. *Collected Shorter Plays*, Faber and Faber 1983.

Theatre I. (Written *c*. 1960.) Collected in *Collected Shorter Plays*, Faber and Faber 1983.

Theatre II. (Written *c*. 1960.) Collected in *Collected Shorter Plays*, Faber and Faber 1983.

Radio I. (Written *c*. 1960.) Collected in *Collected Shorter Plays*, Faber and Faber 1983.

Radio II. (Written *c*. 1960.) Collected in *Collected Shorter Plays*, Faber and Faber 1983.

Collected Shorter Plays. Faber and Faber 1983.

Poetry

Anthology of Mexican Poetry. Translations. (Thames and Hudson 1959.) Reprinted Calder and Boyars 1970.

Poems in English. Collected English poems with some French. (1930–47). John Calder (Publishers) Ltd 1961.

Zone. Translation from Apollinaire. Dolmen Press Dublin, Calder and Boyars London 1972. Collected in *Collected Poems in English and French*, John Calder (Publishers) Ltd 1977.

Collected Poems in English and French. John Calder (Publishers) Ltd 1977: Part I Poems in English; Part II Poems in French (with some translations); Part III Translations from French with the originals from Paul Eluard, Arthur Rimbaud, Guillaume Apollinaire, Sébastien Chamfort.

Criticism

'Dante . . . Bruno. Vico . . Joyce'. Essay on Joyce in *Our Exagmination Round His Factification For Incamination of Work in Progress*. (Shakespeare and Co. 1929.) Faber and Faber 1966.

Proust. Critical study. (Chatto and Windus 1931.) Calder and Boyars 1965. In one volume with *Three Dialogues with Georges Duthuit*.

Three Dialogues with Georges Duthuit. Dialogues on painting and the artistic process. (*Transition* 1949.) Calder and Boyars 1965. In one volume with *Proust*.

Disjecta. Collected criticisms and miscellaneous writings: Part I Essays in Aesthetics; Part II Words about Writers; Part III Words about Painters; Part IV Human Wishes (play fragment). John Calder (Publishers) Ltd 1983.

Beckett Criticism and Memoirs: A short selection

DEIRDRE BAIR. *Samuel Beckett: A Biography*. Jonathan Cape 1978, Picador 1980. This is the only biography of Beckett to have yet appeared and was published without the author's approval, although he did nothing to prevent publication. It is useful as a general guide to Mr Beckett's life and the chronology of the writings. That said, there is little else to recommend the book, which is extremely inaccurate and unscholarly, containing many inventions, fallacies and misinterpretations by the author, many of which have been pointed out by a variety of reviewers.

JOHN CALDER ed. *Beckett at Sixty*. A symposium of reminiscences, new criticism and tributes. Calder and Boyars 1967.

RICHARD COE. *Beckett*. Oliver and Boyd 1964.

RUBY COHN. *Samuel Beckett: The Comic Gamut*. Rutgers University Press 1962.

COLIN DUCKWORTH. *Angels of Darkness*. Allen and Unwin 1972.

MARTIN ESSLIN ed. *Samuel Beckett*. A collection of critical essays. 1965.

MARTIN ESSLIN. *The Theatre of the Absurd*. Penguin 1968.

RAYMOND FEDERMAN. *Journey to Chaos: Samuel Beckett's Early Fiction*. Cambridge University Press 1965.

RAYMOND FEDERMAN and JOHN FLETCHER. *Samuel Beckett: His Works and His Critics*. University of California Press 1970. This is far and away the most important bibliographical guide to Beckett's own works and to writings about him up to the date of publication, listing in addition to complete books important articles, reviews, etc.

JOHN FLETCHER. *The Novels of Samuel Beckett*. Chatto and Windus 1964.

JOHN FLETCHER. *Samuel Beckett's Art*. Chatto and Windus 1967.

JOSEPHINE JACOBSEN and WILLIAM R. MUELLER. *The Testament of Samuel Beckett*. Faber and Faber 1964.

HUGH KENNER. *Samuel Beckett: A Critical Study*. John Calder (Publishers) Ltd 1962. This book is currently out of print in Britain but remains the first and best early study of Samuel Beckett's work.

JAMES KNOWLSON. *Light and Darkness in the Theatre of Samuel Beckett*. Turret Books 1972.

JAMES KNOWLSON and JOHN PILLING. *Frescoes of the Skull*. John Calder (Publishers) Ltd 1979.

JOHN PILLING. *Samuel Beckett*. Routledge and Kegan Paul 1976.

ALEC REID. *All I can manage more than I could*. Dolmen Press 1968.

ALAIN ROBBE-GRILLET. 'Samuel Beckett, or Presence on the Stage'. Essay in *Towards a New Novel*. Calder and Boyars 1965.

EUGENE WEBB. *The Plays of Samuel Beckett*. Peter Owen 1972.

KATHARINE WORTH ed. *Beckett the Shape Changer: A symposium by eight contributors*. Routledge and Kegan Paul 1975.

DOUGAL McMILLAN and MARTHA FEHSENFELD. *Beckett in the Theatre*. John Calder (Publishers) Ltd 1983.

Journal of Beckett Studies. Published twice annually. Contains new Beckett criticism, reviews, photographs and also covers other authors where there is a personal or intellectual connection. John Calder (Publishers) Ltd.

Deirdre Bair
Samuel Beckett £4.95
a biography

Samuel Beckett has always been the most private and mysterious of writers, despite his status in the artistic pantheon and the award of the 1969 Nobel Prize for Literature. There have been many critical studies, but this is the first full biography. Beckett said he would 'neither help nor hinder' Deirdre Bair when she approached him in 1971, proposing to write his biography. This apparently unhelpful pronouncement came to open many doors and uncover much previously unknown information. The result, this masterful biography, illuminates the life of a genius.

'Impressive translation of an enigma into a man' TIME

'Profoundly moving . . . the authentic portrait of a very great writer and a good man' GABRIEL JOSIPOVICI, LISTENER

edited and introduced by John Calder
A William Burroughs Reader £2.50

It is a measure of Burroughs' influence and importance as a writer that the very titles of his books have found their way into contemporary language and consciousness: *The Naked Lunch, The Soft Machine, The Ticket That Exploded, Nova Express, The Wild Boys, Exterminator!* This Reader contains substantial extracts from all Burroughs' work, edited and arranged to provide the perfect introduction to this most ferocious and apocalyptic of visionaries.

'A master of dialogue, a creator of character without contemporary equal, a humorist who gets funnier as his subject-matter gets blacker, and a first-class storyteller' JOHN CALDER

'The most radical innovator in fiction since Joyce, and probably of comparable importance' ANGELA CARTER, GUARDIAN

Samuel Beckett
More Pricks than Kicks £2.50

Beckett's first book – and a compulsively readable introduction to his work. The adventures of a student in Dublin are explored in a wholly original way. With its grim humour and devastating insights the book contains, in embryo, Beckett's whole extraordinary world.

Company £1.50

'Imagine yourself old and reviewing your life. You are at the mercy of your memory, which dins in your ear stories of those scenes that made your life what it was. And if in addition you perceive yourself remembering . . . then you have split yourself yet again: into the voice of memory, the unwilling rememberer, and the unhappy perceiver' NEW YORK TIMES

'There is in it a vivacious sense of despair that tears at the nerve ends. But its real richness lies in its language. What a master Beckett is . . . the finest verbal artist of the twentieth century' PETER TINNISWOOD, THE TIMES

Murphy £1.95

Brilliant tragi-comic novel of an Irishman's adventures in London. By the Nobel prizewinner.

'One of the greatest prose writers of the century' THE TIMES LITERARY SUPPLEMENT

The Beckett Trilogy £2.75
Molloy, Malone Dies, The Unnamable

'Unmistakably a man of genius' OBSERVER

'One of the most remarkable, most original and most haunting prose works of the century . . . concerned with the search for identity and with the true silence which is the end of speech' THE TIMES LITERARY SUPPLEMENT

'The quintessential Beckett . . . folk-sharp and humorous grotesque fantasy' PUNCH

Vladimir Nabokov
Lectures on Literature £3.95

'With a pleasure which is both sensual and intellectual, we shall watch the artist build the castle of cards and watch the castle of cards become a castle of beautiful steel and glass.' For nearly twenty years Nabokov taught a university course on the masterpieces of world literature. An orator, a novelist, a lepidopterist of world renown, he examined literature with a scientific exactitude as well as with a writer's appreciation. Here are his legendary lectures on the Europeans: on Jane Austen, Dickens, Stevenson, Joyce, Flaubert, Proust and Kafka. With an introduction by John Updike.

'A marvellous mixture of casual arrogance (as a man who knows what writing is) and proper humility' A. S. BYATT, THE TIMES

'A collection of sparkling spoken essays but also a minutely organized course' V. S. PRITCHETT

Lectures on Russian Literature £3.95

'Literature must be taken and broken to bits, pushed apart, squashed and then its lovely reek will be smelt in the hollow of the palm, it will be munched and rolled upon the tongue with relish.' Nabokov left his native Russia at the age of twenty to escape what he called 'the bloated octopus of the state'. In this volume are published his lectures on the great nineteenth-century Russian writers: Gogol, Turgenev, Dostoevsky, Tolstoy, Chekov and Gorki.

'I cannot imagine a more rewarding handbook for anyone who appreciates, or hopes to write, fiction' FREDERICK RAPHAEL, SUNDAY TIMES

'A great Russian talking of great Russians' ANTHONY BURGESS

'Unique in the history of literary criticism in its power to grip, astonish and occasionally infuriate' GUARDIAN

Clive James
From the Land of Shadows £2.50

'These literary-critical essays . . . have a kind of freshness about them . . . in the tradition of Hazlitt, Bagehot and Desmond MacCarthy, with a gusto worthy to succeed theirs and a philosopy well set out in the introduction' JOHN BAYLEY, OBSERVER

'James' main strength as a critic of contemporary fiction lies in his wry description . . . we can only be grateful to him for caring, and for keeping us smiling while we learn' TABLET

'His outstanding talent is as a cicerone, guiding the ignorant traveller with patience, knowledge and wit round some favourite literary edifice' THE TIMES LITERARY SUPPLEMENT

'A collection of dignity and coherence' SUNDAY TIMES

Eric Newby
A Traveller's Life £2.95

Eric Newby's life of travel began with strange adventures in prams, forays into the lush jungles of Harrods with his mother and into the perilous slums of darkest Hammersmith on his way to school. Such beginnings aroused his curiosity about more outlandish places, a wanderlust satisfied equally by travels through the London sewers, by bicycle to Italy and through wildest New York. His book chronicles the whole range of situations into which he has thrown himself with characteristic verve and optimism, and his perception of the incongruous is as sharp when travelling abroad in search of high fashion as buyer to a chain of department stores, as it is when recalling his reluctant participation in a tiger shoot in India.

'Eric Newby writes as lightly as he travels. *A Traveller's Life* is a tonic and a pleasure' GUARDIAN

Joyce Johnson
Minor Characters £2.50

Girl met boy on a blind date arranged by Allen Ginsberg. It was January 1957. The girl was Joyce Johnson, the boy Jack Kerouac. It was nine months before *On the Road*. Like Robin Hood's and Peter Pan's, Jack's was a boy gang – women were minor characters at best.

'Joyce Johnson summons up the mythic Greenwich Village of jazz, poetry and black-stockinged Bohemia with infinite ironic grace' ANGELA CARTER

'The love story of Joyce from the Upper Westside who journeys to the Village on the subway . . . and Jack, the confused, mother-tied, suddenly famous road poet . . . a first-rate memoir, very beautiful, very sad' E. L. DOCTOROW

Jan Harold Brunvand
The Vanishing Hitchhiker £1.95
urban legends and their meanings

The take-away chicken that was really a batter-fried rat . . . the carnivorous spider hidden underneath a well-lacquered hairdo, busily eating away at the scalp – these are the stories that always happened to a friend of a relative of the man in the pub. But as Jan Harold Brunvand demonstrates in this entertaining book, they're a great deal more. These tales form the folklore of modern man, some gaining enough credibility to appear regularly as genuine news-stories. So sit back and enjoy the myth and legend of the fast-food joint and the parking lot, the executive lifestyle and the urban jungle, the alligator in the sewer and the madman and the babysitter.

'A string of legends . . . inherently unlikely, even if they did happen to your best friend's best friend' SUNDAY TIMES

Picador

☐	**The Beckett Trilogy**	Samuel Beckett	£2.75p
☐	**Making Love: The Picador Book of Erotic Verse**	edited by Alan Bold	£1.95p
☐	**The Tokyo-Montana Express**	Richard Brautigan	£2.50p
☐	**Bury My Heart at Wounded Knee**	Dee Brown	£3.75p
☐	**Cities of the Red Night**	William Burroughs	£2.50p
☐	**The Road to Oxiana**	Robert Byron	£2.50p
☐	**Our Ancestors**	Italo Calvino	£3.50p
☐	**Auto Da Fé**	Elias Canetti	£2.95p
☐	**Exotic Pleasures**	Peter Carey	£1.50p
☐	**In Patagonia**	Bruce Chatwin	£2.50p
☐	**Sweet Freedom**	Anna Coote and Beatrix Campbell	£1.95p
☐	**Crown Jewel**	Ralph de Boissiere	£2.75p
☐	**Letters from Africa**	Isak Dinesen (Karen Blixen)	£3.95p
☐	**The Price Was High**	F. Scott Fitzgerald	£2.95p
☐	**One Hundred Years of Solitude**	Gabriel Garcia Márquez	£2.95p
☐	**Nothing, Doting, Blindness**	Henry Green	£2.95p
☐	**The Obstacle Race**	Germaine Greer	£5.95p
☐	**Household Tales**	Brothers Grimm	£1.50p
☐	**Meetings with Remarkable Men**	Gurdjieff	£2.75p
☐	**Roots**	Alex Haley	£3.50p
☐	**The Four Great Novels**	Dashiell Hammett	£3.95p
☐	**Growth of the Soil**	Knut Hamsun	£2.95p
☐	**When the Tree Sings**	Stratis Haviaras	£1.95p
☐	**Dispatches**	Michael Herr	£1.95p
☐	**If the War Goes On**	Herman Hesse	£1.75p
☐	**Riddley Walker**	Russell Hoban	£2.50p
☐	**Stories**	Desmond Hogan	£2.50p
☐	**Three Trapped Tigers**	C. Cabrera Infante	£2.95p
☐	**Unreliable Memoirs**	Clive James	£1.95p
☐	**Lantern Lecture**	Adam Mars-Jones	£1.95p
☐	**China Men**	Maxine Hong Kingston	£1.50p
☐	**Bricks to Babel**	Arthur Koestler	£3.95p
☐	**Memoirs of a Survivor**	Doris Lessing	£2.50p
☐	**Albert Camus**	Herbert Lottman	£3.95p
☐	**The Road to Xanadu**	John Livingston Lowes	£1.95p
☐	**The Cement Garden**	Ian McEwan	£1.95p
☐	**The Serial**	Cyra McFadden	£1.75p

☐	**McCarthy's List**	Mary Mackey	£1.95p
☐	**Psychoanalysis: The Impossible Profession**	Janet Malcolm	£1.95p
☐	**Short Lives**	Katinka Matson	£2.50p
☐	**The Snow Leopard**	Peter Matthiessen	£2.95p
☐	**A Short Walk in the Hindu Kush**	Eric Newby	£2.50p
☐	**The Best of Myles**	Flann O' Brien	£2.75p
☐	**Autobiography**	John Cowper Powys	£3.50p
☐	**Hadrian the Seventh**	Fr. Rolfe (Baron Corvo)	£1.25p
☐	**On Broadway**	Damon Runyon	£1.95p
☐	**Midnight's Children**	Salman Rushdie	£3.50p
☐	**Snowblind**	Robert Sabbag	£1.95p
☐	**Awakenings**	Oliver Sacks	£3.95p
☐	**The Best of Saki**	Saki	£1.95p
☐	**The Fate of the Earth**	Jonathan Schell	£1.95p
☐	**Street of Crocodiles**	Bruno Schultz	£1.25p
☐	**Miss Silver's Past**	Josef Skvorecky	£2.50p
☐	**A Flag for Sunrise**	Robert Stone	£2.50p
☐	**Visitants**	Randolph Stow	£2.50p
☐	**Alice Fell**	Emma Tennant	£1.95p
☐	**The Flute-Player**	D. M. Thomas	£2.25p
☐	**The Great Shark Hunt**	Hunter S. Thompson	£3.50p
☐	**Female Friends**	Fay Weldon	£2.50p
☐	**No Particular Place To Go**	Hugo Williams	£1.95p
☐	**The Outsider**	Colin Wilson	£2.50p
☐	**Kandy-Kolored Tangerine-Flake Streamline Baby**	Tom Wolfe	£2.25p
☐	**Mars**	Fritz Zorn	£1.95p

All these books are available at your local bookshop or newsagent, or can be ordered direct from the publisher. Indicate the number of copies required and fill in the form below   8

....

Name_____
(Block letters please)

Address_____

_____

Send to Pan Books (CS Department), Cavaye Place, London SW10 9PG
Please enclose remittance to the value of the cover price plus:
35p for the first book plus 15p per copy for each additional book ordered
to a maximum charge of £1.25 to cover postage and packing
Applicable only in the UK

While every effort is made to keep prices low, it is sometimes
necessary to increase prices at short notice. Pan Books reserve
the right to show on covers and charge new retail prices which
may differ from those advertised in the text or elsewhere